The Ethics of Encounter

May we see Christ in
+ be Christ for
all we encounter
. Peace,
[illegible]

THE ETHICS OF ENCOUNTER

CHRISTIAN NEIGHBOR LOVE AS A PRACTICE OF SOLIDARITY

MARCUS MESCHER

ORBIS BOOKS
Maryknoll, New York 10545

Founded in 1970, Orbis Books endeavors to publish works that enlighten the mind, nourish the spirit, and challenge the conscience. The publishing arm of the Maryknoll Fathers and Brothers, Orbis seeks to explore the global dimensions of the Christian faith and mission, to invite dialogue with diverse cultures and religious traditions, and to serve the cause of reconciliation and peace. The books published reflect the views of their authors and do not represent the official position of the Maryknoll Society. To learn more about Orbis Books, please visit our website at www.orbisbooks.com.

Published by Orbis Books, Box 302, Maryknoll, NY 10545-0302.

Manufactured in the United States of America

Library of Congress Cataloging-in-Publication Data

Names: Mescher, Marcus, author.
Title: The ethics of encounter : christian neighbor love as a practice of solidarity / Marcus Mescher.
Description: Maryknoll, NY : Orbis, 2020. | Includes bibliographical references and index. |
Summary: "The author provides an ethical framework for the culture of encounter
that Pope Francis calls us to build"—Provided by publisher.
Identifiers: LCCN 2019035996 (print) | LCCN 2019035997 (ebook) | ISBN 9781626983762
(paperback) | ISBN 9781608338405 (ebook)
Subjects: LCSH: Interpersonal relations—Religious aspects—Catholic Church. | Love—
Religious aspects—Catholic Church. | Christian life—Catholic authors. | Christian ethics
Catholic authors. |
Christianity and culture.
Classification: LCC BV4597.52 .M47 2020 (print) | LCC BV4597.52 (ebook) | DDC 241/.4—dc23
LC record available at https://lccn.loc.gov/2019035996
LC ebook record available at https://lccn.loc.gov/2019035997

To Anne,
the most grace-filled encounter of my life

Contents

Acknowledgments

I have wanted to write this book for many years, and it has only been possible thanks to countless encounters, relationships, time spent in prayer and reflection, and conversations with far more people than I could mention here. I have been motivated and molded by so many dedicated witnesses to the gospel, gifted teachers, and selfless mentors, especially at Marquette High and Marquette University, at St. Patrick Parish, St. Mary's Visitation, and St. Joseph Catholic Church in Milwaukee, at Boston College, St. Ignatius Parish in Chestnut Hill, and at Bellarmine Chapel in Cincinnati. My profuse thanks to the Society of Jesus—including both those who are ordained and their lay collaborators—for helping me discover the inherent connection between Christian faith and justice, the meaning of *cura personalis*, and the purpose of living *ad majorem Dei gloriam*. I remain very grateful to Terry Brennan, SJ, Thomas Hughson, SJ, John Naus, SJ, and Walter Stohrer, SJ, in particular. My sincere and hearty thanks to the faculty in the Theology Department and School of Theology and Ministry at Boston College for investing in my formation as a moral theologian and person of faith. In particular, I'm profoundly grateful to Steve Pope, Lisa Cahill, David Hollenbach, SJ, Jim Keenan, SJ, Jim Bretzke, SJ, Tom Massaro, SJ, Richard Lennan, and Dan Harrington, SJ. I deeply appreciate so many friends and conversation partners for sharing their wisdom and support, especially Joseph Simmons, SJ, Cole Mannix, Patrick Nevins, Ellen Modica, Kevin Ahern, Meghan Clark, Michael Jaycox, Katie Grimes, Josh Snyder, Nichole Flores, Conor Kelly, Tobias Winright, Julie Rubio, Mark Allman, Greg Carpinello, Dave Johnson, Jack Goldberg, and Ken Overberg, SJ. It's a treat to work with Jill O'Brien at Orbis Books; thank you for your friendship over the last ten years and for your expertise in shepherding this project toward publication. I would like to thank my colleagues at Xavier University for their steadfast support, my students who continually fill me with awe, and my department, college, and university for the research sabbatical in fall 2018 that allowed me to complete much of this manuscript. I would also like to acknowledge the staff of the Xavier University Library for their swift and helpful assistance in providing access to so many articles and books. I am especially appreciative to Josh Snyder, Jim Bretzke, Chris Pramuk, and Jack Goldberg for their careful review and helpful comments in the process of refining this book. I am truly thankful to my brother-in-law

Matthew Glafcke for sharing his artistic talent in the painting that adorns the cover.

Special thanks to my family, the richest encounters of my life and the surest experiences of faith, hope, and love. In particular, I'm indebted to my parents and siblings for their selfless love and dedicated faith. I am enormously grateful to Jane and Dave Blake for their boundless generosity and enthusiastic support. My deepest love and gratitude belong to Noah, Benjamin, and Grace for the gifts and blessings they are for being precisely who they are. The incredible delight, joy, and love I feel for them—and receive from them—is, I know, just a fraction of what God feels for each and every person. And most of all, my endless love and gratitude to Anne for making everything possible: past, present, and future. Your love means more than I can express. I am inspired by the way you incarnate God's healing tenderness in all you do, especially as a wife, mother, and nurse. You have modeled an "ethic of encounter" long before I imagined such a thing might exist.

Introduction

> Next to the Blessed Sacrament itself,
> your neighbor is the holiest object presented to your senses.[1]

To encounter is to live. Each person is the result of an encounter between one's parents and is subsequently shaped by countless encounters with others. These encounters inform our sense of identity and purpose, beliefs and values, deepest fears and hopes. Some encounters are singular, but most are mundane interactions with the people who share our lives: family and friends, neighbors and co-workers, acquaintances and strangers. Some encounters offer affirmation and support; others place demands on us that test our character and resolve. Some encounters produce wisdom while others leave wounds and varying degrees of pain. Some encounters are risky, dangerous, and even deadly. We also shape others by how we encounter them: our gestures, words, and actions can have long-lasting effects on how others see themselves, ourselves, and the world. Even a single comment or action can send powerful messages to others, confirming or undermining their feeling of welcome and safety. All encounters make change possible and sometimes growth, too. Encounters offer a glimpse that there is always more to learn about ourselves, others, and the world.

Each encounter is also an opportunity to become more attentive and responsive to God who is both transcendent (as infinite mystery) and immanent (as always and everywhere present). Coming face-to-face with another person is an encounter with someone "wonderfully made" (Ps 139:14) in the "image and likeness" of God (Gn 1:26). In this way, encounters are sacraments—visible signs of God's invisible grace—such that encountering another person not only reveals the sacred in our midst but also bears an inexhaustible potential for greater discovery. Because God is love (1 Jn 4:8), encounters have the potential to be an experience of love, an invitation to share in the divine life: a Trinitarian communion of love that is offered, received, and returned. When we encounter others, we encounter God. How we treat others is how we treat God; Dorothy Day reflects, "You love

[1]C. S. Lewis, *The Weight of Glory: And Other Addresses* (New York: HarperOne, 1949), 46.

God as much as the one you love the least."[2] Encounter is a willingness to share life together. It involves both an act of reception, in openness to the goodness around us, and service as self-gift, as we strive to meet the needs of others. Where there is hurt or harm, encounter aspires to reconciliation. Encounter is how we heal ourselves and the world.

Such a soaring vision for encountering others can seem exceedingly out of step with our lived experiences, however. Many encounters seem random, trivial, and fleeting. Some may be pleasant but inconsequential. Others may be awkward or confusing, uncomfortable, or even traumatic.[3] Encounter can produce conflict. The etymological root of the word *encounter* is "to meet as an adversary," a meaning that suggests an encounter is a meeting *against* another person. It implies difference if not a clash; the other is not reducible to another me. Every encounter involves a choice: to engage or ignore, to accept or reject. This is a choice each person makes, especially when encountering someone we do not know, the "other." But do we think of ourselves as the stranger or the "other"? Do we ever feel like the one who does not belong? What is it like to feel vulnerable to and perhaps dependent upon the hospitality and generosity of others? How does this enlarge our imagination of how we can better encounter the other in our midst? Every other is a mystery to me, an other I cannot totally understand. Spouses married for years discover there is more to their partner than they knew before—and might ever fully know—indicating that even in this mystical union of two-becoming-one, otherness remains. To encounter another is to be open to a mystery that extends beyond our reach: there is always more to learn about our self, others, and who we are becoming in and through the encounters that we make and miss.

Just as we are shaped by our encounters with others, we also fail to be shaped by those we never encounter. When we withdraw from others, we also keep others from being affected by an encounter with us, a missed opportunity to learn and grow. Aside from rightfully protecting ourselves from those who would harm us, our lives are impoverished by failing to share life with others. Life in America today is marked by social fragmentation and fragility that keep people separate and sometimes fearful of others, especially those who are different. The result is not only a loss of community or a shared commitment to the common good but also rising rates of alienation and loneliness. Social divisions separate individuals and groups across a number of identities, including but not limited to age, abil-

---

[2]Dorothy Day, *On Pilgrimage* (Grand Rapids, MI: Eerdmans, 1999), 247.

[3]On college campuses, for example, too many intimate encounters become an experience of coercion and even violence. By some estimates, close to 90 percent of unwanted sexual encounters take place in a hookup (under the guise of being harmless experimentation or expression). See Donna Freitas, *The End of Sex: How Hookup Culture Is Leaving a Generation Unhappy, Sexually Unfulfilled, and Confused about Intimacy* (New York: Basic Books, 2013), 49.

ity, sex, gender, sexual orientation, race, ethnicity, nationality, legal status, class, geographic location, political affiliation, and religious belief. In view of the volatile and violent state of the world, Mother Teresa's insight rings true: "If we have no peace, it is because we have forgotten that we belong to each other."

If we understand social separation as sin (a failure to love God by loving our neighbor), then redemption lies in encounter. Insofar as social separation is an illness harming individuals and the community, the cure will not be found in papering over our differences in identity, belief, or experience. Neither does the solution lie in calling for civility and tolerance, since "live and let live" just as easily becomes "live and let die," or at least, "live and let suffer." To tolerate the existence of another person deprived of respect and rights does nothing to provide what they need. Neither does tolerance heal the social separation that makes it hard for us to understand, respect, and appreciate those who are different from us. Rather, the cure lies in restoring innate and equal human dignity, repenting for discrimination and exploitation, recognizing our mutual interdependence, and galvanizing a shared commitment to the common good. This requires rebuilding social trust, and trust is impossible without mutual equality, freedom, respect, and responsibility. Given the delicate and divided state of our social context, this reciprocal concern and commitment seem a distant goal. Around the globe, emotions like sadness, anger, and fear are at the highest rates on record.[4]

In the face of these and other experiences of division and isolation, Pope Francis calls the world to foster a culture of encounter that sees Christ in the other, receives Christ through the other, and tries to be Christ for the other. Francis's vision for a culture of encounter aims to bring people together across differences, to celebrate diversity rather than fear it, to enjoy solidarity as life-togetherness, and to promote the global common good. He proposes that building a culture of encounter cuts through the self-interest, cynicism, and "globalization of indifference" that serve as buffers against widespread suffering and injustice.[5] A culture of encounter is the foundation for peace and reconciliation, built by overcoming isolation and distrust.[6] It is inspired by the gospel, which

---

[4]Sadness, anger, and fear were at record levels in 2017, only to rise higher in 2018. See *Gallup 2019 Global Emotions Report*, https://www.gallup.com.

[5]Pope Francis reflects, "Almost without being aware of it, we end up being incapable of feeling compassion at the outcry of the poor, weeping for other people's pain, and feeling a need to help them, as though all this were someone else's responsibility and not our own. The culture of prosperity deadens us; we are thrilled if the market offers us something new to purchase. In the meantime all those lives stunted for lack of opportunity seem a mere spectacle; they fail to move us" (*Evangelii Gaudium*, no. 54; hereinafter *EG*).

[6]In a homily just a few months into his time as pope, Francis describes the culture of encounter as a "beautiful path towards peace." He states, "If we, each doing our own part, if we do good to others, if we meet there, doing good, and we go slowly, gently, little by little, we will make that culture of encounter: we need that so much. We must meet one another doing good. 'But I don't believe,

> tells us constantly to run the risk of a face-to-face encounter with others, with their physical presence which challenges us, with their pain and their pleas, with their joy that infects us in our close and continuous interaction. True faith in the incarnate Son of God is inseparable from self-giving, from membership in the community, from service, from reconciliation with others. The Son of God, by becoming flesh, summoned us to the revolution of tenderness. (*EG*, no. 88)

This "revolution of tenderness" moves us closer to the other, in a posture of open reception, humility, and solidarity. It gives us the strength to keep from "closing our eyes to our neighbor [that] also blinds us to God."[7] Encounter helps the soul feel its worth and worthiness, reminding us that everyone belongs to the family of God. This means that no one should be considered an outsider or outcast, limits that we sometimes place on those we do not know or like. It also requires efforts to heal stigma and shame and to thwart a "throwaway culture" that degrades and excludes certain individuals, communities, and members of creation.[8] Pope Francis explains:

> When we live out a spirituality of drawing nearer to others and seeking their welfare, our hearts are opened wide to the Lord's greatest and most beautiful gifts. Whenever we encounter another person in love, we learn something new about God. Whenever our eyes are opened to acknowledge the other, we grow in the light of faith and knowledge of God. If we want to advance in the spiritual life, then, we must constantly be missionaries. The work of evangelization enriches the mind and the heart; it opens up spiritual horizons; it makes us more and more sensitive to the workings of the Holy Spirit, and it takes us beyond our limited spiritual constructs. A committed missionary knows the joy of being a spring which spills over and refreshes others. Only the person who feels happiness in seeking the good of others, in desiring their happiness, can be a missionary. (*EG*, no. 272)

Pope Francis makes this appeal—to encounter God and cooperate with God as missionaries—to the world's one billion Catholics and two billion Christians, but this is not an exclusively Christian duty. A culture of encounter draws from biblical themes embraced by Jews, Christians, and Muslims alike. This includes

---

Father, I am an atheist!' But do good: we will meet one another there." Pope Francis, "Pope at Mass: Culture of Encounter Is the Foundation of Peace," Vatican Radio, May 22, 2013, vaticannews.va.

[7]Pope Benedict XVI, *Deus Caritas Est*, no. 230.

[8]Pope Francis, *Laudato Si'*, no. 22.

the work of Jewish philosophers like Martin Buber and Emmanuel Lévinas. Buber is best known for his philosophy of dialogue rooted in relationships of "I-Thou," replacing the "I-It" that renders the other an object rather than a subject.[9] Lévinas described the other's otherness as infinite, a portal into the infinity of the Divine, representing a moral priority that supersedes self-interest.[10] The Jewish discipline of *tikkun olam*, "to heal the world," involves a commitment to reconciling social divisions and unjust inequalities. Hospitality and special concern for the marginalized members of a community have long been central practices for Jewish people: the command to "love your neighbor" is repeated twice in the Jewish Scriptures, whereas the command to love the stranger, the widow, and the orphan—those denied status and security—is repeated at least thirty-six times.[11] Likewise, the Quran is filled with dozens and dozens of verses about honoring the neighbor, showing hospitality to the stranger, and serving those in need.[12] Inspired by verse 21:108, the poet Rumi writes that Muhammad came to bring intimacy and compassion among the people of God.[13] Muslims call on Allah, the Infinitely Good and Most Merciful, "Names with which daily human acts are consecrated" because the "aim of the Quranic revelation has also been to create a compassionate society."[14] As someone passes by, a Muslim prays, "inna lilla hai wa inna illahai rajaeoon," which means "from God we are and to God we must return." A culture of encounter resonates with other spiritual traditions as well. Practitioners of yoga are familiar with the word *namaste*, but they may not know it means "the divine in me recognizes the divine in you." Followers of Buddhism aspire to treat every other person with respect and compassion.[15] A

---

[9]Martin Buber, *I and Thou*, trans. Walter Kaufmann (New York: Touchstone, 1970). I-Thou is manifest through mutual presence, openness, and connection; it receives the freedom and individuality of the other.

[10]Lévinas explains, the "dimension of the divine opens forth from the human face . . . God rises to his supreme and ultimate presence as correlative of the justice rendered unto men." He concludes that the other "is indispensable for my relation with God." He later adds, "The Other who dominates me in his transcendence is thus the stranger, the widow, the orphan, to whom I am [always already] obligated." See Emmanuel Lévinas, *Totality and Infinity: An Essay on Exteriority* (Pittsburgh: Duquesne University Press, 1994), 78, 215.

[11]Jonathan Sacks, *To Heal a Fractured World: The Ethics of Responsibility* (New York: Schocken Books, 2005), 103. Often this command is linked with the reminder to the Israelites that they know what it is like to be a stranger from their years of enslavement in Egypt (see, for example, Ex 23:9 and Dt 10:19).

[12]For example, verse 4:36 of the Quran reads, "Worship Allah and associate nothing with Him, and to parents do good, and to relatives, orphans, the needy, the near neighbor, the neighbor farther away, the companion at your side, the traveler." See also 19:97, 59:9.

[13]Seyyed Hossein Nasr, *The Heart of Islam: Enduring Values for Humanity* (New York: HarperOne, 2004), 204–05.

[14]Ibid., 209.

[15]Thich Nhat Hanh describes approaching the other as you would a family member, or a beloved

culture of encounter can be considered a practice of the Golden Rule, shared by countless religions and moral codes: treat others as you would like to be treated. Perhaps the Platinum Rule provides an improvement: treat others as they would like to be treated.[16]

Pope Francis has repeatedly called on political and religious leaders as well as people of all beliefs and lifestyles to build a culture of encounter. He often describes a culture of encounter as involving the tender caress of mercy, the inclusive fidelity of solidarity, and the persistence to hope for a new future, one where everyone belongs and flourishes.[17] Even though an encounter might be envisioned as taking place between two individuals, a culture of encounter implies a collective approach, a commitment shared by people who facilitate encounter by cultivating dispositions, which become habits, which become normative practices for community life. In this way, a culture of encounter should be envisioned less as dyadic (wherein one person encounters another person), and more as a collective endeavor to break down walls, build bridges, and create opportunities for meaningful gatherings. This is an urgent task in light of how many people express disappointment with their encounters at work or church, in their neighborhoods, and even among friends.[18] Contemplating a culture of encounter is an opportunity to rethink how we connect with others and recalibrate our expectations for ourselves and others. It is also a charge to dismantle the beliefs and practices that generate distrust, division, and isolation. We must shatter the illusions that blind us to our shared belonging and interdependence.

ENCOUNTERING GOD IN AN UNEXPECTED PLACE

When I think about the encounters that have most deeply shaped the person I am today, I am amazed at the variety of circumstances: some encounters were by sheer accident—some by substantial good fortune, others by some degree of misfortune—while others were well planned; some encounters were embedded

---

child. If people welcomed the other as "my darling" this would lead to radical interpersonal and structural change. Among his many books, see Thich Nhat Hanh, *Love in Action: Writings on Nonviolent Social Change* (Berkeley, CA: Parallax Press, 1993).

[16]The Platinum Rule was popularized by Dave Kerpen in his book *The Art of People: 11 Simple People Skills That Will Get You Everything You Want* (New York: Crown Business, 2016). Or consider Wendell Berry's version: treat those downstream as you would have those upstream treat you.

[17]Pope Francis, "The Only Future Worth Building Includes Everyone" [Video file] (April 2017), https://www.ted.com.

[18]According to a 2013 study, three-quarters of respondents expressed dissatisfaction with their friends. See "The State of Friendship in America 2013: A Crisis of Confidence," *Lifeboat*, May 21, 2013.

in long-term relationships, others quite singular and profound. One of the most formative encounters of my life happened in a garbage dump in the Dominican Republic. I was seventeen years old and part of a team of ten students commissioned by my all-boys, Jesuit high school to help build a school for a rural community, Comedero Abajo. To prepare for our time in the *campo*, we learned about Dominican culture in the capital city, Santo Domingo. We visited a lighthouse built to commemorate the five-hundredth anniversary of Christopher Columbus's landing on the island, and shortly after that, we took a trip to the city dump. I did not understand why we were driving through piles of garbage, but soon I began to see that people were living there. The Jesuit priest who led our program, Terry Brennan, SJ, explained that these people were so poor that they were forced to make their homes among other people's refuse. I do not think I have ever felt so distant from people so physically close to me. Here I was, a white, middle-class boy from the suburbs of Milwaukee, riding in an air-conditioned van while dozens of Dominicans hunted through garbage for anything they could eat, use, or sell. Then Fr. Brennan stopped the van and told us to get out. We opened the van doors and were hit with a wave of heat, stench, and smoke. The dump was perpetually on fire to make room for more garbage. The intense heat and smells were sickening, but we were not able to dwell on that for long because in mere moments we were tackled by children who lived there—kids wearing rags who hugged us like we were old friends. They grabbed our hands and turned us into human jungle gyms, and we played tag until we were exhausted, conversing as best we could across the language barrier. After some time, a man approached Fr. Brennan and asked him if he would bless his home. So we walked through the garbage, greeting people as they searched for anything of value amid the smoldering trash. When we reached the man's home, we found a small shelter in a hill of garbage, which was divided into two areas: on the right, some old clothing and linens that made for a sleeping area for his family; on the left, a table, a chair, and a framed picture of the Sacred Heart of Jesus. I did a double take. It was the exact same image that adorned a wall in my home parish.

I am ashamed to admit this, but it took that image of Jesus to feel connected to the people living in the garbage dump, to see them as brothers and sisters, not strangers. The image enabled me to recognize God's presence in the garbage dump and in the people we met. I have never been able to forget that moment or the weight of the discovery that, in the eyes of God, we are all equals who belong to each other. But the man who had invited us into his home already recognized this. As soon as we all squeezed in together, he grabbed Fr. Brennan's hand and another student's hand and insisted, "hermanos, rezemos" (brothers, let us pray). We bowed our heads and recited the Our Father in Spanish. In the van, it felt like we lived in a separate world from these Dominicans. Now, we felt like long-lost family.

I often reflect on that icon of the Sacred Heart and what it might be like for Jesus to look through that image at us, in a world marred by sinful divisions and unjust inequalities. How have we made it so hard to recognize each other as belonging to a single human family, as sharing in the same level of dignity, as bound together by one source and destiny? I imagine God's heart breaking for those cast aside and left behind while others pursue an agenda guided by self-interest and security. What does God want for the people living in this dump? For me? For all of us?

It is not an overstatement to say that that single encounter changed the trajectory of my life. It shaped my college aspirations, the courses I took, how I spent my free time, the conversations I initiated, and the friendships I made. It motivated me to apply to graduate school and a career dedicated to Catholic social thought.[19] I would not be the same person without that encounter; it has been a defining lens for how I see myself and others. Now, personally and professionally, I often evaluate my decisions in light of the people I met in the Dominican Republic, as I feel accountable to them. By carrying them in my heart and mind, I hope that this one-time encounter can initiate a life commitment to practicing solidarity. My purpose in writing this book is to propose how a culture of encounter can become a step along the way toward building a culture of solidarity.[20]

GENERATING SOLIDARITY

I imagine my experience in the Dominican Republic twenty years ago as reflecting what Pope Francis has in mind when he speaks of a culture of encounter. However, Pope Francis has not articulated what a culture of encounter entails at the individual, social, and institutional levels. As the title of this book implies, I am proposing what the ethics of encounter involves in a more comprehensive manner: a framework for practicing encounter that affirms innate and equal human dignity, practices neighbor love, heals social divisions, and fosters social trust through mutual respect and responsibility. I envision this as a dynamic and diverse process with steps advancing from encountering others, to accompanying others, to meaningful exchanges with others, to cultivating the kind of rapport and tenderness that animate an embrace of others, thus building an inclusive belonging and accountability that generates solidarity.

---

[19] I found it particularly inspiring to read Roberto Goizueta's assertion that "the poor deserve the very best scholarship," as he writes in *Caminemos con Jesús: Toward a Hispanic/Latino Theology of Accompaniment* (Maryknoll, NY: Orbis Books, 1995), xi.

[20] Pope Francis has discussed a culture of solidarity in a number of settings, including in his July 25, 2013, Address to the Community of Varginha, Brazil, w2.vatican.va. At times I will use culture of belonging and culture of solidarity interchangeably.

The word *solidarity* is commonly used to convey a sense of unity or strength in numbers. In Catholic social teaching, solidarity takes on a more nuanced meaning as a moral principle rooted in human interdependence. The classic definition of solidarity describes it as "social charity" for the just ordering of society and the universal common good, "that is to say to the good of all and of each individual, because we are all really responsible for all."[21] The common good signifies the social, political, and economic conditions that facilitate the comprehensive flourishing of people and communities. This includes certain rights (like access to education, housing, nutrition, healthcare, and employment) as well as protections from certain deprivations or threats that would undermine the safety, agency, and relationships necessary for peace, integral development, sustainability, and justice. Solidarity is a crucial ingredient of the common good because it fosters the welcome, affinity, agreement, and accountability that aspires for an expansive—even global—common good, instead of a parochial or patriotic agenda motivated more by self-interest or security. In addition to proposing a vision of interdependence, solidarity also requires "learning how to see social problems in new ways that allow for the development of new models and structures" in the political, economic, and social realms.[22]

In addition to these social and structural dimensions, solidarity is also a Christian virtue, a personal disposition and habit of cultivating "total gratuity, forgiveness and reconciliation" for the sake of building ever more inclusive communion in the world.[23] When solidarity is adopted on the individual, social, and structural levels, it "pushes us to build a fully human community through practicing respect for human rights."[24] For this reason, the ethics of encounter entails building a culture of encounter that honors the dignity of each person, fostering right-relationships with others, and moving toward creating a culture of solidarity that results from the just ordering of social, economic, and political systems and structures. The

[21]*Catechism of the Catholic Church*, nos. 1939–41; *Sollicitudo Rei Socialis*, no. 38.

[22]Rebecca Todd Peters, *Solidarity Ethics: Transformation in a Globalized World* (Minneapolis: Fortress Press, 2014), 10. Peters proposes an ethic of solidarity that involves understanding social location and personal privilege, building relationships with people across lines of difference, and engaging in structural change.

[23]Pope John Paul II explains that solidarity is to include everyone, aiming for an encompassing unity that "is a reflection of the intimate life of God, one God in three Persons, is what we Christians mean by the word 'communion.' This specifically Christian communion, jealously preserved, extended and enriched with the Lord's help, is the soul of the Church's vocation to be a 'sacrament,' in the sense already indicated. Solidarity therefore must play its part in the realization of this divine plan, both on the level of individuals and on the level of national and international society" (*Sollicitudo Rei Socialis*, no. 40).

[24]Meghan J. Clark, *The Vision of Catholic Social Thought: The Virtue of Solidarity and the Praxis of Human Rights* (Minneapolis: Fortress Press, 2014), 8.

ultimate goal for the ethics of encounter is to construct a culture of mutual respect and responsibility, healthy interdependence, and inclusive belonging robust enough to overcome exclusion, heal division, and dismantle unjust inequalities.

Solidarity is a key principle in Catholic social thought, a body of teachings drawn from Scripture and church teaching to construct a vision for the integral flourishing of individuals, communities, and the planet. These principles include human dignity and rights, environmental stewardship, the preferential option for the poor, and the common good.[25] However, the great failure of Catholic social teaching (aside from its lamentable reputation for being the church's "best kept secret") is that it exhorts people to adopt universal principles into their life without consistently describing how these ideas can be practiced by individuals and families or integrated into schools, parishes, and other institutions. Out of the many hundreds of pages that constitute the canon of Catholic social teaching, only a few paragraphs are dedicated to material focusing on how to learn and live these tenets. Not only does solidarity become a vague term—often confused with togetherness or unity that defines "us" against "them"—but it gets lost in abstraction without being applied to concrete dispositions, actions, relationships, and structures. *The Ethics of Encounter* provides a blueprint for living Catholic social teaching in everyday life. In the pages that follow, I propose how the ethics of encounter fulfills the duties of Christian neighbor love by practicing solidarity on the personal, social, and structural levels.

STRUCTURE OF THE BOOK

This book proceeds in five steps. Chapter 1 addresses some of the chief experiences of social separation in our country today. This includes hyperpartisanship and polarization, social sorting into lifestyle enclaves, racial tension and segregation, class divides, and other forms of discrimination by sex, gender, sexual orientation, and religion. In a time when too few of our political and religious leaders denounce white supremacy and Christian nationalism, this is an important moment to acknowledge the anxiety, fear, threats, and violence generated by these hateful beliefs and words. Innate human dignity and solidarity are irreconcilable with mantras like "America First!" and worldviews that stifle compassion and refuse responsibility for migrants and refugees forced to flee their homes. These social trends contribute to moral malaise, *anomie*, and a pathological permis-

[25]See, for example, Thomas Massaro, SJ, *Living Justice: Catholic Social Teaching in Action* (Lanham, MD: Rowman & Littlefield, 2016), 81–122.

siveness that grows numb to suffering and injustice.[26] This chapter then pivots to examine some of the root causes of these divisive viewpoints and practices. In particular, I highlight the problem of tolerance for the way it makes room—but fails to take responsibility—for the other. The philosophy of Charles Taylor helps us better understand obstacles to building a culture of encounter in light of the prominence of the "buffered self," a view of people free to disengage from their social context and duties.[27] This trend is linked to the rise of secularism and the declining influence of religion, which has contributed to confusion and disagreement about moral norms. Then, the "buffered self" is contrasted with a "networked self" or the "connected self," in light of the state of hyperconnectivity afforded by digital technology, the internet, and social media. Finally, I consider some of the alienating effects of these digital tools and structures, including the unprecedented rise of social isolation and loneliness.

Chapter 2 draws on the example of the Good Samaritan—among the most well-known stories from the Bible—in order to propose a "theology of neighbor" that guides the dynamic process of moving from encounter, to accompaniment, to exchange, to embrace, and ultimately toward cultivating mutual care and concern and inclusive belonging with others. Popularly, the Good Samaritan is a story about a moral hero, someone who helps another in a personal emergency. But this passage is better understood as an essential way to love God and neighbor, as it is framed in the gospel (Lk 10:25–27). This story makes it impossible to see the world as "us versus them" or "left versus right" (among other labels), instead asserting—with the moral core of the biblical tradition that reminds us that we encounter God through encountering others, including those we might pity, deride, or fear—that there is no "us and them," but only "us." There is a strong coherence between Luke 10:25–37 and Matthew 25:31–46: to emulate the Samaritan by going out of one's way and into the ditch to draw near another in need, a person can see Christ in, receive Christ from, and be Christ to the least and lost. An encounter is an epiphany: Christ meets Christ.[28] Strength and weakness meet. Love and hope can overcome fear and division. A culture of encounter relies on a conversion to the sacrament of our neighbor and a commitment to imagine—in creative fidelity—how we can "go and do likewise" (Lk 10:37) according to our abilities, limitations, and circumstances.

Chapter 3 outlines the ethics of encounter informed by the Samaritan's ac-

---

[26]Émile Durkheim defined "anomie" as "normlessness," a product of excessive individualism and social disconnection. See, for example, *The Division of Labor in Society* (1893) and *Suicide: A Study in Sociology* (1897).

[27]See Charles Taylor, *A Secular Age* (Cambridge, MA: Harvard University Press, 2007).

[28]James Finley, *Merton's Palace of Nowhere* (Notre Dame, IN: Ave Maria Press, 1978), 68.

tions on the road to Jericho in displaying courage, mercy, generosity, humility, and fidelity. Taken together, these five virtues inspire Christian neighbor love to realize boundary-breaking solidarity. The ethics of encounter is also inspired by Gustavo Gutiérrez's analysis of the Samaritan's actions, including his claim that there can be no solidarity without friendship with the poor, marginalized, and vulnerable. Gutiérrez's emphasis on friendship provides a practical framework for assessing the moral demands of solidarity, especially in relation to one's preexisting relationships and responsibilities. By exercising the practical wisdom of prudence, people discern how to order these dispositions and habits in their life by honoring commitments to friends and family while also seeking to forge mutual and inclusive bonds of belonging.

Chapter 4 proposes what it will take to practice the ethics of encounter. This means applying courage, mercy, generosity, humility, and fidelity to attitudes and actions in order to cultivate a culture of encounter with others. This process begins with courage as an interior spiritual discipline of being more amenable to drawing near to others and receiving them. Next, mercy inspires the work necessary to combat implicit bias and more intentionally develop positive attitudes and associations for those who are unfamiliar or unknown. Then, generosity is exercised through clear, effective, and meaningful conversation in order to more graciously engage in conversation across differences. Humility shapes the next step, attending to the kinds of formation that take place in the *habitus* of our interactions and shared practices. Finally, fidelity is illustrated through the example of Fr. Greg Boyle, SJ, and his work with gang members at Homeboy Industries in Los Angeles. Boyle's words and actions provide a living witness for how to mend what is broken in and around us, giving us a powerful template for how a culture of encounter can lead to an inclusive culture of belonging that makes everyone feel safe, valued, respected, and loved.

Chapter 5 presents a vision of the personal and social transformation that is possible when Christian neighbor love and solidarity bring the ethics of encounter into existing relationships and communities of belonging. This begins by considering family life, the foundation for church and society, as well as local businesses and parishes. Next, I outline how a culture of encounter can be mediated through a screen by applying the ethics of encounter to the content and connections engaged through digital technology, the internet, and social media. Finally, it would be tragically nearsighted to restrict the ethics of encounter to human interactions. Given that environmental degradation may well be the most urgent moral crisis of our time, this book concludes by exploring how a culture of belonging can include nonhuman creation. Encountering nature and being a neighbor to nature are vital ways to not only encounter God, but also to construct a more integral solidarity that mends our broken bond with nonhuman creation.

In the end, the ethics of encounter is envisioned as a practice of hope, a way to respond to our vocation to be Christ's ambassadors of reconciliation (2 Cor 5:18–20), healing the wounds in ourselves, our relationships, our communities, and the world. This is what it means to love God and neighbor and to be transformed by God's love at work in the world. Trusting in this love, the ethics of encounter guides the way to building a culture of encounter that becomes a culture of inclusive belonging. This is the path to an undivided solidarity, the practice of right relationships that incarnate who God is in the world.

1

The Divided State of America

In his appeal to join in building a culture of encounter, Pope Francis criticizes personal attitudes like selfishness, greed, and fatalism. Individual dispositions help determine whether someone respectfully and compassionately engages the other or ignores the other with cold indifference.[1] However, human agency is never exercised in a vacuum; beliefs and actions are always shaped by one's social context. The social divisions, polarization, and unjust inequalities that mark our social context are not simply the result of individual failure to connect with neighbors or strangers. The world needs a culture of encounter because of the normative images, messages, systems, and structures that influence individuals' perception, emotion, and cognition. While some communities and institutions promote virtuous moral formation, other communities and institutions impede one's ability to know, desire, and choose what is right, good, true, and just.[2] Virtuous structures enhance dispositions and habits ordered toward love, honesty, courage, and empowerment, whereas vicious structures generate dispositions and habits oriented by anxiety, confusion, distrust, and powerlessness. These personal attitudes are acted upon and act into broader systems and structures that perpetuate social separation and subjugation, showing the cyclical relationship between personal and social sin.

This chapter addresses several of the most pressing examples of discrimination and division as well as the social analysis to unearth their root causes. A robust culture of encounter has to move past individuals exercising empathy and

---

[1]Martin Luther King lamented the "appalling silence of the good people" as among the most tragic obstacles to justice. See "Address at the Fourth Annual Institute on Nonviolence and Social Change at Bethel Baptist Church" (December 3, 1959).

[2]Daniel J. Daly offers a perceptive assessment of structures that are hospitable and hostile to virtue in his essay, "Structures of Virtue and Vice," *New Blackfriars* 92, no. 1039 (2011): 341–57.

compassion, civility and tolerance; these are necessary but woefully inadequate for mending broken relationships and communities. This chapter unpacks a range of social issues, pointing to the need to build a culture of encounter, which are also obstacles for practicing Christian neighbor love and solidarity. It moves forward in five steps: first, by discussing several key examples of social division and their impacts on a variety of groups in America; second, by considering the effects of rising insecurity contributing to the "tumbleweed society," as argued by sociologist Allison Pugh; third, by asserting that tolerance has devolved into a laissez-faire permissiveness undermining mutual respect and responsibility; fourth, by evaluating the cultural anthropology characterized by the "buffered self" in the philosophy of Charles Taylor; and fifth, by contrasting the "buffered self" with a vision of the "networked self" in light of the prominence of digital technology and social media. The chapter concludes by exploring whether and how a culture of encounter can resist the "technocratic paradigm" that conditions us to use technology for coercion and maximizing profit, thus exacerbating social division, anxiety, and ennui.[3]

A FRAYING SOCIAL FABRIC

Social divisions and unjust inequalities have plagued every culture, but American society is currently mired in acute social separation, polarization and hyperpartisanship, deteriorating race relations, increasing class divides, tensions around gender and sexual orientation, rising nationalism and xenophobia, and myriad additional causes of insecurity and distrust. The result is an unraveling social fabric, fractured civic body, and mounting frustration at the ubiquitous "us versus them" tribalism.

This is especially true in the current political sphere, where people, issues, and entire states are categorized into "red" versus "blue." Following the 2016 election, 85 percent of Americans reported feeling that the country is sharply divided.[4] Two years later, nearly nine in ten Americans lamented that the nation remains more divided than at any point in their lifetime.[5] Much of this tension is exacerbated by hyperpartisanship that shifts political differences into disdain for those on the other side of the party line. In a recent poll, roughly half of Democrats described Republicans as ignorant (54 percent) and spiteful (44 percent) while a similar proportion of Republicans described Democrats as ignorant (49 percent) and

---

[3]Pope Francis, *Laudato Si'*, nos. 109–12.

[4]Jennifer Agiesta, "A Nation Divided, and Is It Ever," CNN, November 27, 2016, https://www.cnn.com.

[5]Stephen Hawkins, Daniel Yudkin, Míriam Juan-Torres, and Tim Dixon, "Hidden Tribes: A Study of America's Polarized Landscape" (2018), https://hiddentribes.us.

spiteful (54 percent). Moreover, 61 percent of Democrats labeled Republicans racist, sexist, or bigoted, while 31 percent of Republicans applied these terms to Democrats. Perhaps most concerning of all, more than 20 percent of Republicans (23 percent) and Democrats (21 percent) called members of the other party "evil." Only 4 percent of both parties think the other side is fair, and even fewer describe them as thoughtful or kind.[6] Political activity has become obsessed with winning, eclipsing a shared commitment to the common good.[7]

Polarization is the result of the tug-of-war that tries to accumulate power over one's detestable opponents. Polarization might be considered the "defining characteristic of modern American politics," but most Americans "do not like polarization" and prefer to avoid conflict.[8] Polarization intensifies conflict, and partisanship colors how people see themselves and others, creating categories of "insiders" and "outsiders." When party affiliation becomes a person's "megaidentity," winning and losing become personal. This generates greater bias, intolerance, and anger at those on the other side of the party line.[9] Bipartisan cooperation looks more like weakness, especially as more Americans consume media on television and online that caters to their worldviews. Republicans and Democrats watch different TV networks, losing opportunities to discuss common content, create overlapping worldviews, and collaborate in problem-solving.[10] This also creates substantial "perception gaps" between what people assume about members of the other party and what folks across the political aisle actually believe.[11]

It is little surprise, then, that both Republicans and Democrats prefer to spend time with members of their own party and expect it would be easier to get along with a stranger if they were a member of their own party.[12] Pundits play on political anger and anxiety, training Americans to become more emotionally reactive than to thoughtfully ponder the risks and rewards of certain policies. Conflict-based content draws more viewers than civil conversation and emotional arousal sparks certain content to go viral, but "incivility breeds distrust," reinforcing the distance between who counts as "us" versus those demonized as "them."[13] Normalizing

---

[6]Kim Hart, "Most Democrats See Republicans as Racist, Sexist," Axios, November 12, 2018, https://www.axios.com.

[7]Lilliana Mason, *Uncivil Agreement: How Politics Became Our Identity* (Chicago: University of Chicago Press, 2018), 11–12.

[8]James E. Campbell, *Polarized: Making Sense of a Divided America* (Princeton, NJ: Princeton University Press, 2016), 117, 126.

[9]Mason, *Uncivil Agreement*, 14, 22.

[10]Ibid., 43–44.

[11]Interestingly, those with advanced degrees are even more likely to fall prey to serious misperception about members of the other party. See https://perceptiongap.us/.

[12]Mason, *Uncivil Agreement*, 54–55.

[13]Diana C. Mutz, *In-Your-Face Politics: The Consequences of Uncivil Media* (Princeton, NJ: Princeton University Press, 2015), 43–45, 194.

incivility makes it easier to endure cruel language that casts shame. This heightens insecurity and drives people to seek protection within their chosen tribe. Political action is powered less by one's values than by "the sense that there are other people on [my] side."[14] Partisanship becomes a feedback loop of tribalism that feasts on and spits out "us versus them" antagonism.

This takes the shape of a new kind of prejudice: partyism. Partyism represents a rancor that eclipses other forms of bias; Americans report they would be against their son or daughter marrying someone from the other party and would justify withholding a scholarship from a qualified person from the other party even more than one from another race.[15] This kind of partisan bias provides motivation for processing information about their own party in a positive light while ignoring or rejecting information that might critique their own party and worldview, a form of "motivated reasoning" that confirms their preexisting beliefs.[16] This means that more Americans are confined to echo chambers that expose them to agreeable views and voices, reinforcing the perception that they have reason and a majority on their side. It becomes harder and harder to recognize the validity of other perspectives and to respect those with whom we disagree.

Social separation makes it easier to demonize others across differences, as one rarely encounters someone who looks, thinks, or acts differently. This has been the trend in America for decades, as the "collapse of the American community" has resulted in the decline of social trust.[17] Social capital, or the connective tissue of community, has decreased dramatically since the 1950s, when social bonds were forged through playing bridge or bowling with neighbors, participating in sewing circles, and attending meetings for the Rotary Club, Knights of Columbus, or PTA. Even if people were living in ethnically or religiously homogenous neighborhoods, their interactions in these social clubs and meetings created a diverse social bond.[18] Since Robert Putnam's work to diagnose the decline of social capital nearly twenty years ago, "social sorting" has been on the rise, creating homogenous lifestyle enclaves, "geographies of similar manners, sentiments, and interests."[19] Fewer Americans encounter others across differences—except at

[14]Mason, *Uncivil Agreement*, 121. Mason explains, "We take political action, potentially making real political changes, because we feel close to particular groups of people and want them (and therefore ourselves) to be winners" (ibid., 126).

[15]Marc Hetherington and Jonathan Weiler, *Prius or Pickup? How the Answers to Four Simple Questions Explain America's Great Divide* (Boston: Houghton Mifflin Harcourt, 2018), 119.

[16]Ibid., 134.

[17]Robert Putnam, *Bowling Alone: The Collapse and Revival of American Community* (New York: Simon and Schuster, 2000), 20–21.

[18]Ibid., 23, 103–4.

[19]Bill Bishop, *The Big Sort: Why the Clustering of Like-Minded America Is Tearing Us Apart* (Boston: Mariner, 2009), 71.

work[20]—because of the loss of "middle ring" relationships between the intimate ties of family and friends and the more distant ties of acquaintances.[21] The rise of "homophily" means that Americans are living increasingly segregated lives, not only by race or ethnicity but also by political and economic ideology.[22] This is also true by class, as economic inequality increases. Putnam describes this as "incipient class apartheid," resulting in the kind of segregation that makes it hard for most Americans to know "how the other half lives."[23]

In a time of unprecedented wealth accumulating into the hands of a select few, a "new gilded age" means that the top 1 percent of families take in more than twenty-six times as much as a family in the bottom 99 percent.[24] In addition to this staggering wealth inequality, the economic elite are becoming increasingly socially isolated from the rest of the country. For example, many of the wealthiest Americans have sorted themselves into "superzip clusters" that are largely homogenous in economic, educational, cultural, and in many cases, political terms.[25] American exceptionalism erodes American community, in part because of the "secession of the successful" and because fewer encounters with others across differences makes it much harder to understand and trust others who are different.[26] A "get ahead" mentality endorses fighting your way to the top and makes everyone else a rival if not an outright obstacle to success. In fact, some studies show that as wealth increases, empathy, compassion, and ethical behavior decrease.[27] Self-interest and greed become obstacles to social bonds and shared duties. These trends give credence to the claim that the most powerful Americans "increasingly trade on

[20]Maxine Najle and Robert P. Jones, "The Fate of Pluralism in a Divided Nation," Public Religion Research Institute, February 19, 2019, https://www.prri.org/

[21]Marc J. Dunkelman, *The Vanishing Neighbor: The Transformation of American Community* (New York: W. W. Norton, 2014), 97.

[22]Bishop, *The Big Sort*, 12–13.

[23]Robert Putnam, *Our Kids: The American Dream in Crisis* (New York: Simon & Schuster, 2015), 39, 41. Moreover, Putnam finds evidence of "increasing endogamy" (marrying within one's own social class), which means that "rich Americans and poor Americans are living, learning, and raising children in increasingly separate and unequal worlds, removing stepping-stones to upward mobility," and as result, "members of the upper middle class are less likely to have firsthand knowledge of the lives of poor kids and thus are unable even to recognize the growing opportunity gap" (ibid., 40–41).

[24]Estelle Sommeiller and Mark Price, "The New Gilded Age," Economic Policy Institute, July 29, 2018, https://www.epi.org.

[25]Nearly 40 percent of those living in these "superzip" clusters abide in New York, Washington, DC, Los Angeles, and San Francisco. See Charles Murray, *Coming Apart: The State of White America, 1960–2010* (New York: Crown Forum, 2012), 84–94.

[26]Ibid., 241–44, 252–55. Murray points out that social trust is "eroded by ethnic diversity," inauspicious for the future in light of demographic shifts toward majority-minority status shortly after 2040.

[27]See, for example, Paul K. Piff, Daniel M. Stancato, Stéphane Côté, Rodolfo Mendoza-Denton, and Dacher Keltner, "Higher Social Class Predicts Increased Unethical Behavior," *Proceedings of the National Academy of Sciences of the United States of America* 109, no. 11 (March 13, 2012): 4086–91.

the perks of their privileged positions without regard to the seemliness of that behavior," abdicating their responsibilities to the common good.[28]

On the other end of the spectrum, a growing number of Americans are simply trying to survive. One hundred forty-three million Americans live below or near the federal poverty line, and as this number grows, the percentage of impoverished citizens increases from 20 to almost 50 percent.[29] Christians are twice as likely as non-Christians to blame the poor for their state in life.[30] This judgment points to a failure to understand the complex circumstances and structural inequalities that often contribute to economic deprivation. For example, wages have not increased in proportion to inflation or costs of living since the 1960s.[31] Many employees have seen pensions cut, retirement funds slashed, and health care costs skyrocket.[32] Forty percent of Americans do not have the necessary funds to cover an unexpected expense of four hundred dollars.[33] A 2017 CareerBuilder survey found that almost 80 percent of US workers live paycheck to paycheck to make ends meet. More than one in four workers do not set aside any savings each month. Three in four say they are in debt, and more than half think that will always be true. A majority of minimum-wage workers say they have to work more than one job to make ends meet.[34] Americans are living with more debt than ever before, as student loan debt, car loan debt, credit card debt, and mortgage debt have collectively surpassed thirteen trillion dollars.[35] That does not include medical debt, a burden carried by one in five Americans and the leading cause of personal bankruptcy in the United States.[36] These financial burdens push people to work harder, caught in a vicious cycle of production and consumption. Time for leisure and play seems expendable, even while time for rest is essential for mental health and emotional wellbeing. All of this contributes to anxiety at home, insecurity at work, and an overall sense of scarcity that makes generosity or hospitality to strangers too much to expect. Politicians play on these insecurities to

---

[28]Murray, *Coming Apart*, 298.

[29]Tavis Smiley and Cornel West, *The Rich and the Rest of Us: A Poverty Manifesto* (New York: SmileyBooks, 2012), 9.

[30]Julie Zauzmer, "Christians Are More Than Twice as Likely to Blame a Person's Poverty on Lack of Effort," *Washington Post*, August 3, 2017, www.washingtonpost.com.

[31]Drew Desilver, "For Most U.S. Workers, Real Wages Have Barely Budged in Decades," Pew Research Center, August 7, 2018.

[32]Zachary Tracer, "Rising Health-Insurance Costs Are Eating into Employees' Paycheck Gains," Bloomberg, September 19, 2017.

[33]Anna Bahney, "40% of Americans Can't Cover a $400 Emergency Expense," CNN, May 22, 2018.

[34]"Living Paycheck to Paycheck Is a Way of Life for Majority of U.S. Workers, According to New CareerBuilder Survey," CareerBuilder, August 24, 2017.

[35]Ben Lane, "Americans Now Have More Debt Than Ever Before," HousingWire, August 14, 2018.

[36]Chris Coffey, "Nearly 1 in 5 Americans Has Crippling Medical Debt," NBC Chicago, March 12, 2018.

justify xenophobia and "America First" policies that boost agendas oriented by self-interest and exclusion.

These examples of social and economic separation contribute to racial segregation and inequality as well. Racial tension and injustice continue to persist in our country. A few years ago, researchers found that three-quarters of white Americans do not have a single black friend, while two-thirds of black Americans say they do not have any white friends.[37] This should not be all that shocking, in light of the geographical segregation by race that persists in America. The marginalization of people of color—especially African Americans, Latinos, and indigenous people—means that these families have access to only a fraction of the resources, freedom of choice, and accumulated wealth as compared to most white Americans.[38] People of color are more stuck than mobile in terms of social, economic, and political rights.[39] They also endure other effects of racism on a daily basis, which pushes them to the peripheries of status and power.

Discrimination and injustice are also experienced by people because of their sex, gender, and sexual orientation. For example, women have long been deprived of equal rights in social and economic sectors. Many women are responsible for full-time care for children, which is rarely compensated. A growing number also care for parents and other family members, work that typically receives low remuneration. Occupational segregation persists, limiting women in a variety of professional fields. Wage gaps persist for women compared to men, as well as women of color compared to white women. While some progress has been made, research shows that pay parity for white women will not be achieved until the year 2059. Black women will have to wait until 2119, and Hispanic women will have to wait until 2224 for pay equity to be extended to them.[40] Women are 38 percent more likely to live in poverty than men. Two-thirds of poor seniors are women, and one-third of families led by a single mother live in poverty.[41] Women face even worse conditions in other countries.[42]

The #MeToo movement has revealed the harassment women face in a variety of settings. Women are typically marginalized from free and equal exercise of

---

[37]Daniel Cox, Juhem Navarro-Rivera, and Robert P. Jones, "Race and Americans' Social Networks," Public Religion Research Institute, August 28, 2014.

[38]Angela Hanks, Danyelle Solomon, and Christian E. Weller, "Systemic Inequality," Center for American Progress, February 21, 2018.

[39]Richard Florida, "The Geography of America's Mobile and 'Stuck,' Mapped," City Lab, March 5, 2019.

[40]Institute for Women's Policy Research, https://iwpr.org/issue/employment-education-economic-change/pay-equity-discrimination/.

[41]Kayla Patrick, "Poverty among Women and Families," National Women's Law Center, September 2017.

[42]Christine Firer Hinze, *Glass Ceilings and Dirt Floors: Women, Work, and the Global Economy* (Mahwah, NJ: Paulist Press, 2015).

power and influence, are often made to feel unsafe or out of place, and are forced to deal with a variety of sexist double standards. For example, boys and men are socialized to be strong, assertive, aggressive, ambitious, and outspoken. We compliment men with these traits for their courage, character, and leadership. However, when women share these same characteristics, they are often labeled as power hungry, obsessive, bossy, pushy, and vain. Derogatory words like "bitch" or "feminazi" are intended to "put women in their place," that is, to force them to be polite, deferential, and service oriented. Our social context has desensitized us to the scandalous reality that so many women feel unsafe in so many places, including but not limited to home and work. Women disproportionately endure stalking and unwanted sexual advances. One in three women will suffer sexual violence and one in five women will be raped in their lifetime.[43] Thirty-eight million American women have experienced intimate partner violence; every day, three women are killed by a current or former male partner in the United States, one of the reasons why the United States is among the ten most dangerous countries in the world for women.[44] Black women experience intimate partner violence at rates 35 percent higher than white women. Ten million children are exposed to domestic violence every year.[45] Globally, women are more likely to be killed by an intimate partner or family member than a stranger.[46]

LGBTQ individuals widely endure prejudice, exclusion, and unequal legal protection. For example, more than fifteen states do not extend nondiscrimination laws to cover all who identify as LGBTQ.[47] LGBTQ individuals often face bullying in school, work, churches, and even families. Churches that are expected to affirm innate human dignity and inclusive solidarity are sometimes the reason why people express heterosexist and homophobic views. Some congregations and schools fire their LGBTQ employees while turning a blind eye to the sins of their cis-gender, heterosexual employees.[48] Of the one-and-a-half million teens experiencing homelessness, 40 percent are LGBTQ. Forty-six percent left home because they were rejected for their sexual orientation or gender identity, and 32 percent left to flee physical, emotional, or sexual abuse at home.[49] One in five

[43]National Sexual Violence Resource Center, https://www.nsvrc.org/statistics.

[44]David Brennan, "U.S. in Top 10 Most Dangerous Countries for Women, Report Finds," *Newsweek*, June 26, 2018.

[45]Alanna Vaglios, "30 Shocking Domestic Violence Statistics That Remind Us It's an Epidemic," *Huffington Post*, October 23, 2014.

[46]UNODC, *Global Study on Homicide 2018* (2018).

[47]Rich Bellis, "Here's Everywhere in the US Where You Can Still Get Fired for Being Gay or Trans," Fast Company, August 28, 2017.

[48]Michael O'Loughlin, "Firing of LGBT Catholic Church Workers Raises Hard (and New) Questions," *America*, February 13, 2018.

[49]Jaimie Seaton, "Homeless Rates for LGBT Teens Are Alarming, but Parents Can Make a Difference," *Washington Post*, March 29, 2017.

LGBTQ youth attempted suicide in the past year, an indictment of the shame and stigma that result from widespread discrimination and rejection.[50] Given that sex, gender, sexual orientation, race, ethnicity, and class overlap, there are some people who experience far more discrimination and injustice because of these complex and interrelated categories of identity.[51]

Hate crimes have increased 17 percent since 2016, targeting racial, ethnic, and religious minorities.[52] Anti-Semitism and Islamophobia continue to rise as well.[53] Migrants, refugees, and those seeking asylum are being turned away from our national borders, separated from family members, and detained indefinitely in appalling conditions that some compare to concentration camps.[54] Indifference to the plight of noncitizens betrays repeated commands in Scripture to provide hospitality to strangers (see, for example, Dt 10:19, Lv 19:33–34, Mt 25:35, Rom 12:13, and Heb 13:1–3). While some people and groups are outraged and grow more outspoken against such exclusion, violence, and injustice, our fraying social fabric is making it harder to foster the agreement and accountability necessary for creating change.

AN AGE OF INSECURITY

If people feel anxious and helpless, they will more readily turn to rage and blame. Sociologist Allison Pugh identifies economic anxiety as a major contributor to our fraying social fabric, which she describes in terms of a "tumbleweed society" that leaves people feeling destabilized and displaced. For example, a lack of job security impacts how we think of men who have traditionally been considered the breadwinners for families. It also creates new challenges for women, who may have more economic autonomy and flexibility, but still shoulder most of the responsibilities for dependent care. Overall, economic insecurity thwarts social mobility and makes it more difficult for people to decide whether to leave or endure unhealthy relationships at home. In spite of mounting stress at home and work, companies and the state mostly escape blame. Employees come to expect less from their employers and largely feel "not anger but shame, not indignation

---

[50]"National Survey on LGBTQ Youth Mental Health 2019," The Trevor Project, https://www.thetrevorproject.org.

[51]Kimberlé Crenshaw, "The Urgency of Intersectionality" [Video file] (October 2016), https://www.ted.com.

[52]John Eligon, "Hate Crimes Increase for Third Consecutive Year, FBI Reports," *New York Times*, November 13, 2018.

[53]Randy Rosenthal, "Why We Need to Pay Attention to the Rise of Anti-Semitism in America Now," *Washington Post*, February 15, 2019.

[54]Jonathan M. Katz, "Not Every Concentration Camp Is Auschwitz," *Slate*, June 20, 2018.

but grief, not outrage but sorrow."[55] More and more people seek to be distracted or disconnected from these negative emotions and desperate conditions. To cope, they build a "moral wall" between work and home, trying to focus on what they can control at home, seeing how little power they have to determine their future at work.[56]

A common finding is that Americans facing social change and economic uncertainty find refuge in a "circle the wagons" mentality that turns inward on the family unit. They seek comfort in "a belief in the righteousness of the family,"[57] focusing on "traditional family morality,"[58] that reduces the scope of moral concern to the domestic household. This affects how parents interact with their children and what they expect from their children: whereas well-educated and job-secure parents have the freedom and resources to cultivate creativity, self-direction, and self-esteem in their children, these "promotive" strategies for success are not shared by job-insecure parents who focus more on discipline, conformity, and other "preventative strategies" to keep their children out of trouble.[59] This, too, exacerbates social separation, since affluent parents are inclined to overindulge their children, while parents who are struggling financially can barely provide for their own. To reduce their mental and emotional load, affluent parents depersonalize others, which leads to estrangement. This makes it easier to ignore the needs of others as well as social duties that extend beyond the family unit. We expect others to deliver on these responsibilities, sometimes even outsourcing the "emotional labor" of caring about other people.[60]

On the one hand, this makes perfect sense: when life is unpredictable, it is necessary to focus on what you can control. But on the other hand, if we have more and more families that prioritize the good of their own unit ahead of everyone else, we fall prey to what Edward Banfield described sixty years ago: "amoral familism" that maximizes the self-interest of one's own family and assumes that other families are doing the same.[61] Americans are becoming less aware of the needs of others and their obligation to others or are actively "redefining and reducing" expecta-

---

[55]Allison J. Pugh, *The Tumbleweed Society: Working and Caring in an Age of Insecurity* (New York: Oxford University Press, 2015), 32.

[56]Ibid., 51.

[57]Jennifer Sherman, *Those Who Work, Those Who Don't: Poverty, Morality, and Family in Rural America* (Minneapolis: University of Minnesota Press, 2009), 187.

[58]Tex Sample, *Working Class Rage: A Field Guide to White Anger and Pain* (Nashville: Abingdon, 2018), 48.

[59]Putnam, *Our Kids*, 121.

[60]Arlie Russell Hochschild, *The Outsourced Self: Intimate Life in Market Times* (New York: Metropolitan Books, 2012), 55–56, 177–78.

[61]Edward C. Banfield, *The Moral Basis of a Backward Society* (Glencoe, IL: Free Press, 1958), 85.

tions for and from them.[62] In the end, this reflects an overall trend of "shrinking understandings of what we owe each other."[63]

This produces a social withdrawal, a growing trend of isolation and loneliness. Nearly 30 percent of Americans report feeling lonely, a figure that continues to rise in the face of so many ways to connect, including through digital technology and social media.[64] Among older adults, this rate reaches over 40 percent, almost three times higher than in the 1970s.[65] This is even widespread among young people, who seem like "virtual hermits," tethered to their screens, still feeling alone.[66] The collapse of community means that loneliness is taking root in new places. Hyperpartisanship and polarization leave people feeling overwhelmed and disempowered. Attacks from political and religious leaders leave people in minority groups feeling not only rejected and excluded, but afraid for their safety and sequestered from the interactions and status of community life. Loneliness results in "painful feelings of not belonging and disconnectedness from and abandonment by others."[67] Feeling lonely is desolation; it is akin to feeling unworthy, unimportant, and unloved. It contributes to illness and early death.[68]

Loneliness is a personal and social experience of exclusion. It is the exact opposite of a culture of encounter that seeks to move from accompaniment to exchange to embrace to inclusive belonging. Loneliness is the absence of meaningful connection, a kind of displacement that can leave one feeling lost, unsupported, and unsure of one's identity and purpose.[69] It is a function of a "tumbleweed society," the result of feeling insecure and unmoored from community life. Paying attention to loneliness is important not only to heed the mental and emotional state of a growing number of Americans but also to consider the cultural rituals, exercise of power, covert and overt tensions and conflict, and marginalization that contribute to this rising trend of loneliness.[70] Individualism,

---

[62]Pugh, *The Tumbleweed Society*, 80. Pugh finds evidence of new language to create different categories of relationships and responsibilities, like "bar friends" versus "real friends" (ibid., 82–83).

[63]Ibid., 86.

[64]Olga Khazan, "How Loneliness Begets Loneliness," *The Atlantic*, April 6, 2017.

[65]Michael Harris, *Solitude: In Pursuit of a Singular Life in a Crowded World* (London: Random House, 2017), 32.

[66]"The Youth of Today," *The Economist*, January 13, 2018, 52.

[67]Gerald Arbuckle, Loneliness: Insights for Healing in a Fragmented World (Maryknoll, NY: Orbis Books: 2018), xiv.

[68]Julianne Holt-Lunstad, Timothy B. Smith, Mark Baker, Tyler Harris, and David Stephenson, "Loneliness and Social Isolation as Risk Factors for Mortality: A Meta-Analytic Review," *Perspectives on Psychological Science* 10, no. 2 (2015): 227–37.

[69]John T. Cacioppo and William Patrick, *Loneliness: Human Nature and the Need for Social Connection* (New York: W. W. Norton, 2008).

[70]Arbuckle, *Loneliness*, 33–40. See also Carol Graham, *Happiness for All? Unequal Hopes and Lives in Pursuit of the American Dream* (Princeton, NJ: Princeton University Press, 2017).

self-interest, and competition contribute to the "rat race" that leave people feeling like they are fighting against the other, rather than able to receive and learn from the other.[71] How can we expect Americans to understand the needs of others and deliver on their obligations to others when they have less and less interaction with those who are other? To be fair, these concerns about social separation are not new. Twenty years ago, Robert Putnam lamented the decline of "social capital" necessary to bridge and bond individuals in social networks, where people are formed by norms like reciprocity and trust. Social capital is vital for overcoming self-interest, "us versus them" categories, and "civic malaise" that undermine social commitments.[72] Around the same time, Gertrude Himmelfarb warned that pervasive social divisions create an "ethics gap" causing "moral disarray."[73] This has yielded the *anomie* Durkheim warned of more than a century ago, a loss of social connection necessary for the norms that rely on shared agreement and accountability.[74] Permissiveness is destroying the virtue of tolerance.

THE PROBLEM OF TOLERANCE

Not every analysis of American culture finds division and distrust on the rise. Sociologist Alan Wolfe argues instead that America is united and stabilized by its middle class, insisting that concerns about class inequality and social division are overblown. He proposes that middle-class Americans are united by a "quiet faith" and "morality writ small" that place high value on individual freedom, personal accountability, nonjudgmentalism, and modest virtue.[75] He explains that self-interest and disinterested tolerance for others helps individuals avoid conflict. Wolfe summarizes this shared morality in a hypothetical "Eleventh Commandment:" "Thou shalt not judge."[76] His findings are corroborated by subsequent reports that show Americans are shifting to increasingly more permissive moral judgments.[77] A morality of "do no harm" eclipses one that emphasizes delivering on obligations to others.

---

[71]Philip Slater writes, "each race leads only to a new one," in *Pursuit of Loneliness: American Culture at the Breaking Point* (Boston: Beacon, 1990), 9.

[72]Putnam, *Bowling Alone*, 20–21.

[73]Gertrude Himmelfarb, *One Nation, Two Cultures* (New York: Alfred A. Knopf, 1999), 116–17.

[74]Émile Durkheim, *The Division of Labor in Society* (1893) and *Suicide: A Study in Sociology* (1897).

[75]Alan Wolfe, *One Nation, After All: What Middle-Class Americans Really Think About God, Country, Family, Racism, Welfare, Immigration, Homosexuality, Work, the Right, the Left, and Each Other* (New York: Penguin Books, 1998), 290. Wolfe explains that a "morality writ small" is middle-class morality that "should be modest in its ambitions and quiet in its proclamations."

[76]Ibid., 54.

[77]Jeffrey M. Jones, "Americans Hold Record Liberal Views on Most Moral Issues," Gallup, May 11, 2017.

The problem with this kind of "live and let live" mentality is that it can become "live and let suffer" or even "live and let die." This trend seems to be growing even more prominent when looking at the moral views of young people, many of whom invoke an "I do me, you do you" credo that takes on the appearance of tolerance but actually promotes moral relativism. Moral relativism, by definition, means that each person gets to decide what is true and good. This raises the question of whether it is possible to pursue the common good, a shared vision of the good life, or even "speak of a community at all."[78] Christian Smith, drawing on data from the National Study of Youth and Religion, finds ample evidence that moral individualism is common among young people today, as 60 percent of emerging adults indicated that morality is a matter of personal choice or opinion, and one-third said they did not know what makes anything morally right or wrong.[79] Smith and his colleagues also report high rates of civic disengagement among young Americans. Sixty-nine percent said they were "not political in any way," compared to only 4 percent who considered themselves to be actively political, a group that was almost exclusively male.[80] Radical nonjudgmentalism and tolerance undermine basic moral norms necessary for communal living; without agreement and accountability, morality becomes a free-for-all. Social disengagement and civic withdrawal become symptoms of self-interest and self-preservation that undermine moral norms, social responsibility, and the common good.[81] In other words, the prominence of tolerance and nonjudgmentalism weakens social courage and endangers moral duty. The status quo lets too many of us absolve ourselves from the unjust policies and practices that cause the suffering of our neighbors near and far.

Nonetheless, Americans value tolerance. They report higher tolerance for hate speech,[82] even as more grow weary with the silencing effects of "political

---

[78]David Hollenbach, *The Common Good and Christian Ethics* (Cambridge: Cambridge University Press, 2002), 22.

[79]See Christian Smith et al., *Lost in Transition: The Dark Side of Emerging Adulthood* (Oxford: Oxford University Press, 2011), 21, 36.

[80]Smith and colleagues observe that this data was collected in 2008, a year that is typically touted for empowering youth involvement in politics. National Study of Youth and Religion data reveal that most emerging adults feel "disempowered, apathetic, and sometimes even despairing when it comes to the larger social, civic, and political world beyond their own private lives." See ibid., 196, 206–08.

[81]Wolfe states, "Society requires a common morality capable of softening and guiding the unchecked desires of its citizens *and* a system of rights capable of protecting minorities and enhancing the self-development of all. Yet neither conservatives nor liberals generally believe that people themselves can be trusted to play much of a role in finding the balance between those two imperatives." Alan Wolfe, *Moral Freedom: The Search for Virtue in a World of Choice* (New York: W. W. Norton, 2002), 15–16.

[82]Richard Wike, "5 Ways Americans and Europeans Are Different," Pew Research Center, April 19, 2016.

correctness."[83] When Americans lament the state of moral values in our country, a lack of tolerance is cited as the most important moral problem.[84] American parents are united in what values they want to pass on to their children: a strong work ethic and personal responsibility come first, followed by socially oriented values like empathy, helping others, and tolerance.[85] Tolerance may be widely recognized as a social good, but it remains mostly vague and flaccid. It raises serious questions about the limits of restraint and how best to respond to objectionable beliefs or actions. Calls for tolerance can blunt prophetic words and actions seeking justice. Martin Luther King Jr. explained that the greatest obstacle to the Civil Rights Movement was not the KKK but "the white moderate who is more devoted to order than to justice . . . who constantly says, 'I agree with you in the goal you seek, but I can't agree with your methods of direct action.' "[86] In response to critics of the "Catonsville Nine" (who stole 378 draft files from the draft board in Catonsville, Maryland, and, in a liturgical ritual, burned them with homemade napalm on May 17, 1968), the Jesuit priest and peace activist Dan Berrigan, SJ, stated: "Forgive us, dear friends, for this fracture of good order, for the crime of burning paper, instead of children." When tolerance becomes the greatest good, it can become a totalizing force to coerce people to conform, to be complacent with an unjust status quo. Excessive tolerance can mute moral outrage and repudiate noncompliance, sanitizing and endorsing cooperation with evil. This vicious form of tolerance risks violating the freedom of conscience, the "most secret core and sanctuary" of the individual where one hears the voice of God.[87]

Indiscriminate tolerance fosters moral compromise, similar to relativism that is indifferent to and complicit with what is false or evil.[88] Some lament that widespread tolerance of malice and schadenfreude has actually served to make American society irredeemably intolerant.[89] For example, social media is plagued by public hatemongering and shaming without much resistance from individu-

---

[83]Emily Ekins, "The State of Free Speech and Tolerance in America," Cato Institute, October 31, 2017.

[84]Alyssa Brown, "Americans' Negativity about U.S. Moral Values Inches Back Up," Gallup, May 18, 2012.

[85]Kim Parker, "Families May Differ, but They Share Common Values on Parenting," Pew Research Center, September 18, 2014.

[86]Martin Luther King Jr., "Letter from Birmingham Jail" (dated April 16, 1963), in *A Testament of Hope: The Essential Writings and Speeches of Martin Luther King Jr.* (New York: HarperOne, 1986), 289–302.

[87]*Gaudium et Spes*, no. 16.

[88]See, for example, Joseph Cardinal Ratzinger, *Truth and Tolerance: Christian Belief and World Religions*, trans. Henry Taylor (San Francisco: Ignatius Press, 2003), 210–14.

[89]David French, "America Is Intolerably Intolerant," *National Review*, December 12, 2018.

als, groups, or the platforms used to spout dehumanizing speech.[90] Freedom of speech is invoked to insist that even disrespectful or offensive speech should be tolerated. Tolerance is too often distorted and abused while some push the limits of what others can and will endure, producing bystanders who remain silent in the face of threats and deception. "Live and let live" allows for a retreat from minimum standards of the good, like kindness and forgiveness. When cowardice finds protection in tolerance, we are guilty of a "traitorous moral flabbiness" that has converted virtue into vice.[91] When excessive tolerance is normalized, it can force people to endure harmful beliefs or actions, creating a "moral culture of oppression" that undermines human dignity and the common good.[92]

A significant problem with the popular understanding of tolerance is that it makes space for the other but takes no responsibility for his or her well-being. It presumes the other has the same access to resources, range of choice, and exercise of agency. It can be used as a shield to hide indifference to the subjugation and suffering of others. When the other is marginalized, oppressed, or otherwise prevented from full and equal participation in social life, tolerance—as it is commonly understood today—endorses passive acceptance of social sins like exclusion and inequality. Today's popular notion of tolerance too easily devolves into wishing for autonomy and peace without any commitment to acting toward these ends for others. This opposes tolerance as moral philosophers understand it: as a stance that is crucial for equal respect and freedom and that makes claims on each of us.[93] But tolerance can become passive acceptance when it is divorced from empathy, especially when empathy provides the cure for judgmentalism that divides people into camps of right and wrong, us and them.[94] Tolerance is too often viewed as a unilateral action, a permissive acceptance of others. Insofar as it is impossible to predict the actions of others or enforce tolerable actions by others, tolerance is a necessary but insufficient moral norm.

In the Christian moral tradition, tolerance cannot be considered apart from the command to "love your neighbor as yourself." Tolerance is a virtue (sometimes referred to as forbearance), empowering love to endure difficulty and suffering, thus emulating Jesus's patience, self-denial, and "priceless kindness" (Rom 2:4, 15:1–4). Tolerance is patient with difference and even tension. It makes room

---

[90] Louise Matsakis, "Twitter Releases New Policy on 'Dehumanizing Speech'," *Wired*, September 25, 2018.

[91] John R. Bowlin, *Tolerance among the Virtues* (Princeton, NJ: Princeton University Press, 2016), 30.

[92] Ibid., 65.

[93] See, for example, John Rawls, *A Theory of Justice* (Cambridge, MA: Belknap Press, 1971), 214–21.

[94] Jonathan Haidt, *The Righteous Mind: Why Good People Are Divided by Politics and Religion* (New York: Vintage Books, 2012), 58.

for the other, even in the face of disagreement, without becoming so passive or uncritical that it must bear any or all burdens. As a virtue, it is a mean between extremes of deficiency and excess, just as hope is the proper midpoint between despair and presumption, and being courageous is the ideal balance between being cowardly and being brazen. Tolerance seeks harmony between the respective extremes of what would be harmless and harmful to endure. It counters the vice of intolerance that withdraws from others, coerces others, or expels others from belonging. Tolerance also opposes the vice of acquiescence that subjects the self to being a doormat, stripping a person of dignity, agency, and self-care. As part of an ongoing discernment, tolerance helps a person to integrate proper commitments to patience, self-denial, and forbearance so that self-gift does not become self-annihilation. Tolerance cannot be considered only as a matter of self-restraint or of ways to resist fear, hatred, and violence. It must also be recognized as crucial for promoting virtuous behavior and communities. For these reasons, tolerance requires prudent judgment about what should be tolerated (the beliefs, actions, and relationships that foster unity, peace, and the common good) just as much as what should be considered intolerable (threats to self-care, courage, and justice, for example). This means that tolerance cannot be conflated with nonjudgmentalism, though that is how it is popularly conceived.

Tolerance attends to the other in a spirit of empathy, understanding, and cooperation. Tolerance is not the same as "I do me, you do you," because such a credo denies mutual responsibility and accountability. This "live and let live" mentality is a symptom of social cowardice that undermines the shared commitments necessary for the common good. The problem of tolerance is the widespread endorsement of permissiveness that accepts disrespect, creates social distance, and normalizes injustice. We are facing problems too big for tolerance to handle.[95]

THE BUFFERED SELF

As philosopher Charles Taylor sees it, social separation is the future of Western civilization. It is fostered by a "social imaginary," a phrase Taylor uses to describe social beliefs, practices, and structures that influence "the ways people imagine their social existence, how they fit together with others, how things go on between them and their fellows, the expectations that are normally met, and the deeper normative notions and images that underlie these expectations."[96] The social imagi-

---

[95]Hollenbach, *The Common Good and Christian Ethics*, 32–61.

[96]Charles Taylor, "Modern Social Imaginaries," *Public Culture* 14, no. 1 (2002): 91–124. Taylor explains that a "social imaginary" is social in two ways: it is shared and it is about society. See Charles Taylor, *A Secular Age* (Cambridge, MA: Belknap Press, 2007), 323.

nary is a crucial factor in moral formation because it shapes what people believe is socially valued, the scope of obligation, and what can reasonably be expected from social participation. Taylor argues that declining rates of religious belief and shared moral norms contribute to more prominent expressions of self-interest and self-preservation, which he calls "expressive individualism." Shared religious belief and practice used to foster connections between individuals and groups provide a sense of belonging and purpose. In times of hardship or uncertainty, religion was often a source of reassurance and hope. But in the current age, a so-called secular age, as Taylor sees it, religion holds much less cultural sway for society as a whole, even while it informs the identity and mission of individuals and groups. When religion and other social institutions bond people together, they share commitments that temper freedom and self-interest. But in a secular age, the "buffered self" replaces a "bonded self" or "porous self."[97] Whereas the bonded self shares social identity and duties (and the porous self is shaped by one's social context), the buffered self values invulnerability, self-possession, and personal achievement.

The buffered self is more insulated from encounters with and obligations to others. Taylor warns that the predominant social imaginary also contributes to blindness and insensitivity, moral malaise and mutual fragilization.[98] The "fragilization" Taylor describes weakens social ties such that the social order is held together by a "sociability of strangers," individuals who associate for mutual benefit.[99] This resonates with what sociologists refer to as "weak ties" or "loose connections" that describe the decrease in time spent together, emotional intensity, and expected reciprocity in most social contexts.[100] Without strong social bonds marked by mutual respect, trust, and accountability, the self-protecting buffered self can pursue self-interest, protected by moral relativism that makes no claim on a person to sacrifice for the common good. Taylor's insights are helpful for understanding why the social fabric has frayed so quickly and also why social courage and social responsibility seem to be lacking in the face of widespread struggle and suffering. A buffered self is less likely to feel empathy and a sense of obligation to others than a bonded self.

Moreover, the buffered self is likely unaware and perhaps indifferent to the geographic tensions that undermine shared civic identity and responsibility. Much has been made of the urban–rural divide in America and the differences between those who live on the coasts and the rest of us who reside in the "flyover states."[101]

---

[97]Taylor, *A Secular Age*, 61.

[98]Ibid., 300–304.

[99]Ibid., 575–78.

[100]Robert Wuthnow, *Loose Connections: Joining Together in America's Fragmented Communities* (Cambridge, MA: Harvard University Press, 2002).

[101]Rachel Premack, "8 Things 'Coasties' Get Wrong about the Midwest, According to People

Place-based-umbrage is generated by feeling misunderstood and misrepresented, a sentiment that is shared in both cities and the countryside.[102] Rural resentment is real—especially when directed toward politicians and other elites—and it also cannot be extricated from racism and xenophobia, given the homogenous nature of rural communities in comparison with cities and suburbs. Even patriotism often covers for distrust of diversity.[103] This should not be all that shocking, given the racial segregation that persists in America. The physical marginalization of people of color—especially African Americans—demonstrates "the fatal couplings of place and race in our society" that leaves black individuals and families with only a fraction of the access to resources, freedom of choice, and accumulated wealth enjoyed by most white Americans.[104]

This is among the biggest deficiencies in Taylor's analysis: he ignores the role of race and ethnicity in a culture of buffered selves. The unspoken fact of the matter is that Taylor's buffered self is white. This is less a claim about skin color or ideology than it is about the perception of space that idealizes purity and sameness, concealing rather than revealing social problems. Segregated schools, neighborhoods, businesses, and health care facilities become networks of skewed opportunities along racial lines. When whiteness is normative (as is the case in the United States, historically, culturally, and institutionally[105]), space is constructed to enforce white privilege, ensuring freedom and social mobility for whites while imposing unfair obstacles on people of color, especially African Americans.[106]

Whiteness is more than skin color; the racialization of space means that racism is built into systems and structures that funnel unfair advantages to whites while people of color are left behind.[107] Spatial segregation leaves many white Americans

---

Who Live There," *Business Insider*, June 11, 2018; Duane Townsend, "America Is Held Hostage by Flyover States," *The Hill*, December 12, 2016.

[102]Kim Parker et al., "What Unites and Divides Urban, Suburban, and Rural Communities," Pew Research Center, May 22, 2018.

[103]Tex Sample, *Working Class Rage: A Field Guide to White Anger and Pain* (Nashville: Abingdon, 2018), 53, 72–73.

[104]George Lipsitz, *How Racism Takes Place* (Philadelphia: Temple University Press, 2011), 5.

[105]Ta-Nehisi Coates writes, "In America, it is traditional to destroy the black body—it is *heritage*. Enslavement was not merely the antiseptic borrowing of labor . . . [it was also] casual wrath and random manglings, the gashing of heads and brains blown out over the river as the body seeks to escape. It must be rape so regular as to be industrial . . . It could only be the employment of carriage whips, tongs, iron pokers, handsaws, stones, paperweights, or whatever might be handy to break the black body, the black family, the black community, the black nation." He continues, "The plunder of black life was drilled into this country in its infancy and reinforced across its history, so that plunder has become an heirloom, an intelligence, a sentience, a default setting to which, likely to the end of our days, we must invariably return." See Ta-Nehisi Coates, *Between the World and Me* (New York: Spiegel & Grau, 2015), 103–4, 111.

[106]Lipsitz, *How Racism Takes Place*, 29, 36.

[107]Spatial segregation also applies to African Americans, Latinx, Asian Americans, and Native

oblivious and perhaps indifferent to their unearned privileges as well as the deep divides that exist between neighborhoods and schools because of "redlining," the problem of gerrymandering and voter suppression, or the school-to-prison pipeline fueling the mass incarceration of African Americans.[108] People who invoke colorblindness may in fact be blind to the lack of freedom, resources, and status in nonwhite spaces.[109] Many white Americans may not question why most people assume whites deserve to live in the suburbs while people of color deserve to live in ghettos, or why housing policies financially reward whiteness and discriminate against people of color, or how these practices subsidize the concentration of wealth, produce sprawl, waste resources, and divert social costs to nonwhite neighborhoods.[110] These are tough issues to explore, as just talking about race in America is fraught with difficulty, given the fear of many white people of being labeled a "racist." Most of us assume that the real racists are others, extremists, like members of the KKK. Ignorance and anxiety keep us from understanding the scope and impact of "white innocence" (obliviousness to white privilege and supremacy) and our participation—whether conscious or not—in antiblack racism.[111]

This is not to suggest that every white person is and inevitably will be racist; instead, it speaks to the way in which social distance lulls white Americans into complacency and complicity with policies and structures that defy racial justice. For example, the racial wealth gap, if left unaddressed at the present trend, will mean that in 2053, the median white household wealth will be $137,000 and the median black household wealth will be zero.[112] People of color are more likely to be forced to deal with urban food deserts, underperforming schools, unfair housing practices, and much harsher drug enforcement than what is typical for the suburbs. All these issues reinforce segregation and poverty, exacerbate social fragmentation, and generate the conditions for criminal activity.[113] Ra-

---

Americans. One example of people of color being left behind is wealth inheritance, which determines life chances even more than college degrees, marital status, number of children, or employment. In *The Hidden Cost of Being African American*, Thomas Shapiro finds that the wealth gap between whites and people of color quadrupled between 1984 and 2007. Lipsitz reports that more than one-fourth of African American families "have no assets at all" (*How Racism Takes Place*, 4).

[108]Michelle Alexander, *The New Jim Crow: Mass Incarceration in the Age of Colorblindness* (New York: New Press, 2010).

[109]Mary McClintock Fulkerson describes the phenomenon of "obliviousness" in a white American, middle-class context with regard to white privilege, racism, and the marginalization of disabled people. See McClintock Fulkerson, "A Place to Appear: Ecclesiology as If Bodies Mattered," *Theology Today* 64 (2007): 159–71.

[110]Lipsitz, *How Racism Takes Place*, 28.

[111]See George Yancy, *Backlash: What Happens When We Talk Honestly about Racism in America* (Lanham, MD: Rowman & Littlefield, 2018), 14.

[112]Chuck Collins, Dedrick Asante-Muhammed, Emanuel Nieves, and Josh Hoxie, "The Road to Zero Wealth," Institute for Policy Studies, September 11, 2017.

[113]Lipsitz, *How Racism Takes Place*, 37.

cial disparities distort the criminal justice system, fueled by moral panic and a preference for punishment over mercy, resulting in African Americans suffering disproportionately from an immoral system.[114] For these reasons, it is imperative to state explicitly that racism "is not incidental, aberrant, or individual, but rather collective, cumulative, and continuing."[115] How can we expect Americans to understand the needs of and obligations to their neighbors when they have less and less interaction with them?

Whereas Taylor discusses a disembodied "social imaginary," it would be more accurate to address the "white spatial imaginary" that frames American society through specific social, political, and moral patterns of place.[116] Taylor's buffered self unconsciously assumes the pervasive power of white supremacy. White supremacy is not simply a matter of whites fearing people of color; it is the benefit of a corrupt system that deprives and disempowers people of color. It is the unearned financial security that "provides whites with a floor below which they cannot fall."[117] To condemn whiteness is not tantamount to condemning all white people. Whiteness is more a condition than a color, the advantage and security of segregation that benefits from diminishing or even demonizing people of color. As Lipsitz explains, while "the white spatial imaginary originates mainly in appeals to the financial interests of whites rather than to simple fears of otherness, over time it produces a fearful relationship to the specter of Blackness. This possessive investment in whiteness guarantees that the 'not free' is 'not me.' "[118] The buffered self lives in a dream that convinces white people to believe it is better to "live white than live free."[119]

This is what makes white supremacy so dangerous: it is so much more than personal ignorance, fear, or prejudice. It is the abuse of power, the exercise of social, economic, and political (and often religious[120]) practices and policies to

---

[114]Bryan Stevenson, *Just Mercy: A Story of Justice and Redemption* (New York: Spiegel & Grau, 2014).

[115]Lipsitz, How Racism Takes Place, 41. Given the pervasive and pernicious effects of slavery, Jim Crow, and antiblack racism, Ta-Nehisi Coates argues compellingly for reparations in his essay, "The Case for Reparations," The Atlantic, June 2014.

[116]Lipsitz explains, "The while spatial imaginary portrays the properly gendered prosperous suburban home as the privileged moral geography of the nation. Widespread, costly, and often counterproductive practices of surveillance, regulation, and incarceration become justified as forms of frontier defense against demonized people of color" (Lipsitz, *How Racism Takes Place*, 13).

[117]Ibid., 36.

[118]Ibid., 37.

[119]Coates, *Between the World and Me*, 143. Coates suggests it is unlikely that white people will become aware of "their need to be white, to talk like they are white, to think that they are white, which is to think that they are beyond the design flaws of humanity, [and what whiteness] has done to the world" (ibid., 146).

[120]Katie Walker Grimes, *Christ Divided: Antiblackness as Corporate Vice* (Minneapolis: Fortress Press, 2017).

organize the spaces we occupy and the choices we consider that make people of color more vulnerable and less in control of their future. For example, because of discriminatory—and sometimes predatory—lending and investment practices, black families are more likely to rent than own their home. This means a less secure living arrangement and a smaller chance at building equity for later in life or to pass down to one's children. In light of the many disadvantages people of color face, they often develop relationships and practices that foster mutual support and reciprocal assistance; their shared spaces—like barbershops and hair salons, for example[121]—illustrate a black spatial imaginary rooted in solidarity, marked much more by bonded or porous selves than buffered selves. The same is often true for many immigrant communities as well.[122] White supremacy is a primary driver of social separation (by class, race, and ethnicity) and unjust inequalities.

Identifying whiteness as an unjust exercise of power is not intended to ignore the poverty or social marginalization experienced by some white people. Indeed, race and class are bound together in a complex relationship in the United States.[123] Whatever one thinks of when they hear the word "poor," it is clear that poverty does not discriminate by ethnicity, race, or geography; in fact, poverty has grown the most in suburban settings since 2000.[124] Cultural separation is fomented by white upper- and middle-class Americans who associate mostly with people who look like them, think like them, and act like them. Cultural divides are being further buttressed thanks to rising endogamy (marrying within one's social class) and homogamy (interbreeding of individuals with like characteristics).[125] Moreover, at the same time that racial segregation has been decreasing over the last forty years, socioeconomic segregation has been increasing.[126] Combining this analysis of race and class, it is evident that Taylor's discussion of expressive individualism and the prominence of the buffered self is much more accurate for white upper-

---

[121]Lipsitz, *How Racism Takes Place*, 58.

[122]For example, kin networks among Latinx immigrants extend beyond the nuclear family, creating communities of *familismo*. See Kristin E. Heyer, *Kinship across Borders: A Christian Ethic of Immigration* (Washington, DC: Georgetown University Press, 2012), 81–87; Nichole M. Flores, "Latina/o Families: Solidarity and the Common Good," *Journal of the Society of Christian Ethics* 33, no. 2 (2013): 57–72.

[123]See, for example, Monica McDermott, *Working-Class White: The Making and Unmaking of Race Relations* (Berkeley: University of California Press, 2006).

[124]See Kim Parker, Juliana Menasce Horowitz, Anna Brown, Richard Fry, D'vera Cohn, and Ruth Igielnik, "What Unites and Divides Urban, Suburban, and Rural Communities," Pew Research Center, May 22, 2018.

[125]Putnam, *Our Kids*, 40; Murray, *Coming Apart*, 61.

[126]Douglas Massey and his colleagues report on the "secession of the successful" by measuring how "the well-educated and the affluent increasingly segmented themselves off from the rest of American society." See Douglas Massey, Jonathan Rothwell, and Thurston Domina, "The Changing Bases of Segregation in the United States," *Annals, American Academy of Political and Social Science* 626 (2009): 74–90, at 85.

and middle-class Americans than for anyone else. Taken together, these patterns of choice and cultural trends destabilize robust and diverse local communities.

A SECULAR AGE

The rise of the buffered self coincides with the decline of religiosity in the West. Taylor's reference to secularism alludes to a threefold rise in secularization: the separation of church and state, exclusive humanism (that excludes any reference to transcendence), and a tolerant plurality of diverse beliefs and practices.[127] Taylor identifies these forms of secularity to illustrate a key change in human values and the vision of flourishing. Secular social imaginaries, according to Taylor, have shifted the "good" toward a more interior and private concern. This is one reason why he laments "the world we have lost, one in which spiritual forces impinge on porous agents, in which the social was grounded in the sacred and secular time in higher times."[128] Corresponding losses include convictions of belief, belonging, and shared responsibilities. Human flourishing has become disconnected from any reference to "something higher which humans should reverence or love or acknowledge."[129]

In contrast to the previous age of the bonded self and the porous self, the buffered self is free to pursue self-interest, autonomy, and invulnerability. The buffered self possesses a new ability to disengage with the world, allowing the buffered self to "avoid distressing or tempting experiences." The buffered self is a master of one's own meaning, free from social or religious coercion.[130] The present social imaginary creates a vision for personal flourishing that relies on the ability to "opt-out" of unwelcome obligations.[131] For these reasons, Taylor's concern about ascending secularism is not just to lament the loss of religious traditionalism. Religion—through shared beliefs, individual practices, and collective rituals—bonds people together across differences of age and ability, class and status, race and ethnicity, sex and gender. The decline of religious belief in the United States, however, corresponds with fewer opportunities to encounter and build relationships across these demographic differences. In the United States, the rapid growth of the "nones"—those who do not identify as religious—now claims almost a quarter of the adult population.[132] Three-quarters of Americans identify as spiritual, while

[127]Taylor, *A Secular Age*, 2–3.
[128]Ibid., 61.
[129]Ibid., 245.
[130]Ibid., 38.
[131]Ibid., 35, 41.
[132]Michael Lipka, "A Closer Look at America's Rapidly Growing Religious 'Nones,'" Pew Research Center, May 13, 2015.

only 54 percent think of themselves as religious.[133] Confidence in organized religion has fallen from 68 percent to 38 percent in the last forty years.[134] More than half of Americans say it is not necessary to believe in God to be moral.[135] As church attendance continues to decline—only about a third of Americans worship weekly, and another third attend rarely or never—this means fewer people participate in services designed to bond folks together in shared belief and practices.[136] Insofar as ritual can be understood as the language of community, participation in these shared practices is instrumental for communicating identity and purpose. These trends point to less-frequent experiences that bond people together in common identity, mutual support, and accountability.

Attending religious services has long been an opportunity to encounter others. Declining church attendance means fewer interactions with others who share beliefs and purpose, a trend that is combined with local church demographics that do more to reinforce social division than to bridge differences. It has been more than fifty years since Dr. Martin Luther King declared eleven o'clock on Sunday morning "the most segregated hour of America," and yet faith communities have become only marginally more diverse and inclusive.[137] Of all religious Americans, Catholics are the most likely to attend a racially diverse worship service, but this only applies to one in five Catholics overall.[138] When believers engage in "church shopping" to find worship that matches their taste in content and style, they often reinforce social sorting into homogenous lifestyle enclaves.

Moreover, religion is unique among social institutions for the way it calls individuals and communities to conversion, to a departure from self-interest and apathetic disregard for the suffering of others. Christianity's call to conversion, wisdom, and compassion is domesticated by the pervasive social imaginary of therapeutic healing. Charles Taylor describes this in terms of the prevalence of "the immanent frame," wherein the present order appears "closed" and thus eclipses the transcendent and possibilities for transformation. According to Taylor, these "closed world structures" obfuscate theological concepts like "sacramental vision" and minimize the perceived import and influence of agapic actions.[139] As Taylor

---

[133]Michael Lipka and Claire Gecewicz, "More Americans Now Say They're Spiritual but Not Religious," Pew Research Center, September 6, 2017.

[134]Lydia Saad, "Military, Small Business, Police Still Stir Most Confidence," Gallup, June 28, 2018.

[135]Gregory A. Smith, "A Growing Share of Americans Say It's Not Necessary to Believe in God to Be Moral," Pew Research Center, October 16, 2017.

[136]"Why Americans Go (and Don't Go) to Religious Services," Pew Research Center, August 1, 2018.

[137]Michael Lipka, "Many U.S. Congregations Are Still Racially Segregated but Things Are Changing," Pew Research Center, December 8, 2014.

[138]See Robert D. Putnam and David E. Campbell, *American Grace: How Religion Divides and Unites Us* (New York: Simon & Schuster, 2010), 292.

[139]Taylor understands these "closed world structures" as "ways of restricting our grasp of things

sees it, in this immanent frame people are encouraged to soothe their scruples and find healing for their insecurities and inadequacies instead of confronting the reality of their moral failures. This poses a significant ethical problem because, as Taylor argues, without a healthy sense of sin, the "link between sacrifice and religion is broken."[140]

Christian Smith and his colleagues at the National Survey of Youth and Religion report that many young people have replaced religion with a "moral therapeutic deism," asking only that people be nice or kind. Moral therapeutic deism is an individualistic and morally relativistic ethos that prizes personal subjectivity, feeling, and self-fulfillment at the expense of shared moral norms and obligations.[141] At first blush, this view seems harmless: young people say they believe that "God wants people to be good, nice, and fair to each other," and that "the central goal of life is to be happy and to feel good about one's self."[142] However, moral therapeutic deism defies any normative understanding of good or evil, which is necessary for establishing common agreement and accountability. In moral therapeutic deism, a person can be self-indulgent without any thought of social or ecological responsibility. Community is an add-on and often an encumbrance.[143] The privatization of religious and moral demands betrays the moral core of the biblical tradition that repeatedly commands God's people to work for justice, "the early form of God's holiness."[144] If all God wants is for me to be happy, then I can be content to focus on my own comfort, status, and achievement. There is little room—or need—for moral duty or social responsibility in such a worldview.

The decline of religion in America is related to a decline in morality. Smith and his colleagues detect in today's young people a deep confusion and disorientation when it comes to morality. Moral duties are viewed as inessential to character formation or spiritual maturity; they are considered to be "largely avoidable displeasures to be escaped in order to realize a pleasurable life of happiness and

---

which are not recognized as such" (Taylor, *A Secular Age*, 551). For example, the priority of reason, empiricism, and private faith has led to what Taylor describes as the "excarnation" of Christianity. This is problematic, as Taylor points out, for achieving the highest standard of the New Testament, the bowel-wrenching pity displayed by the Samaritan (ibid., 554).

[140] Ibid., 649.

[141] Christian Smith with Melinda Lundquist Denton, *Soul Searching: The Religious and Spiritual Lives of American Teenagers* (Oxford: Oxford University Press, 2005), 162.

[142] Ibid., 162–63.

[143] As an example, two-thirds of those surveyed say involvement in congregations is unnecessary to be religious (ibid., 76). More to the point, Smith finds a surprising lack of civic engagement among emerging adults, with very few claiming to be active in their neighborhood or local organizations, or politically aware and invested. Smith argues that digital technology and social media make it easier to create a state of "nearly total submersion of self into fluidly constructed, private networks of technologically managed intimates and associates." See Smith et al., *Lost in Transition*, 223.

[144] Walter Brueggemann, *The Covenanted Self: Explorations in Law and Covenant*, ed. Patrick D. Miller (Minneapolis: Fortress Press, 1999), 48–58.

positive self-esteem."[145] Two-thirds of emerging adults were unable to consistently and coherently respond to questions about moral dilemmas in their lives. Instead, they made sporadic appeals to generic platitudes like "do no harm," the Golden Rule, or Karma, without being able to describe how these relate to religious and ethical systems. As many as 60 percent of emerging adults say their morality is situational, with roughly half explaining that they determine what is moral based on whether it might hurt someone.[146] Smith and his colleagues contend that emerging adults demonstrate very little concern for religious obligation or love for God; rather, their moral motivation is social order, efficiency, and prosperity under the safeguard of tolerance. Smith and his colleagues conclude that parents and educators have done an "awful job when it comes to moral education and formation."[147]

These trends indicate the rise of a domesticated form of Christianity that dilutes the demands of discipleship.[148] Domesticated Christianity in the United States is privatized, banal, and oblivious to the needs of others, and enables self-exculpating deceptions about one's complicity in others' suffering. Like the "cheap grace" denounced by Dietrich Bonhoeffer as "the mortal enemy" of the church, domesticated Christianity shirks the "cost" of discipleship.[149] In a country that touts high rates of religiosity and enjoys its status as the most prosperous and powerful in the world, these critiques need to be confronted by American Christians today.[150]

---

[145]Smith and Denton, *Soul Searching*, 173.

[146]These statistics are reported by Christian Smith in *What Is a Person?: Rethinking Humanity, Social Life, and the Moral Good from the Person Up* (Chicago: University of Chicago Press, 2010), 38–39, 59.

[147]Smith et al., *Lost in Transition*, 60. This is also true among Catholic emerging adults, for whom "morality is simply not a pressing issue for many of them" (Smith and Denton, *Soul Searching*, 215).

[148]I use "domesticated Christianity" in reference to what I understand to be an American version of what Johann Baptist Metz denounced as "*bourgeois* Christianity." Metz described this phenomenon among "those who already have, those with secure possessions, the people in this world who already have abundant prospects and a rich future." See Johann Baptist Metz, *The Emergent Church* (New York: Crossroad, 1981), 2.

[149]Bonhoeffer describes "cheap grace" as "grace without a price, without costs" that allows Christians to "live the same way the world does" without practicing self-denial or any of the demands of following Jesus Christ. Most concisely, "Cheap grace is that grace which we bestow on ourselves." See Dietrich Bonhoeffer, *Discipleship*, ed. Geffrey B. Kelly and John D. Godsey, trans. Barbara Green and Reinhard Krauss (Minneapolis: Fortress Press, 2001), 43–45.

[150]Americans continue to report high rates of religious faith, despite trends of secularization and the rise of the religiously unaffiliated. Nonetheless, rising numbers of the unaffiliated cannot be ignored. Neither can their critiques of religious institutions. The unaffiliated complain that churches are too concerned with money and power, too focused on rules, and overly involved in politics. Religiously unaffiliated Americans are slightly less likely to affirm institutional religions for their ability to strengthen community bonds and help needy members of society, and are much more doubtful (relative to the general public and religiously affiliated Americans) about organized religion's ability to protect and strengthen morality. See "'Nones' on the Rise: One-in-Five Adults Have No Religious Affiliation," Pew Forum on Religion and Public Life, October 2012.

Disciples should resist the kinds of self-referential piety that evade responsibility for (to say nothing of solidarity with) our neighbors, especially those who suffer the most from the policies and practices that maintain the status quo. Christians need to acknowledge that their overreliance on episodes of charity-from-a-distance (i.e., making donations to social services and religious organizations that directly serve the poor instead of taking up this work themselves) does little to ameliorate the present situation, and, furthermore, falls short of their duties in love and justice. As Maureen O'Connell argues, "Most Americans are 'compassionate by proxy,'"[151] instead of being personally invested in showing compassion for others in need.

In addition to inviting individuals and groups to reflect on their struggles with sin, authentic religion also issues a prophetic critique of social patterns and policies that deny human dignity, betray the care and commitment that grounds inclusive solidarity, and undermine the duties of each and all to the common good. The prophetic vision of Christianity, which builds on the Torah and prophets like Amos, Micah, and Isaiah, ought to shake people out of complacency in response to an unjust status quo. This vision interrupts the dominant paradigm of scarcity, or the "kingdom of paucity," that produces anxiety, animosity, and aggression in America.[152] This includes the vast accumulation of wealth by a select few, unchecked consumerism and materialism, as well as the exploitation of workers and natural resources. These are all features of free market capitalism, the dominant economic ideology in the world today. When people uncritically accept such a degrading and exploitative system, it makes it more difficult to confront the beliefs, practices, and structures that contribute to a "winner take all" mentality that withholds excessive privilege, power, and affluence from all but a select few.[153] Prophetic Christianity destabilizes this system through gratitude and generosity, repenting and atoning for exploitation, inclusive neighbor love, and work for justice. This is not from a distance, but by standing with those who are being abused by the status quo, as Jesus did (Lk 4:16–21, 6:20–26). Complacent Christians are an indication of an anemic religion that has become a weapon against the vulnerable and marginalized. This reveals a religion that has strayed from the moral core of the biblical tradition that

---

[151]Maureen O'Connell, *Compassion: Loving Our Neighbor in an Age of Globalization* (Maryknoll, NY: Orbis Books, 2009), 20. She notes that Martin Luther King Jr. used the term *compassionate by proxy* in order "to describe a superficial suffering with others that demands little in terms of commitment of material resources or dedication of the self" (ibid.). Saint Augustine is credited with writing, "Charity is no substitute for justice withheld."

[152]Walter Brueggemann, *The Journey to the Common Good* (Louisville, KY: Westminster John Knox Press, 2010), 29–32.

[153]Some take exception to the critique of the most successful individuals, given their philanthropy and humanitarian assistance. Upon closer inspection, however, these initiatives make only modest improvements and largely ensure the perpetuation of an inequitable status quo. See Anand Giridharadas, *Winners Take All: The Elite Charade of Changing the World* (New York: Alfred A. Knopf, 2018).

makes clear that our relationship with God is measured by how we treat those most in need (e.g., Ex 22:20–26; Lv 19:9–10; Dt 15:4–11; Is 58:5–7; Mt 25:31–46).

In the current age marked by radical self-interest and "amoral familism" that turns people inward instead of outward, it is easy to see why the "globalization of indifference" abounds. People at the bottom are disdained, accused of laziness or a deficient work ethic. This kind of judgmentalism is not only unfair and untrue, but it blinds people to the exploitation implicit in the system and the degradation that follows from this worldview. Americans take pride in a "rugged individualism" and personal responsibility. But often the cardinal American values—freedom, achievement, prosperity, and power—become idols. Jesus warned against the dangers of wealth (Lk 6:24–25, 16:19–31), knowing that a divided heart cannot serve both God and mammon (Mt 6:24; Lk 16:13). Christianity, which has long been complicit with the accumulation of wealth, has been unable to find effective language to critique excess, the vice of luxury.[154] When so many of our neighbors are fighting for survival, this confirms the claim made more than thirty years ago: that Americans have committed what the "founders of our nation [believed] was the cardinal sin: we have put our own good, as individuals, as groups, as a nation, ahead of the common good."[155] A consumer society is a formation system, shaping identity and status into measures of production and consumption; personhood disappears.[156] Inherent human dignity is eclipsed by market exchange: what good can you do for me? If the answer is nothing, then you are of no use to me. This makes it less outrageous when people are discarded, abandoned, or forgotten in the "throwaway culture" that Pope Francis laments.[157]

MORE ALONE THAN TOGETHER?

Although it has merit in some views of Western culture, Taylor's "buffered self" does not adequately account for the constant state of connectivity afforded by digital technology, the internet, and social media. It seems more fitting to speak of a "networked self" or a "connected self," or even an "embedded self."[158] Still, at the

[154]David Cloutier, *The Vice of Luxury: Economic Excess in a Consumer Age* (Washington, DC: Georgetown University Press, 2015), 3. See also Elizabeth Hinson-Hasty, *The Problem of Wealth: A Christian Response to a Culture of Affluence* (Maryknoll, NY: Orbis Books, 2018).

[155]Robert N. Bellah, Richard Madsen, William M. Sullivan, Ann Swidler, and Steven M. Tipton, *Habits of the Heart: Individualism and Commitment in American Life* (Berkeley: University of California Press, 1985), 285.

[156]John F. Kavanaugh, *Following Christ in a Consumer Society: The Spirituality of Cultural Resistance* (Maryknoll, NY: Orbis Books, 1981), 4.

[157]Pope Francis, *Laudato Si'*, no. 43.

[158]Sociologist Barry Wellman describes this in terms of a "networked individualism." This phrase expresses a tension between the digital ties between people tempered by a neoliberal conception

same time that we can tap into unprecedented connection, we are also experiencing a surge in isolation and loneliness. Digital technology, the internet, and social media have created a social context of hyperconnectivity. The average American uses a screen (desktop, laptop, tablet, or phone) more than eleven hours a day, which is more hours than we sleep.[159] This includes time for work and school, but it also represents a growing amount of time for entertainment (whether streaming videos, watching TV, or using a specific app) and mindless distraction. There are many valuable tools among these technologies, providing shortcuts and services that make life easier, faster, and more efficient. Apps can be used for a variety of benefits, including mental health, tracking physical fitness, and even facilitating spiritual disciplines like reading Scripture and taking time for prayer. Digital networks have made new business contacts and opportunities possible, including prospects for entrepreneurship. These technologies have helped forge meaningful and in some cases life-changing connections for people across great distances. Gaming provides a platform for cooperation and competition among friends and strangers. Families and friends can video conference, talk, and text to stay in contact even when they are traveling or studying, working, living, or deployed abroad. Websites like YouTube and apps like Instagram open portals to encounter others with unprecedented diversity, variety, and range of choice. Those who are socially marginalized—especially the young and old, LGBTQ individuals, and people with disabilities—can find communities of support and understanding online. People who are isolated and lonely, including those who experience mental illness and endure suicidal ideation, can access assistance more easily through a screen than perhaps they might in person. Alternatively, however, the anonymity of the digital realm can make it easier to spew hateful rhetoric without many (if any) consequences. Social media algorithms designed to present users with content they are inclined to engage with can create echo chambers filled with the same perspectives and ideas that reinforce our beliefs and worldview. Even though a culture of encounter is certainly taking place online, it is not always mediated by mutual respect, is not guaranteed to reach across real differences, and does not consistently reflect a culture of belonging that seeks to include and empower everyone.

From the outset, it should be stated that digital technology, the internet, and social media are tools. Independently, they are neither good nor bad. Paradoxically, neither are they neutral, since they are not used in a vacuum but in particular

---

of the self that maintains autonomy. He describes the resulting virtual communities as "ego-centric networks." See Barry Wellman, "The Rise of Networked Individualism," in *Community Networks Online*, ed. Leigh Keeble (London: Taylor & Francis, 2001), 17–42.

[159]Quentin Fottrell, "People Spend Most of Their Waking Hours Staring at Screens," Market Watch, August 4, 2018.

social contexts, shaped by specific cultural norms, and used by agents with distinct intentions. These tools form and deform human perception, desires, and choices. Their impact includes certain examples of empowerment and inclusion as well as serious examples of moral failure and sin.[160] Take, for example, the camera on a smartphone. While it might just as easily be used to FaceTime between grandparents and grandchildren, it can also be used as a tool to coerce a stranger, acquaintance, friend, or romantic partner to send nude pictures (a practice called sexting). While some couples engage in this practice freely, there are other individuals who feel pressure from their partners, peers, or supervisors to take and share such images. This is especially true among young adults, impacting roughly one in seven teens.[161] Even while they feel social pressure to participate, they find it "morally wrong," "disgusting," and "degrading" to send and receive these explicit images. They fully understand that it is a dangerous practice, since images can be saved and disseminated to an unlimited number of people without a person's consent.[162] When it is possible to share such intimate images and hack passwords, it is hard to have a genuine sense of privacy or security, thanks to these digital tools and structures. This can contribute to rising rates of anxiety, fear, and even vengeance.[163]

The way these digital technologies degrade sexual identity and intimacy does not end there. Pornography is now viewed more on tablets and phones than any other device, and pornographic websites like Pornhub attract about thirty billion visits per year (one hundred million visits per day, roughly a thousand visits per second, with more than 40 percent of traffic coming from the United States). For some, pornography is almost harder to avoid than find: nearly 80 percent of men under thirty watch porn regularly, and more than 20 percent of viewers are women; the average age of first exposure is eleven. Despite its popularity, watching porn produces a number of negative effects on mental health, lowers sex drive, can become addictive, and is cited as a reason for marital problems in a growing

---

[160]On the impact of such tools or structures on human agency and culpability—especially for the negative influences of structures that impose "value blindness" on individuals—see Josef Fuchs, *Moral Demands and Personal Obligations*, trans. Brian McNeil (Washington, DC: Georgetown University Press, 1993), 67.

[161]Sheri Madigan and Jeff Temple, "1 in 7 Teens Are Sexting, New Research Finds," CBS News, February 26, 2018.

[162]Donna Freitas, *The Happiness Effect: How Social Media Is Driving a Generation to Appear Perfect at Any Cost* (Oxford: Oxford University Press, 2017), 207–08.

[163]A 2016 study found that one in twenty-five Americans was the victim of "revenge porn," the nonconsensual sharing of nude pictures. Victims of this practice typically describe mental and emotional trauma similar to that of a survivor of sexual violence. See Amanda Lenhart, Michelle Ybarra, and Myeshia Price-Feeney, "Nonconsensual Image Sharing," Center for Innovative Public Health Research, December 13, 2016.

percentage of divorce cases.[164] As Gail Dines points out, the most popular pornography is not just nudity or sex; 88 percent of scenes depict at least one verbal or physical act of aggression toward women, with an average of at least twelve violent acts per scene. The normalization of objectifying and violating women (and in some cases, children) not only degrades human dignity and wounds the human family, but it desensitizes viewers to the scourge of violence.[165] This example—though unpleasant—points to the need to confront unjust systems and structures (including industries that profit from and legislation that permits these dehumanizing practices), which cannot be accomplished by calls to practice civility, tolerance, or kindness.

Despite all the opportunities to connect and engage through screens, one surprising outcome has been that more time spent on social media leads to higher rates of feeling insecure, isolated, and lonely.[166] Researchers have found that time spent on social media has a direct causal link to decreased mental and emotional well-being.[167] In some cases the reason is that social media is flooded with images of people who look like they are always happy, social, and successful. This makes it easier for more of us to feel like we cannot measure up, that we do not belong, that it is unacceptable to be vulnerable in sharing honestly about one's mental or emotional state, or to ask others for help.[168] It has left more people—especially younger generations—feeling fragile and afraid to fail.[169] Nevertheless, people struggle to put their screens down. Screens have a drug-like effect on the brain, which is concerning for those under age twenty-five, whose brains are still developing.[170] Psychologist Sherry Turkle describes this digital milieu as fashioning a mentality of "I share, therefore I am," resulting in a delicate identity that demands constant validation by others.[171] The result is a rising trend toward narcissism

---

[164]These and other statistics are available at https://www.thebabbleout.com.

[165]Gail Dines argues that most Americans' idea of pornography is "twenty years out of date." See Gail Dines, *Pornland: How Porn Has Hijacked Our Sexuality* (Boston: Beacon Press, 2010), xviii–xxii.

[166]Sherry Turkle, *Alone Together: Why We Expect More from Technology and Less from Each Other* (New York: Basic Books, 2011), 157.

[167]Michelle W. Berger, "Social Media Use Increases Depression and Loneliness," Penn Today, November 9, 2018.

[168]A poignant example of this is Madison Holleran, as described in Kate Fagan's book, *What Made Maddy Run: The Secret Struggles and Tragic Death of an All-American Teen* (New York: Hachette Book, 2017).

[169]Jean M. Twenge, *iGen: Why Today's Super-Connected Kids Are Growing Up Less Rebellious, More Tolerant, Less Happy—and Completely Unprepared for Adulthood* (New York: Atria, 2017). Twenge explores the "sudden, cataclysmic shift downward in life satisfaction" and mental illness (ibid., 96–116).

[170]Research shows the brain responds to screens as it would cocaine and detects elevated dopamine levels similar to what is experienced during sex. See, for example, Nicholas Kardaras, *Glow Kids: How Screen Addiction Is Hijacking Our Kids—And How to Break the Trance* (New York: St. Martin's Press, 2016).

[171]Turkle, *Alone Together*, 302. She describes this mentality as a kind of narcissism that "cannot

among social media users,[172] compounding a decline in empathy among young people by 40 percent.[173] Nonstop surveillance—which comes from always being connected and ready to share—exacerbates vulnerability and a feeling of being constantly judged. Social media can aggravate insecurity among users because "anything they say or do can easily be taken out of context" by "audiences [that] are invisible" to them.[174]

These digital tools and structures have produced more psychologically demanding conditions for connection. The ubiquity of screens can make it feel like one is living in a state of constant diversion or endless busyness, a "world of continual partial attention."[175] For example, Snapchat—a photo- and video-sharing app popular among those age thirty-five and younger—boasts three hundred million users (188 million per day), who create three billion images and view ten billion videos each day. Insofar as the average Snapchat user has exchanged anywhere between 10,000 and 400,000 photos with friends, how else can this trend be described other than as a "distraction sickness"?[176] Brains become used to—and actually crave—connection and interruption, making it difficult to concentrate on subjects and other people.[177] When everyone is tethered to a screen, there is pressure to be "constantly on," since interacting online is critical for gaining social acceptance and status.[178] This means a growing number of users endure the effects of "technostress"[179] and feel trapped in a "cycle

---

tolerate the complex demands of other people but tries to relate to them by distorting who they are and splitting off what it needs, what it can use" (ibid., 177).

[172]Ibid., 241–48. These views are corroborated by reports by Soraya Mehdizadeh, "Self-Presentation 2.0: Narcissism and Self-Esteem on Facebook," *Cyberpsychology, Behavior, and Social Networking* 13, no. 4 (August 2010): 357–64; and Elliot T. Panek, Yioryos Nardis, and Sara Konrath, "Mirror or Megaphone?: How Relationships between Narcissism and Social Networking Site Use Differ on Facebook and Twitter," *Computers in Human Behavior* 29, no. 5 (September 2013): 2004–12.

[173]Sara H. Konrath, Edward H. O'Brien, and Courtney Hsing, "Changes in Dispositional Empathy in American College Students Over Time: A Meta-Analysis," *Personality and Social Psychology Review* 15, no. 2 (May 2011): 180–98.

[174]danah boyd, *It's Complicated: The Social Lives of Networked Teens* (New Haven, CT: Yale University Press, 2014), 53.

[175]See Turkle, *Alone Together*, 155–61.

[176]Andrew Sullivan, "I Used to Be a Human Being," *New York Magazine*, September 2016.

[177]Turkle, *Alone Together*, 171, 227.

[178]Freitas, *The Happiness Effect*, 217. Freitas finds that many users describe having a "love–hate" relationship with their phones for this reason.

[179]"Technostress" is described as the psychological and physical effects of this constant connectivity, sometimes manifested through decrease of appetite, insomnia, and suppressed immune activity. See John Palfrey and Urs Gasser, *Born Digital: Understanding the First Generation of Digital Natives* (New York: Basic Books, 2008), 190. They also attribute "technostress"—potentially a "major health hazard for most digital natives"—to concerns about personal safety, especially in light of instances of online bullying. These issues can be exacerbated because of the gap that exists between digital natives' understanding of technoculture (the good and bad) and their parents, who may not be aware of these issues or how to appropriately respond (see ibid., 109–10, 186–87).

of responsiveness."[180] Users are not always cognizant of the "impact imprint" of their digital tools and apps.[181] Even though there are apps that can help us limit our time with a screen, using that technology to limit our use of social media technology might be considered yet another example of becoming dependent on the technology itself.

This dependence can also spill into social status and acceptance. Social media trains users to compare themselves against others' profiles, producing envy of the highlight reels of others' fun, successful lifestyles, and social influence. Users lament the pressure to appear perfect, popular, and happy, even if that is not how they feel.[182] They spend numerous hours on the endless task of "impression management,"[183] even going back to filter out any undesirable digital interactions to "clean up" their digital presence.[184] By prioritizing the state of connection over the actual quality of the content or people being engaged, people unconsciously contribute to making personhood both cheap and overglorified.[185] The temptation to commodify people is difficult to avoid in an era in which they feel their identities are linked to a mobile device (a product designed to be purchased, used, disposed of, and replaced in a short period of time).[186] It does not help that so much of life—both online and offline—is shaped by the market, making it difficult to avoid transaction-like exchanges, self-interested and instrumental approaches to connecting with others, and rampant commercialization to maximize profits.

---

[180]This is observed among those who seek nonstop availability for and from their personal and work contacts (e.g., constantly checking emails and texts in such a way that it consumes evening hours and even vacation days). See Leslie A. Perlow, *Sleeping with Your Smartphone* (Cambridge, MA: Harvard Business Review Press, 2012), 7.

[181]The phrase "impact imprint" refers to the manner in which technologies transfer "their essential qualities" to their users. See Nancy K. Baym, *Personal Connections in the Digital Age* (Malden, MA: Polity Press, 2010), 26.

[182]Freitas, *The Happiness Effect*, 6–15. Freitas describes how users feel pressured to project an idealized version of their lives through constant crafting, cultivating, and curating a more desirable image.

[183]boyd, *It's Complicated*, 47. Here, boyd cites sociologist Erving Goffman, who uses this term to describe the "social rituals involved in self-presentation" created by individuals in the context of wider groups (which establish norms for what might be considered popular, funny, sexy, etc.).

[184]Freitas describes the "Facebook Cleanup" as an attempt to remove anything that reveals negative emotions, mean comments, unpopular or divisive opinions (e.g., about religion or politics), embarrassing or illicit behavior, and posts that garnered few "likes" or "favorites," which makes someone look boring, silly, and otherwise unpopular (Freitas, *The Happiness Effect*, 48).

[185]This is the viewpoint of Michael Bugeja in *Interpersonal Divide: The Search for Community in a Technological Age* (Oxford: Oxford University Press, 2005), 99–100. This is due in part to the influence of corporate marketing and its corresponding commodification of human activity in the digital realm.

[186]Phones, in particular, are symbolically rich objects that serve as a "repository of personal history," designed to capture and save some of life's most intimate experiences—only to be thrown away and replaced. See Rich Ling, *New Tech, New Ties: How Mobile Communication Is Reshaping Cohesion* (Cambridge, MA: MIT Press, 2008), 97.

All of this contributes to the "soft new totalitarianism of consumerism" and the electronic "colonization of the lifeworld."[187] Since so many internet-based services are free, the trade-off for corporate interests is personal information, considered the highly desired "oil" of the digital age.[188] As the saying goes, if a product is free, then the user is the product. While not all digital users are content to surrender their privacy, a growing number—including many young people who grew up with digital technologies—show little concern about the potential impact on their identities and relationships.[189]

The constant state of digital connection masks a growing sense of social isolation and loneliness in our country. For a culture of encounter to find traction in and through these experiences of social separation and unjust inequality, it will have to overcome the individualism that sees the other as an inconvenience, obstacle, or threat. It will have to combat the social, economic, political, and religious beliefs and practices of exclusion. In a pluralistic society, differences and disagreement are unavoidable. But conflict does not automatically equate with abuse. Disparate beliefs, perspectives, and experiences do not mean that we have to abandon efforts to affirm human dignity, rights and responsibilities, and mutual empowerment for integral flourishing. In fact, we cannot really talk about a community in any real sense if we fail to include diverse views, values, and voices.

Given the divided state of America today, calls for civility, tolerance, and empathy are necessary but insufficient for engendering neighbor love in the pursuit of justice and solidarity. The biblical vision for holiness and right relationship with God admonishes every person to work for a more just, equitable, and inclusive community. As the prophet Micah summarizes, "You have been told, O mortal, what is good, and what the LORD requires of you: only to do justice and to love goodness, and to walk humbly with your God" (Mi 6:8). Every person is expected to care for their neighbor through acts of hospitality and solidarity, extending God's welcome to all.[190] No people should be made to feel like they do not belong, or that they are unworthy of love, respect, and participation. This requires more

---

[187]Felicia Wu Song quoting Benjamin Barber and Jürgen Habermas, respectively. See Felicia Wu Song, *Virtual Communities: Bowling Alone, Online Together* (New York: Peter Lang, 2009), 78.

[188]Newton Lee, *Facebook Nation: Total Information Awareness* (Tujunga, CA: Springer, 2013), 61. "Data mining," that is, the collection of digital user habit information by corporations, is used both to improve targeted advertising to attract new customers and to track consumers' behavior to find ways to entice them to "stickier" brand loyalty. The result is a considerable loss of digital user privacy; in fact, some believe that Facebook's data mining tactics mean that it has effectively "murdered privacy." See Patrick W. Watson, "This Is the End of Privacy as We Know It," *Forbes*, April 26, 2018.

[189]Palfrey and Gasser describe the "net effect of the digital age" as "paradoxical": on the one hand, digital users have more power and access to create images of themselves, while on the other hand, they have less control over how others perceive them (*Born Digital*, 19–20).

[190]See, for example, Dt 10:19; Lv 27:19; Jer 7:5–7; Mt 5:43–44, 23:11–12; Lk 9:23, 12:48, 22:26; Mk 8:31–10:45; Rom 13:8–10; Phil 2:3–4.

than making room for the other. It means drawing near the other—intentionally choosing encounter—with courage, mercy, generosity, humility, and fidelity that make meaningful connection and inclusive community possible. Building a culture of encounter will require a shift from tolerance that creates distance to the tenderness that generates intimacy, and a move from the unilateral gift of charity to the mutuality of solidarity.

2

A Theology of Neighbor

In Scripture, encounters often reveal a God of surprises. Sometimes God appears as a stranger, like the three men who visit Abraham and Sarah, and promise them a son, Isaac (Gn 18:1–15). These and other encounters likely inspired the author of the Letter to the Hebrews to assert, "Let mutual love continue. Do not neglect to show hospitality to strangers, for by doing that some have entertained angels without knowing it" (Heb 13:1–2). The Incarnation is a singular encounter between God and humanity, as Jesus is fully human, fully divine, and a unique, dynamic, and mysterious union of both humanity and divinity. This encounter takes place in history far from the center of status and power. In the Incarnation, God becomes poor for us (2 Cor 8:9). Jesus was a poor, dark-skinned, Middle Eastern Jew from a backwater town occupied and oppressed by the Roman Empire, who was executed as a threat to that empire. Encounter changes history.

Over and again, Scripture reveals that God is to be encountered in the world, to shatter expectations, and to usher in radical transformation. Jesus's teaching and healing ministry reflect many such encounters. He met his disciples where they were, called them to follow him, and they immediately left what they were doing (e.g., in Mk 1:16–20). Often these encounters reveal Jesus's identity and mission, helping others understand (such as in Mt 18:1–5). Sometimes these encounters yielded conversion, forgiveness, and miraculous healings (as in Jn 8:1–11). Other times they generated rejection (Lk 4:16–30), conflict (Mk 2:13–17), temptation (Lk 4:1–13), and even betrayal (Mk 14:10–11, 43–50). Jesus's encounters with others typically sparked a profound change and growth for the people and communities involved, like the Samaritan woman at the well, whose testimony about Jesus led many other Samaritans to believe in him (Jn 4:1–40). There were even some encounters that changed Jesus, as with the Syrophoenician woman (Mk 7:24–30; cf. Mt 15:21–28). These encounters illustrate that Christ walks with us, just as the disciples unexpectedly encounter the Risen Christ on the road to Emmaus (Lk 24:13–35). Even though they did not recognize him at the time, they reflect back on their experience, recalling, "Were not our hearts burning?" These encounters depict the nearness of God, a God who desires to encounter us and be encountered by us. They communicate God's hope for us to see and receive Christ in the other and to be Christ for and with the other. Encounter is the pathway to discovering and advancing a unity where there is neither Jew nor Greek, slave or free person, male or female, "for you are all one in Christ Jesus" (Gal 3:28) because "Christ is all and in all" (Col 3:11).

Jesus's best-known tale, the story of the Good Samaritan, points to both the duty to encounter others as well as the transformative possibilities of encounter with others. Even though so many people are familiar with the gist of the story, the meaning of this passage is poorly grasped. Instead of being used normatively for the Christian moral life, the Samaritan's example is often invoked in American culture as expressing a humanitarian ideal in emergency situations,[1] as an inspiration for community service,[2] and as heroic—and thus exceptional, rather than normative. Even the customary title "the parable of the Good Samaritan" is a misnomer and will therefore be avoided in this book.[3] This all provides evidence for the present need to revisit and reexamine this popular but widely misunderstood paradigmatic example of what it means to love God by being a loving neighbor through initiating encounter with others.[4]

---

[1]A Google search of "Good Samaritan" routinely yields news stories of people who stop to offer roadside assistance. Alternatively, when people are in trouble and no one stops to help, people ask, "Where is the Good Samaritan?" One poignant example would be the death of Walter Vance, who collapsed and later died during a 2011 "Black Friday" early-morning rush at a Target store in West Virginia. In an interview with CNN, one of Vance's co-workers expressed her incredulity that no one helped someone so obviously in need. She asked, "Where is the Good Samaritan side of people?" See "Black Friday Shoppers Ignore Dying Man," CNN, November 28, 2011.

[2]Sociologist Robert Wuthnow reports that in one study of people involved in community service, half of those who do not identify as religious and two-thirds of churchgoers cited the story of the Good Samaritan as part of their motivation to serve. See Robert Wuthnow, *Acts of Compassion: Caring for Others and Helping Ourselves* (Princeton, NJ: Princeton University Press, 1993), 161.

[3]Several commentators object to calling Luke 10:25–37 the "Parable of the Good Samaritan." One reason is that the phrase *Good Samaritan* does not appear in the biblical text. Another reason is because it is not a parable by definition (the etymology of "parable" implies a comparison); it is an example story, not a simile or metaphor (about the Reign of God, for instance). Also, this story should not be completely separated from the one that follows about Jesus's visit with Mary and Martha (vv. 38–42), since together these passages depict what it means to love God and neighbor. See Charles Talbert, *Reading Luke: A Literary and Theological Commentary on the Third Gospel* (New York: Crossroad, 1982), 120.

[4]Although widespread familiarity with this passage can be an asset in making it accessible, it can also reduce the "critical distance" necessary to receive the text free from these preconceived expectations and biases. As New Testament scholar Sandra Schneiders notes, the biblical text "must maintain its identity, its 'strangeness' which both gifts and challenges the reader. It must be allowed to say what

For a culture of encounter to honor the dignity of the other, we have to first construct a theology of the other. Since the word *other* implies difference and perhaps also strangeness, it is better to use the word *neighbor* in connection with the "Greatest Commandment" to "love your neighbor as yourself." When we practice inclusive neighbor love, we make solidarity real. This chapter employs Luke 10:25–37 as a generative theme to depict a "theology of neighbor." The Samaritan is not only an example of what it means to encounter God in the other but also what it means to reveal God's presence and power for the other. This illustrates that God is to be found in love expressed in terms of solidarity, a love that seeks unity across differences. The unique purchase of this passage extends beyond the Samaritan's actions to Jesus's parting words to the lawyer, the command to "go and do likewise." This means that Christians are not confined to precisely imitate the Samaritan's actions, but rather to instead adopt the "analogical imagination" that creatively envisions how one might apply the Samaritan's characteristics to their own lives.[5] Doing "likewise" is to emulate the Samaritan's courage, mercy, generosity, humility, and fidelity. This provides the foundation for the ethics of encounter (to be discussed at length in the next chapter) that guides the dynamic process that begins with encounter and moves to accompaniment to exchange to embrace and toward the ultimate goal: solidarity expressed through mutuality and inclusive belonging.

Luke 10:25–37 is a source of wisdom for Christian discipleship not because it is such a familiar story, but because Jesus is responding to a question about inheriting eternal life (v. 25), a matter of ultimate concern for any religious person then or now. Framed by a question about eternal life, the Samaritan's example and Jesus's parting words to "go and do likewise" cannot be interpreted as relevant only for emergencies, random acts of kindness, or a select few moral heroes. Rather, with this story, Jesus teaches that the deepest longings of the human heart and the profoundest meaning of life are fulfilled more by doing than knowing.[6]

This passage is especially germane for today's social divides and unjust inequalities because the details of the characters involved and the setting of this story specifically reference and render illegitimate social, religious, and ethnic biases and boundaries. This example story is as much about the central function of love in Christian discipleship as it is a call to more fully realize bonds of human

---

it says, regardless of whether this is comfortable or assimilable by the reader." See Sandra Schneiders, *Biblical Interpretation and Christian Ethics* (Cambridge: Cambridge University Press, 1993), 171.

[5]David Tracy, *The Analogical Imagination: Christian Theology and the Culture of Pluralism* (New York: Crossroad, 1981).

[6]Jesus says "*do* this, and you will live" (v. 28; emphasis added). The Samaritan's example shows what is implied by this command to *do*. It also illustrates Luke's view that disciples ought to focus on doing the law rather than discussing it. The reward for *doing* is living well, both now and eternally (cf. 10:25, 18:18). Note the parallel with the Last Judgment scene in Matthew 25:31–46.

solidarity. As Ada María Isasi-Díaz contends, "salvation depends on love of neighbor, and because love of neighbor today should be expressed through solidarity, solidarity can and should be considered the *sine qua non* of salvation."[7] Typical exhortations to "love your neighbor as yourself" fail to effectively communicate the depth of the challenge to be a Samaritan-like neighbor who is moved by compassion at the sight of others' suffering, and who responds with courage, mercy, generosity, humility, and fidelity to break social barriers in the spirit of solidarity. Solidarity requires more than friendship or "social charity."[8] Solidarity aspires to cultivate inclusive friendships, but it remains incomplete unless and until people generate a shared commitment to building a just ordering of society for the unity and integral development of the human family in right relationship. Moreover, Gustavo Gutiérrez interprets the Samaritan as embodying not only the principle of solidarity, but the moral obligation known as "the preferential option for the poor."[9] To go out of our way and into the ditch, as the Samaritan does, is to meet the needs of the poor, vulnerable, and marginalized—those pushed to the peripheries of society—and to stand with them, just as God does (e.g., Ex 22:20–26; Lv 19:9–10; Dt 15:4–11; and Is 58:5–7). This is what it means to practice a theology of neighbor, to seek and to reveal God in encountering others, especially those considered "other." As Luke contends, this is precisely what a disciple must do in order to inherit eternal life. This chapter proceeds in the following steps: it first puts this passage in broader biblical context, then provides a detailed exegesis of Jesus's story about the Samaritan, and next unpacks what a theology of neighbor entails. Finally, this chapter proposes how conversion to the sacrament of our neighbor can orient individuals toward building a culture of encounter.

BIBLICAL CONTEXT

Luke 10:25–37 should first be situated in the context of the two-volume work (the Gospel of Luke and the Acts of the Apostles) attributed to this evangelist. Luke writes for a primarily Gentile audience, "a group of late first-century churches

---

[7]Ada María Isasi-Díaz, "Solidarity: Love of Neighbor in the 21st Century," in *Lift Every Voice: Constructing Christian Theologies from the Underside*, ed. Susan Brooks Thistlethwaite and Mary Potter Engel (Maryknoll, NY: Orbis Books, 1998), 30–39, at 31.

[8]*Catechism of the Catholic Church*, no. 1939.

[9]This principle of Catholic social teaching is informed by Jesus's teaching in Matthew 25:31–46 as well as a number of other passages in Scripture that show God's special concern and commitment to the most vulnerable members of society. This claim has been articulated by popes and bishops since the beginning of the canon of Catholic social teaching; see, for example, *Rerum Novarum*, no. 37. In short, it claims that the needs of the poor and vulnerable merit a higher priority or preference over those with greater stability, security, and resources.

of diverse social composition," comprising people from "different ethnic and religious backgrounds, social status, and wealth."[10] Luke tells Jesus's story to provide guidance for action for those seeking to follow "the way" of discipleship.[11] Luke often refers to the Christian life as a journey, and discipleship is called "the way" in several instances in the Acts of the Apostles (e.g., 9:2, 18:25, 19:9), meant to signify a lifelong pilgrimage seeking to imitate Jesus, empowered by the Holy Spirit.[12] Discipleship is inherently communal, a shared process in which to discern how to grow in collaboration with the Holy Spirit in order to build right relationships between the self and God and others, forming a vibrant and inclusive community. It is worth noting that the Greek word for community, *koinōnia,* also refers to "partnership," implying both interpersonal right relationship and cooperation with the Holy Spirit.[13] When Luke 10:25–37 ends with "go and do likewise," the expectation is that this is a shared project for all disciples who can rely on the Spirit's presence and power in order to become more like the Samaritan.

Luke addresses typical gospel themes like repentance for sins, the cost of discipleship, and the Reign of God. He also pays special attention to the lowly and marginalized, highlighted in the Magnificat of Mary (1:46–55) and the commencement of Jesus's public ministry, wherein Jesus announces good news to the poor, release for the captives, and freedom for the oppressed (4:18–21). Sharon Ringe points out that this gospel is more inclined to "talk *about* the poor" and also "*to* the well-to-do" concerning their responsibilities to and for the poor.[14] In the Acts of the Apostles, Luke demonstrates his intention to address more privileged members of the early Christian communities about their responsibilities to needier disciples. This is part of Luke's aim to praise these communities' devotion to prayer, Eucharistic meals, and sharing of possessions such that "there was no needy person among them" (e.g., Acts 2:42–47, 4:32–35). Luke's description intends to communicate that these disciples exemplify an accurate following of

---

[10]Robert C. Tannehill, *Luke* (Nashville: Abingdon, 1996), 24.

[11]Richard B. Hays, *The Moral Vision of the New Testament: Community, Cross, New Creation; A Contemporary Introduction to New Testament Ethics* (San Francisco: HarperSanFrancisco, 1996), 134–35; Richard A. Burridge, *Imitating Jesus: An Inclusive Approach to New Testament Ethics* (Grand Rapids, MI: Eerdmans, 2007), 280–82.

[12]Commentators seem to agree that the parting words of the passage, "go and do likewise," though attributed to Jesus by Luke, may be a Lucan redaction. This expresses Luke's desire for his audience to respond in action "with imagination and conviction, and not through one's own strength but through the power of the Holy Spirit." Talbert, *Reading Luke,* 5.

[13]John Koenig explains, "In the great majority of passages where the *koinōnia* words appear, the meaning has to do with human participation in a blessing or task of higher reality that is directed by God." Partnership suggests "cooperation in a divine project." John Koenig, *New Testament Hospitality* (Philadelphia: Fortress Press, 1985), 9.

[14]Sharon Ringe, "Luke's Gospel: 'Good News to the Poor' for the Non-Poor," in *The New Testament: Introducing the Way of Discipleship,* ed. Wes Howard-Brook and Sharon Ringe (Maryknoll, NY: Orbis Books, 2002), 65.

"the way" and also signals the presence and power of the Holy Spirit at work in their midst.

Luke 10:25–37 comes after passages on following Jesus (9:57–10:24) and before a section on prayer (11:1–13) in Jesus's teaching and healing ministry on his way to Jerusalem (19:44), the site of his passion, death, and resurrection. Luke describes Jesus and the disciples being denied a hospitable reception by Samaritans (9:52) to highlight the ethnic and religious tensions that existed between Jews and Samaritans. The chiastic pattern in Luke's writing includes a parallel with 18:18–23, when the question is again posed to Jesus, "What must I do to inherit eternal life?" In that scene, Jesus encounters a wealthy official who poses this question and professes his faithful observance of the commandments. Jesus replies, "There is still one thing left for you: sell all that you have and distribute it to the poor, and you will have a treasure in heaven. Then come, follow me" (v. 22). This even more radical demand fits with Luke's objective to instruct disciples on the proper use of possessions.[15] Luke 18:18–23 issues a warning about the ways in which possessions can become obstacles to following Jesus and inheriting eternal life.

Although this story about the Samaritan is unique to Luke, the command to "love your neighbor as yourself" is also mentioned in Mark 12:28–34 and Matthew 22:34–40. However, in Luke's version (10:27), the command to love God and neighbor is a single command, making no room for debate about a "first" or "second" priority between the two.[16] Mark and Matthew join two distinct passages from the Hebrew Scriptures (Dt 6:5 and Lv 19:18), but commentators do not agree as to whether Luke's combination of love of God and love of neighbor into a single command is novel. The fact that Luke places this summary statement in the mouth of the lawyer, affirmed by Jesus without further qualification, suggests a common contemporary understanding that loving God is incomplete if it does not also include loving others as oneself.[17] Luke Timothy Johnson thus

---

[15]Commentators infer that a Samaritan traveling on the road to Jericho was likely a merchant, and thus a man of relative wealth. Luke's detailed description of the Samaritan's care of the victim in the ditch is a model for how possessions are to be used in service of those in need (note links to Acts 2:42–47, 4:32–35). See Joseph Fitzmyer, *The Gospel According to Luke X–XXIV*, AB 28A (Garden City, NY: Doubleday, 1985), 888. Burridge sums this up by stating, "The motivation behind the sharing of wealth is always love" and adds that this sharing should not exclude anyone (Burridge, *Imitating Jesus*, 264).

[16]It is worth noting that in John's Gospel, there is no commandment to love God, only the "new commandment" to "love one another as I have loved you" (Jn 13:34). This theme is repeated in the First Letter of John (3:11). See also the clarification that one cannot love God without also loving one's neighbor (1 Jn 4:20–21).

[17]Fitzmyer confirms this as normative for Christian discipleship; Luke's claim is to demand "the same attitude toward one's neighbor as toward Yahweh" and that "No love of God is complete without that of one's neighbor" (Fitzmyer, *The Gospel According to Luke*, 878).

contends that "'love of neighbor' has the same force as 'love for God.'"[18]

Here it is appropriate to clarify what the word "love" means in this context. In English, the word "love" is much like a miscellaneous kitchen drawer: it holds way more than it should. It can refer to the devotion between romantic partners; affection between family members; or the feelings one has for their favorite movie, artist, food, or other inanimate object, like their phone. In Scripture, piety revolves around love for God and neighbor. But the "love" that is commanded does not denote strong feelings, benevolent service, or supererogatory acts. Neither is it an exhortation to charitable giving offered from surplus or as a matter of convenience. Luke 10:25–37 depicts how love is the basis for holiness, or right relationship with God, which implies justice. Justice is viewed as intrapersonal and interpersonal right relationship. In the Hebrew Scriptures—beginning in the Pentateuch—Israel receives both covenant and law as the way to share *shalom* with God and one another. *Shalom* is often translated into English as "peace," but it is better translated as the wholeness and fullness of life in harmony and right relationship. Deuteronomy 6:5, part of the *Shema*, best captures how Israel is called to "love the Lord, your God, with all your heart, and with all your soul, and with all your strength." "Love" in the Hebrew Scriptures is conditioned by its sociocultural context, wherein love is a term for political loyalty between two parties. The words for *love*, most often *'ahav* or *khesedh*, are not fully expressed by the English word *love*, but are also sometimes meant to convey friendship, loyalty, and kindness. In describing Israel's orientation toward God, "love means whole-hearted obedience, exclusive worship, and conscientious observation of covenant law in order to follow God's demands for righteousness in the covenant community."[19]

This righteousness is fulfilled through fidelity to the demands of covenant relationships with God and neighbor expressed in love and justice. This means emulating Yahweh, who is revealed as the defender of the oppressed (e.g., Ex 3:7–8; Dt 10:18; Ps 82:3–4). Israel is commanded to offer hospitality for strangers, fairly resolve conflicts, facilitate reconciliation within or between kin and clan, and strive to overcome abuse, violence, and vengeance in order to establish peace.[20]

---

[18]Luke Timothy Johnson, *The Gospel of Luke* (Collegeville, MN: Liturgical, 1991), 174.

[19]This included an affective dimension oriented toward God, since "Only actions rooted in affective commitment express genuine love for God." See Katharine Doob Sakenfeld, "Love in the OT," in *The New Interpreter's Dictionary of the Bible* (Nashville: Abingdon Press, 2006), 3:713–18, at 716.

[20]In the Hebrew Scriptures, *shalom* requires *mishpat* (justice) and *tsedheq* (righteousness), which are almost used synonymously, though some commentators suggest *mishpat* may carry a more theoretical sense of "rightness," whereas *tsedheq* is closely linked with *doing* righteousness (that is, living *khesedh*, covenantal love, loyalty to God and others). Rabbi Jonathan Sacks explains that love (*khesedh*) *and* justice (*mishpat*/*tsedheq*) together constitute the *darkhei shalom* ("ways of peace"), the project of *tikkun olam*, that is, mending or perfecting the world. See Jonathan Sacks, *To Heal a*

God's covenant partners aspire to an imitation of divine love and justice in human relationships, that is, steadfast loyalty to one another marked by mercy, forgiveness, and repairing relationships, while accounting for the reality of finitude and sin. This calls for special protections for the most vulnerable members of society: widows, orphans, and the poor (e.g., Ex 22:21–22; Dt 14:29, 15:7; Ps 103:6).

In the Christian Scriptures, which are not meant to be oppositional or supersessionist to the Hebrew Scriptures, "love" most often appears as the Greek words *agape* or *philia*.[21] In most cases, love in the Christian Scriptures carries many meanings, from reciprocal loyalties and commitments, to submission of one to another for the sake of unity and solidarity, to the kind of emotion marked by living for others and the enjoyment of friendship. Love as a word and theme appears much more in the Christian Scriptures than the Hebrew Scriptures, but this does not mean that it replaces the covenantal concern for justice.[22]

This is true especially because another word, *dikaiosynē*, gets even more attention and emphasis in the New Testament, appearing in various forms roughly three hundred times in the Christian Scriptures.[23] *Dikaiosynē* is difficult to translate into English because of its varied meanings. It connotes "righteousness" in terms of being upright, honest, and correct; it means "justice" in terms of equity, fairness, or integrity; it can also convey, less frequently, "purity," "judgment," "blamelessness," "mercy," or "compassion." In Greek literature, its most consistent use and meaning is the fulfillment of one's duty.[24] *Dikaiosynē* is inadequately understood as "righteousness" alone because it can be misinterpreted to mean "self-righteousness." Despite this, in nearly every instance, *dikaiosynē* and its related forms are translated as "right," "righteous," or "righteousness" in the *New Revised Standard Version* of the New Testament. *Dikaiosynē* can best be summarized as describing who God is and what God wants for God's people. In his teaching and healing ministry, Jesus Christ is the sacrament of *dikaiosynē* in the world.

Dikaiosynē is relevant for eternal life because God's righteousness is expressed

---

Fractured World: The Ethics of Responsibility (New York: Schocken Books, 2005), 46, 72, 98.

[21]These words are not exclusive to Christian theology. Although distinctions can be made between *agape* (traditionally interpreted as the most selfless love), *philia* (fraternal love), and *eros* (desirous love), this is a difficult and sometimes inappropriate aim. For more on navigating these versions of love, see John S. Kloppenborg, "Love in the NT," in *The New Interpreter's Dictionary of the Bible*, 3:703–13.

[22]Anders Nygren famously claimed that Jesus's emphasis on spontaneous love and generosity renders concern for justice "obsolete and invalidated." See Anders Nygren, *Agape and Eros*, trans. Philip P. Watson (London: S.P.C.K., 1954), 90. Nygren specifically alludes to the example of the Samaritan to prove his thesis that "the whole content of Scripture is Caritas" (ibid., 62, 456).

[23]See Marion L. Soards, "Righteousness in the NT," in *The New Interpreter's Dictionary of the Bible*, 4:813–18.

[24]See Jutta Leonhardt-Balzer, "Righteousness in Early Jewish Literature," in *The New Interpreter's Dictionary of the Bible*, 4:807–13.

not only in salvation as a one-time gift but also in the ongoing process of sanctification.[25] A domesticated Christian faith might interpret this to mean that God's grace is meant for individual obedience and private piety. Responding to the call to *dikaiosynē* means to strive to be more like God, but not in an other-worldly sense of private perfectionism. To be "perfect as your heavenly Father is perfect" (Mt 5:48) means to be wholeheartedly faithful to God and to promote right relationship with God and others precisely because the Triune God—Father, Son, and Holy Spirit—exists as a communion of love that is offered, received, and returned. In this way, the Trinity reminds us that to become more like God is to resist whatever forms of discrimination, oppression, or injustice thwart inclusive, mutual, and just relationships. To be holy or Godlike is to practice merciful love and liberation for and with others, building community so that more people can share in the fullness of life.[26]

In this way, *dikaiosynē* is also important for solidarity and the preferential option for the poor, vulnerable, and marginalized. Practicing *dikaiosynē* means standing with those who hunger and thirst for *dikaiosynē* (Mt 5:6). It means transcending social, political, and religious boundaries and recognizing the neighbor in the most remote place or the most difficult condition.[27] Thus, *shalom* and *dikaiosynē* do not make love and justice competing claims or relegate love and justice to separate spheres of influence. Instead, they call for a return gift of love and commitment to justice in response to God, who is a community of shared, gratuitous love.[28]

God, who is the perfection of *dikaiosynē*, is to be recognized and shared among people. This is a notable theme in the Gospel of Matthew, ranging from the

---

[25]See, for example, Romans 6:13–23. John Donahue, SJ, calls for more attention to Paul's linking faith with justice. Too often it is dismissed as a justification/sanctification matter, or an "interim ethic," and what is lost is Christ's demand to take responsibility for the world, as in Romans 8:21–23 and Galatians 6:2, for example. See John R. Donahue, "What Does the Lord Require? A Bibliographical Essay on the Bible and Social Justice," *Studies in the Spirituality of Jesuits* (St. Louis, MO: Institute of Jesuit Sources, 2000), 55–56.

[26]New Testament expert Ernst Käsemann writes, "Perfection in this context is nothing like the formation of character up to its last possibilities in the endless way of approximating the highest. Here, perfection (and this is constitutive) exists only in relation to the other, be it the neighbor or the enemy, and of course in the sense of radical service, undivided surrender." See Ernst Käsemann, "The Sermon on the Mount—A Private Affair?" in *On Being a Disciple of the Crucified Nazarene*, trans. Rudolf Landau and Wolfgang Kraus (Grand Rapids, MI: Eerdmans, 2010), 126.

[27]Käsemann writes, "The Beatitudes do not allow for closed societies. They open hearts and heads to a service that transcends earthly boundaries, perceives the neighbor in the most distant place, and never concedes to tyrants the right to the earth, which belongs to God." See "The Fourth Beatitude (Matthew 5:6)," in *On Being a Disciple*, 152. This resonates with Johann Baptist Metz's question, "Do we share the sufferings of others, or do we just believe in this sharing, remaining under the cloak of a belief in 'sympathy' as apathetic as ever?" See Johann Baptist Metz, *The Emergent Church*, trans. Peter Mann (New York: Crossroad, 1981), 3.

[28]For more on this, see Gustavo Gutiérrez, *We Drink from Our Own Wells: The Spiritual Journey of a People*, trans. Matthew J. O'Connell (Maryknoll, NY: Orbis Books, 2003), 108–9.

Beatitudes (5:1–12) to the Last Judgment scene (25:31–46). It is also evident in Luke 10:25–42, which combines the story about the Samaritan with Jesus's visit with Mary and Martha. After Martha busies herself with "much service" while her sister Mary sits at the feet of Jesus and listens to him, Martha complains to Jesus. But Jesus replies by saying, "Mary has chosen the better part and it will not be taken from her" (v. 42). Although it seems confusing to praise the Samaritan's servant actions in verses 29–37 and then criticize Martha's service in verses 38–42, Luke invites his audience to hold these two passages together. Doing so demonstrates a discipleship for *dikaiosynē* that balances action and contemplation in seeking union with God and neighbor.

Jesus's story about the Samaritan has many unique features that merit extra study. At the same time, this passage is only one small part of a broad and diverse theological and moral vision constructed by Scripture and tradition. For his part, Luke puts an exclamation point on this passage to encapsulate the disciples' mission to the Gentile world: to inherit eternal life is to be like the Samaritan. All who hear are called to "go and do likewise."

WHO IS MY NEIGHBOR?

The lawyer is not content to ask his question about eternal life and have his own answer confirmed by Jesus. He presses further, "wanting to justify himself" (Luke 10:29), and asks, "And who is my neighbor?"[29] Since this is such a well-known story, this question seems perfectly innocent to modern ears. But the lawyer would have known the appropriate definition of neighbor, or *plēsion*: the word means "one who is near."[30] Given the collectivistic societies that marked the Mediterranean world during Jesus's time, group identity and support were of paramount importance. Jesus's Jewish contemporaries would have known that "neighbor" applies to all those bound in covenant with Yahweh because they shared common blood, land, language, way of life, and worship. Daily life was marked by relations of mutual entitlements among such insiders.[31]

---

[29]Note that "justify" is one of the *dik*-stem words derived from *dikaiosynē*.

[30]The lawyer's question is essentially, "Who is my near one?" By this he wants to learn the limits of proximity and, thus, the acceptable limits for his attention and responsibility. In John 4:5, as Jesus passes through Samaria, *plēsion* refers to a nearby plot of land that Jacob had given Joseph (the location of Jacob's well, where Jesus interacts with the Samaritan woman in vv. 7–26). If a dimension of nonhuman creation can be considered a neighbor (like a field), perhaps neighbor love can be shared between humans and nonhumans. On recognizing nonhuman creation as covenant partners in right relationship and the corresponding rights and responsibilities due nonhuman creation, see my essay "Neighbor to Nature," in *Green Discipleship*, ed. Tobias Winright (Winona, MN: Anselm Academic, 2011), 200–217.

[31]Bruce Malina explains that "neighbor" referred to "the widest circle of all Israel," marked by

In antiquity, there were three concentric circles of relations: neighbors, nonneighbors, and enemies. Although reciprocal relations among neighbors were crucial in daily life, covenant law extended obligations to nonneighbors as well. It is worth repeating that the mandate to "love your neighbor" is repeated twice in the Hebrew Scriptures, but the command to love the stranger, the widow, or orphan—the most defenseless—is reiterated more than thirty-five times.[32] Nonetheless, there were different expectations for treatment of insiders relative to outsiders. Though strangers and sojourners should be granted hospitality, much more was expected from and for fellow Israelites. Rabbis vigorously debated the scope and limits of these obligations. For example, some taught that it was acceptable to make exceptions and restrict duties to sinners and enemies, since to offer aid to such people could be seen as condoning their sins (e.g., Ecclus 6:13).

Jesus's teaching and healing ministry did not allow for any such loopholes. At length, Luke describes Jesus's rejection of limited obligations based on reciprocal relationships (see 6:27–36). Jesus demands that his followers love even their enemies, asking, "If you love those who love you, what credit is that to you?" (v. 32). Villagers would know who would be included among their neighbors, but the lawyer asks Jesus for his interpretation of who is included as *plēsion*. The lawyer's question is not so innocent; it is a self-interested, ethnocentric, limit-seeking attempt to learn the minimum requirement for adherence to the law and eligibility for eternal life.[33] It is asked in a similar spirit as asking a police officer, "How much over the speed limit can I drive without getting a ticket?" Focusing on limits—how much we can get away with, or how little we must do—is the wrong way to approach faith and love, as Jesus's response shows.

Jesus's story about the Samaritan illustrates why the question "who is my neighbor?" is the wrong question to ask. The question seeks a limit: who are the people I am less obligated—or not obligated at all—to help? It implies there is a nonneighbor, a person beyond one's moral concern. Jesus turns this question upside down by subverting distinctions between "near" and "far." He tells the story of a man who was traveling from Jerusalem to Jericho and "fell into the hands"

"bonds of generalized reciprocity" wherein neighbors "act like fictive kin." Accordingly, the purpose of the command to "love your neighbor" is to maintain social harmony and prevent conflict within the ingroup, since "Neighbors and conflict are sort of a contradiction." See Bruce J. Malina, "Neighbor," in *The New Interpreter's Dictionary of the Bible*, 4:251–52.

[32]Sacks, *To Heal a Fractured World*, 103.

[33]Charles Talbert offers the following question to illustrate what he interprets as the lawyer's intention: "How can I spot others who belong to God's people so that I can love them?" (Talbert *Reading Luke*, 122).

To clarify, even if the lawyer's question is not exactly innocent, it is still significant. As Malina explains, "The difficulty in antiquity was to consider people beyond the outermost rim of the ingroup as anything other than enemy, as a different species, as not belonging to the ethnocentric human race constituted of self and one's neighbors." See Malina, "Neighbor," 4:252.

of robbers who stripped him, beat him, robbed him, and left him "half dead" (v. 30).[34] The robbers are literally "near" to the traveler but act exactly the opposite of being a neighbor. A priest and later a Levite, upon seeing the robbers' victim, pass by on the opposite side of the road. Jesus intentionally describes the way these men—who have a religious duty to be loving neighbors—move farther away from the victim. In Greek, the priest and Levite's movement is described as *antiparechomai,* containing two prepositions meaning "not" and "beside," to signify their failure to act as neighbors. Some interpreters excuse the priest and Levite from helping the man in need because they could not risk defilement and the seven days' lost wages spent to be purified.[35] This overlooks the fact that the Mishnah explicitly makes exceptions for neglected corpses and that the law could be broken in matters of life and death.[36] Moreover, since Samaritans followed the same legal tradition as the priest and Levite, if it had applied to the two religious leaders, it would also have been a valid excuse for the Samaritan. This observation does not suggest an anticlerical or anti-Semitic intent, but instead serves as an indictment of moral myopia, the "phenomenon of avoidance" of those who ignore the law and fail to act in love for another person in need.[37] Pope Francis points to the priest and Levite as representing the "globalization of indifference" that continues to creep into hearts around the world today.[38]

---

[34]Interestingly, this is the only story or teaching of Jesus that is geographically specified. Jesus's audience would have known that the road to Jericho descends more than three thousand feet over eighteen miles and was a notoriously unsafe passage, susceptible to ambush and robbery. In fact, this road was known as the "Bloody Pass."

[35]See Leviticus 21:1–4.

[36]See *m. Nazir* 7.1, as cited by Bernard Brandon Scott in *Hear Then the Parable: A Commentary on the Parables of Jesus* (Minneapolis: Fortress Press, 1989), 195–96. Herman Hendrickx summarizes the scene this way: the priest and Levite "were required to stop. According to oral law, they either had to bury the dead or give life-sustaining assistance to someone in need." See Herman Hendrickx, *The Third Gospel for the Third World* (Collegeville, MN: Michael Glazier, 1996), 3A:66.

[37]It would also be a mistake to read this passage as anticlerical because Jesus shows respect for the role of priests in Luke 5:14 and 17:14; for example. Fitzmyer asserts this is not anti-Semitic, as this would be an inaccurate (and anachronistic) way of importing issues "that were not really Luke's concern" (Fitzmyer, *The Gospel According to Luke X–XXIV,* 885). On the "phenomenon of avoidance," see James Breech, *The Silence of Jesus: The Authentic Voice of the Historical Man* (Philadelphia: Fortress Press, 1983), 176. Gerald Schlabach proposes that Christians today consider the priest and Levite as victims "trapped in a religious system that numbed their hearts even as it overwhelmed them with obligations." He sees these figures as a relevant challenge to ordained, vowed, and lay leaders who are overcommitted and unable to love the neighbors right in front of them. See Gerald Schlabach, *And Who Is My Neighbor? Poverty, Privilege, and the Gospel of Christ* (Scottdale, PA: Herald Press, 1990), 43.

[38]In a homily at Lampedusa, Pope Francis invokes this passage before preaching, "we see our brother half dead on the side of the road, and perhaps we say to ourselves: 'poor soul . . . !' and then go on our way. It's not our responsibility, and with that we feel reassured, assuaged. The culture of comfort, which makes us think only of ourselves, makes us insensitive to the cries of other people, makes us live in soap bubbles which, however lovely, are insubstantial; they offer a fleeting and

Given the fact that the first two characters are religious leaders, many in Jesus's audience were likely expecting the next person in the story to be a lay Israelite. Jesus's selection of a Samaritan as the third figure would have been shocking to his audience because of the volatile hostility between Jews and Samaritans at the time. A Samaritan would have been considered an enemy because of a complicated and partially shared religious history and practice. The enmity between Jews and Samaritans dates back to 722 BCE, when the Assyrians conquered the northern kingdom, exiled most of the Israelites, and the newcomers intermarried with those left behind. Religious Jews from the southern kingdom believed this new population to be racially corrupt, morally bankrupt, theologically insufficient, and therefore unworthy of the salvation promised to the covenanted people. The Assyrian conquest interrupted the belief and practice of those in the northern kingdom; as a result, Samaritans had their own version of the Pentateuch and maintained religious worship on Mount Gerizim in Shechem (whereas Jews from Judea insist that true worship takes place in the temple in Jerusalem).[39] Jews cursed Samaritans publicly and prayed that God would not allow them a share in eternal life. Given that this story is told in response to a question about what a person must do to inherit eternal life, Jesus's audience would have thus felt nothing but disdain at the mention of a Samaritan in this story.[40] It is difficult to translate what a "Samaritan" would be for us today, but one has to imagine the kind of person who would make your stomach turn and skin crawl.

The rancor between Jews and Samaritans strikes at the core of Jesus's intent with this story.[41] If Jesus had intended only to reinforce the current understanding of loving one's neighbor, it would have been sufficient for a lay Israelite to tend to the robbers' victim. If Jesus wanted to reiterate his previous call to love one's enemy (Lk 6:27–36), then the man lying in the ditch would have been a Samaritan, and a lay Israelite would have been the appropriate figure to stop and offer aid.

---

empty illusion which results in indifference to others; indeed, it even leads to the globalization of indifference." Pope Francis, "Visit to Lampedusa Homily," July 8, 2013, w2.vatican.va.

[39]Sirach 50:25–26 denounces the "degenerate" people who worship in Shechem, categorizing them with the same loathing as that directed toward the Edomites and Philistines.

[40]In the gospels, Luke and John are the only authors to incorporate Samaritans into their accounts. Luke's portrayal of Samaritans is ambiguous: Jesus is refused hospitality in a Samaritan town (9:51–56), but in a later scene, when he cures ten lepers, the only one to return with words of thanks is a Samaritan (17:15–19). John also depicts Samaritans in an ambiguous light: on the one hand, the word "Samaritan" is an epithet among Jews (8:48), and Jews and Samaritans would share nothing in common (4:9); on the other hand, Samaritans sometimes model receptivity to Jesus's message when Jews do not (4:39–41).

[41]John L. McKenzie writes, there is "no deeper break of human relations in the contemporary world than the feud of Jews and Samaritans, and the breadth and depth of Jesus' doctrine of love could demand no greater act of a Jew than to accept a Samaritan," in *Dictionary of the Bible* (London: Geoffrey Chapman, 1965), 766.

Insofar as the priest and Levite are presumably the victim's own religious leaders, the Samaritan's actions are shocking because this odious outsider does precisely what would have been expected of those considered the moral exemplars.[42] Jesus's audience would have been utterly scandalized to hear such a despised figure be the one to uphold the law. Some biblical scholars have even wagered that had the victim been conscious, he likely would have refused the Samaritan's assistance since "Any self-respecting, pious Jew in a ditch would rather be left for dead than be helped by such a person."[43]

The Samaritan's actions are all the more powerful because he acts this way in a setting where he is a hated enemy. The road to Jericho was notoriously unsafe, due in part to the fact that it descends more than three thousand feet in less than twenty miles. All the switchback curves made for easy ambush, so Jesus's audience would have felt zero sympathy for the man who is beaten, stripped, and robbed. If the man who is left for dead was foolish enough to travel this dangerous path alone, the same would be true for the Samaritan, especially since he would have been targeted precisely because he was such a despised outcast in this territory. The Samaritan, whom commentators surmise was likely a merchant returning from Jerusalem, would be facing great risk of theft. Going out of his way in drawing near to the man lying in the ditch would have made him an easy target for ambush or might make him look like the one responsible for the beating and robbery in the first place. Moreover, Jesus's audience would have considered the Samaritan's act of bringing the wounded man to an inn to be sheer folly.[44] Given the serious threat of danger the Samaritan faces at every step along the way, it may be more appropriate to call this the story of the "Foolish Samaritan."[45] Of course, Jesus is not teaching his disciples to endorse a foolish or reckless ethic. Rather, Jesus aims to break open the closed world of his contemporaries. He does so by using this

[42]Frank Stern writes, "the priest and Levite had broken the very laws they were expected to uphold." See Frank Stern, *A Rabbi Looks at Jesus' Parables* (New York: Rowman & Littlefield, 2006), 214.

[43]Sylvia C. Keesmaat, "Strange Neighbors and Risky Care," in *The Challenge of Jesus' Parables*, ed. Richard N. Longenecker (Grand Rapids, MI: Eerdmans, 2000), 282.

[44]Kenneth Bailey claims, "An American cultural equivalent would be a Plains Indian in 1875 walking into Dodge City with a scalped cowboy on his horse, checking into a room over the local saloon, and staying the night to take care of him." See Kenneth Bailey, *Through Peasant Eyes: More Lucan Parables, Their Culture and Style* (Grand Rapids, MI: Eerdmans, 1980), 52.

[45]This is the claim of Douglas E. Oakman, who imagines Jesus's audience laughing at the Samaritan's unexpected and perhaps even foolish generosity. This is a reason, according to Oakman, for considering the passage as Christological and soteriological. He imagines Jesus concluding the story with, "And the Kingdom of God is like this," to describe how God's Reign is marked by such generosity in such unlikely places. (Incidentally, if this were the original intention of the story, it would then be appropriately considered a parable.) See Douglas E. Oakman, "Was Jesus a Peasant? Implications for Reading the Jesus Tradition (Luke 10:30–35)," in *The Social World of the New Testament: Insights and Models*, ed. Jerome H. Neyrey and Eric C. Stewart (Peabody, MA: Hendrickson, 2008), 125–40.

renegade outsider—the last person expected—to be the moral exemplar. The Samaritan represents a "world shatterer" and "the stimulus towards creating a new world. In this respect, he is the instrument of the God who is wholly Other, who cannot be identified with any object of this world, not even the Temple of Jerusalem."[46] This is a story about smashing the limits of one's moral imagination, which is why "Who is my neighbor?" is the wrong question to ask. God is to be found in every other and especially those considered "other." For this reason, distinguishing duties between those who are "near" and those who are "far" misses the point; all are called to participate in ever-more-inclusive communion for right relationship and solidarity.[47]

After concluding the story about the Samaritan, Jesus drives his point home by issuing his own question to the lawyer. He asks, "Which of these three, do you think, was a neighbor to the man who fell into the hands of the robbers?" (v. 36). The lawyer is so embarrassed that the despised Samaritan is the one who inherits eternal life that he cannot bring himself to say the word "Samaritan." Instead, he confesses, "The one who showed mercy."[48] But Jesus is doing more than defining neighbor relations through merciful action. He is changing the question. The lawyer posed a hypothetical question about the limits of one's duty to others. Jesus responds by asking who was neighbor *to* the person in need, thereby shifting the focus on "neighbor" from an object of obligation to a proactively loving subject. This makes "Who is my neighbor?" a less important question than "To whom am I a neighbor?" or even "How neighborly am I?"[49]

A THEOLOGY OF NEIGHBOR

The command to love God and neighbor is the summation of the law and prophets. The human person is made in the image and likeness of God, reveal-

---

[46]J. Ian H. McDonald, "Alien Grace: The Parable of the Good Samaritan," in *Jesus and His Parables: Interpreting the Parables of Jesus Today*, ed. V. George Shillington (Edinburgh: T&T Clark, 1997), 50.

[47]This point is made emphatically in Paul's letter to the Galatians (3:26–28).

[48]This connects back to Jesus's previous teaching abolishing reciprocal duties to love only those who offer love and reemphasizing the new command to love even enemies. By instructing his disciples to "Be merciful, just as your Father is merciful" (Lk 6:36), Jesus claims that human compassion is to imitate God's mercy (see also: Lv 19:2; Dt 10:17–19; Mt 5:48). Eduard Lohse adds that part of what is novel here is that even though Hellenistic and Jewish culture would have agreed that one should help another in need—even another considered unworthy or an enemy—the motivation would not have been described as an attitude of "love." See Eduard Lohse, *Theological Ethics of the New Testament*, trans. M. Eugene Boring (Minneapolis: Fortress Press, 1991), 56.

[49]Ian McFarland points out, "Jesus' counter-question redirects attention from the status of others to that of the lawyer himself" in McFarland, "Who Is My Neighbor? The Good Samaritan as a Source for Theological Anthropology," *Modern Theology* 17, no. 1 (January 2001): 57–66.

ing inherent dignity and value. To encounter another person is to encounter the Divine in our midst. As Matthew 25:31–46 illustrates, not only is it true that God can be found in every person, but Jesus identifies himself precisely with those pushed to the peripheries of society. Pope Francis insists, "Every stranger who knocks at our door is an opportunity for an encounter with Jesus Christ, who identifies with the welcomed and rejected strangers of every age."[50] How we treat the most vulnerable and needy is how we treat Jesus. Luke 10:25–37 adds to the biblical tradition of loving God by loving others through the unique details of this passage. A "theology of neighbor" expresses the religious and moral obligation to cultivate a culture of encounter through dignity and respect for all. Not only is every person to be considered a neighbor, but everyone is called to *be* the kind of neighbor depicted in the Samaritan's actions.

A theology of neighbor is framed by five observations drawn from Luke 10:25–37. First, not only is "neighbor" redefined, but love of neighbor now knows no boundaries. As Augustine asserts, "all people are to be recognized as neighbors."[51] This is a major reason why the Samaritan's example is crucial for asserting that Christian neighbor love is incomplete unless and until it leads to inclusive solidarity. Through this story, Jesus makes clear that the bonds of human filiation exclude no one and that moreover, no person is immune from the duties implied by neighborly relationships and responsibilities. In the face of social sins that foment division, exclusion, and unjust inequalities, the story of the Samaritan echoes the prophetic call to be "repairers of the breach" (Is 58:12).

A second, related point is that it is always and everywhere a duty to act as a neighbor. Put differently, there are no loopholes to avoid acting neighborly. This is suggested by the command to "go and do likewise." The challenge of the Samaritan's example is not necessarily to seek out a road like the one to Jericho, but rather to be the kind of person who goes out of his or her way and draws near those in need. This means being open to receive others—no matter who they are, what they look like or believe, or how they live—in order to build mutually respectful, responsible, and inclusive relationships, thus widening the scope of belonging. To "go and do likewise" is to be someone who builds bridges across social separation and subjugation. This can and should be done in one's own context: healing wounds, righting wrongs, working for *shalom* and *dikaiosynē* to foster right relationships, solidarity, and the just ordering of society. This is what

---

[50]Pope Francis, "104th World Day of Migrants and Refugees Message," January 14, 2018, w2.vatican.va.

[51]Augustine, *De Doctrina Christiana*, trans. R. P. H. Green (Oxford: Oxford University Press, 1999), bk. I.xxx.32. Moreover, the Samaritan's example "obliterates boundaries that close off compassion or that permit racism or attitudes of superiority" (Klyne Snodgrass, *Stories with Intent: A Comprehensive Guide to the Parables of Jesus* [Grand Rapids, MI: Eerdmans, 2008], 358).

Gustavo Gutiérrez means when he contends, "To know God is to work for justice. There is no other path to reach God."[52]

Third, to be a neighbor means to act with courage, mercy, generosity, humility, and fidelity. As a despised outcast, the Samaritan risked his own safety to tend to the robbers' victim and to enlist others in continuing that care. Perhaps, being a reviled outsider, the Samaritan more readily identified with the man left for dead.[53] Relating to this person in need catalyzes the Samaritan to draw near the man lying in the ditch, in stark contrast with the cold indifference or avoidance demonstrated by the priest and the Levite.[54] In this vulnerable setting, the Samaritan's merciful actions manifest tender concern as expressed in this detailed narrative: far more words are used to describe the Samaritan's actions than any other figure in the gospels, aside from Jesus. Between the bookended verses "Do this and you will live" (Lk 10:28) and "go and do likewise" (v. 37), the Samaritan exemplifies the courage that is required for *doing*. The Samaritan's example makes clear that doing matters more than believing or belonging (a parallel with Mt 25:31–46). Moreover, what matters is doing *like this*. The verbs Jesus uses to describe the Samaritan's care are part of Jesus's response to the lawyer's question: the law is fulfilled in love and meant to exclude no one (see, for example, Rom 13:8, 10; Gal 5:14).[55] Courage gives love the audacity to reach for solidarity.[56]

This is not just because love is what God wants for creation, but love—offered,

---

[52]Gustavo Gutiérrez, *A Theology of Liberation: History, Politics, and Salvation*, Eng. trans. (Maryknoll, NY: Orbis Books, 1988), 156.

[53]Although the Samaritan's own sociocultural context may be a significant factor in inspiring his actions on the road to Jericho, it does not determine his behavior. After all, not all marginalized people empathize with other vulnerable people or groups, just as all those who experience suffering are not always sensitive to others' suffering.

[54]Eduard Lohse states that, insofar as the story about the Samaritan is framed by the command to love God and neighbor, "passing by the half-dead man on the other side is the same as passing by the God who is on the side of the victims of injustice and oppression." See Lohse, *Theological Ethics of the New Testament*, 76.

[55]Frank Matera cites this passage in stating that "The essence of the law for Jesus is love." See Frank Matera, *New Testament Ethics: The Legacies of Jesus and Paul* (Louisville, KY: Westminster John Knox, 1996), 88.

[56]Solidarity is inferred by the boundary-breaking redefinition of neighbor more than the Samaritan's specific actions. The former creates a new category to include all human people, whereas the latter is still paradigmatic of unidirectional aid. Ada María Isasi-Díaz writes, "It is my contention that solidarity, in the original sense of that word, must replace charity as the appropriate Christian behavior—ethical behavior—in our world today. This contention implies a significant paradigmatic shift for Christian behavior for there is an essential difference between solidarity and charity. Charity, the word used most often when talking about love of neighbor, has been implemented mainly though a one-sided giving, a donation, almost always, of what we have in abundance . . . The paradigmatic shift I am proposing calls for solidarity as the appropriate present-day expression of the gospel mandate that we love our neighbor. This commandment, which encapsulates the gospel message, is the goal of Christianity" (Isasi-Díaz, "Solidarity: Love of Neighbor in the 21st Century," 31).

received, and returned in the Trinity—is who God is. Even though the story of the Samaritan is not to be understood as a Christological allegory, one cannot overlook the connections between the Samaritan's compassion and divine mercy.[57] Mercy is the characteristic that makes the Samaritan, like Yahweh and Jesus, who are moved with compassion (Ex 34:6–7; Lk 7:13). This is no small point. In the Hebrew Scriptures, compassion (*rakham*) and mercy (*hesed*) are most often used to describe God's character and purpose. *Hesed* is the very basis for the covenant with Yahweh (Dt 5:2, 10; Hos 2:16–21; Is 55:3) and the manifestation of solidarity between God's people, expressed through fidelity and obligation (2 Sm 7:11–16). *Hesed* defines faithfulness (Hos 6:6; Mi 6:8; see also Mt 12:7, 23:23) and characterizes those who love God (Ru 1:8, 2:20, 3:10). The Hebrew Scriptures make clear that *hesed* is inseparable from justice, judgment, piety, compassion, and salvation (Ps 72:1–4, 82:3, 140:13). These claims are echoed in the Christian Scripture as well. Some biblical scholars have suggested that the word *charis* (grace) is a closer equivalent to *hesed* than the Greek *eleos*, which is translated as "mercy." Identifying mercy with grace reinforces the idea that insofar as grace is God's self-gift, then God makes Godself known through mercy. *Eleos* appears in the New Testament dozens of times to fortify the witness of the Hebrew Scriptures that mercy describes God's own being (Lv 6:36, 15:11–32; 2 Cor 1:3; Eph 2:4) and how God treats God's people (Lk 1:58; 1 Pt 2:10). Jesus's teaching and healing ministry is framed in terms of mercy: it is what he teaches (Mt 5:7) and practices (Mk 5:19). It is the way to love one's neighbor and inherit eternal life (Lk 10:25–37), the standard for unlimited forgiveness (Mt 18:21–35), and what makes faithfulness possible (Rom 12:1–2; 2 Cor 4:1). It is the heart of God's desire for God's people (Mt 9:13, 12:7, 23:23), linked to wisdom (Jas 3:17), and the reason for hope (1 Pt 1:3).[58] The fact that the Samaritan's actions are characterized by mercy—a most Godlike quality—is meant to obliterate the belief that anyone might stand apart from the people of God or be unworthy of giving or receiving mercy. Luke 10:25–37 serves as a clarion call to disciples to overcome the ethnic, social, and religious boundaries that have kept God's people

[57]It should be noted that early commentators from Augustine to the Venerable Bede to Bonaventure did read this passage as a parable about the Reign of God and allegorized it as representing the entire *kerygma*. See *Quaestiones Evangeliorum* II.19; this summary is from Klyne Snodgrass, "From Allegorizing to Allegorizing: A History of the Interpretation of the Parables of Jesus," in *The Challenge of Jesus' Parables* (Grand Rapids, MI: Eerdmans, 2000), 4. Today, aside from a few exceptions, like John Dominic Crossan, who argue that the story is domesticated when read as a moral example story (see John Dominic Crossan, *In Parables: The Challenges of the Historical Jesus* [New York: Harper & Row, 1973], 56), most commentators agree this Christological allegory is not what Luke intends for this passage.

[58]See Sze-Kar Wan, "Mercy," in *The New Interpreter's Dictionary of the Bible*, 4:46–49.

from practicing the kind of inclusive mercy that God shows and requires.[59]

Compassion exemplifies mercy in this passage. Jesus describes the Samaritan's fulfillment of the law as motivated by compassion rather than knowing the right thing to do according to the rules. In Luke 10:33, the word for "compassion" is *splanchnizomai*, a reference to the entrails.[60] When this is translated into English as "pity," this fails to effectively express what is meant here: "being shaken in the depths of the womb or bowels, a wrenching gut reaction" or "his heart was melting."[61] Through this story, compassion serves as the "the optic nerve of Christian vision," providing a new way to see, feel, and act as a neighbor to other neighbors.[62] This new way of seeing cuts through socially constructed barriers and excuses that give reasons not to help. Overall, the Samaritan's compassion serves as the "fulcrum on which the story turns."[63]

In contrast to the lawyer's limit-seeking question, the Samaritan's actions show that love is oriented toward generosity, not minimum standards. Love should be an expression of a desire to help and heal, not motivated by duty. Love seeks union with the other for the well-being of the other, so it is not frugal or patronizing. Love is expressed through abundance, which marks the Samaritan's care at the roadside as well as his overnight stay at the inn, payment for two weeks' worth of care, and promise to return to cover the balance, if incurred. The Samaritan identified with another person in need, recognized him as an equal, and provided the kind of tender care and assurance for complete recovery that might only be expected from family members or close friends. Jesus insists this is the kind of steadfast, tender love that should be shared among neighbors. It is the kind of merciful kindness that God bestows on God's people and expects from and for God's people.[64] It is the fulfillment of everything Jesus had to teach.[65]

---

[59]See, for example, Jeremiah 30:17, Hosea 6:6, and Micah 6:8.

[60]In Proverbs 26:22, this visceral feeling is linked to the womb. In antiquity, the gut was considered the center of the person.

[61]William C. Spohn, *Go and Do Likewise: Jesus and Ethics* (New York: Continuum, 2007), 89; Gutiérrez, *A Theology of Liberation*, 114.

[62]Spohn, *Go and Do Likewise*, 87.

[63]Hendrickx, *The Third Gospel for the Third World*, 70.

[64]In Scripture, God is revealed as merciful and gracious, slow to anger, abounding in steadfast love and faithfulness (Ex 34:6–7). God's character and purpose are expressed as a love that is always faithful and never fails, a love marked by loyalty and tenderness, an overabundance (Jo 2:12; 1 Sm 20:14–17; Is 54:8–10) in goodness that endures for a "thousand generations" (Ex 20:6). God's gratuitous love endures forever and embraces all creation (Dt 7:7–9; Ps 111:4, 136:1; Dn 7:9–14). These themes are also found in the Christian Scriptures (see, for example, Lk 1:58; 2 Cor 1:3; Eph 2:4; 1 Pt 2:10).

[65]So believes Pheme Perkins in *Jesus the Teacher* (Cambridge: Cambridge University Press, 1990), 86. But Perkins acknowledges it is not quite that simple. On the one hand, the point of the story is when it comes to loving one's neighbor and being a loving neighbor, "Nothing is calculated; nothing is too much." On the other hand, Jesus understands that compassion "sets up rather a puzzle. It

Some dismiss the Samaritan's neighborly example as a hyperbolic ideal. But this misreading depicts the Samaritan as an exceptional hero rather than as a paradigm for how to love God by loving others and thereby inherit eternal life. The Samaritan recognizes another person in need and provides the care he is capable of offering. The Samaritan models humility in this story by acting within his means. Humility refers to the truth about ourselves as creatures: people who are intrinsically good, capable of exercising agency, and also limited by finitude. The Samaritan enlists others to join in caring for the man left for dead, and continues along his way. He does not sell all his possessions, disown his family, or abandon his trade. He does not set up camp in the ditch or dedicate his life to the "Jericho Road Development Agency."[66] This passage does not ignore the reality of finitude, question the legitimate pursuit of one's own interests, or neglect one's preexisting relationships. Through this story, Jesus challenges his followers to see in a way that recognizes the need around them and to respond by doing what they can, no more and no less.

The Samaritan also exemplifies fidelity, the loyalty that encompasses the whole family of God. Insofar as justice implies "fidelity to the demands of a [covenant] relationship,"[67] the Samaritan's actions show him to be an agent of justice. Justice delivers to each according to their due, and the Samaritan does his part to deliver justice to the robbers' victim. Justice fits with fidelity to hold us accountable to proximate relationships.[68] Fidelity is a virtuous allegiance to those who are closest to us and rely most consistently upon our care and concern. Although fidelity represents a strong pull toward these close ties, these relations among family members and friends should not be viewed in competition with a more expansive loyalty or solidarity with all of the members of the "household of God" (Eph 2:19).[69]

---

ignores social boundaries and all the reasonable sorts of calculations that people make. It may even cause those who are recipients or witnesses of it some perplexity . . . Jesus understands compassion and love of enemy to be very complex problems." See Pheme Perkins, *Love Commands in the New Testament* (New York: Paulist Press, 1982), 64.

[66]See Maureen H. O'Connell, *Compassion: Loving Our Neighbor in an Age of Globalization* (Maryknoll, NY: Orbis Books, 2009), 183–207. Dr. Martin Luther King Jr. believed disciples *should* strive to transform the road to Jericho to resist and reform these life-threatening conditions as part of their commitment to justice. King preached this assertion at Riverside Church in New York City on April 4, 1967, one year before his assassination.

[67]John Donahue, SJ, "Biblical Perspectives on Justice," in *The Faith That Does Justice: Examining the Christian Sources for Social Change*, ed. John C. Haughey, SJ (Eugene, OR: Wipf and Stock, 1977), 68–112, at 69.

[68]James F. Keenan, SJ, highlights the importance of fidelity for ordering claims of love and justice. He points out that doing justice for one's child would be different than doing justice for a stranger and argues that justice more appropriately pertains to the general relations with neighbors, whereas fidelity is a more apt virtue for family and friends. See "Proposing Cardinal Virtues," *Theological Studies* 56 (1995): 723–26.

[69]Ken and Michael Himes evaluate whether particular allegiances—like to one's country—are

Fidelity virtuously harmonizes one's commitments between the particular and universal. Practicing fidelity leads to other virtues like humility and temperance in striving for simplicity and moderate levels of consumption.[70] Fidelity ensures that we are properly attached to people and things, in the right way, for the right reasons, and ordered to the right ends. Balancing the demands of our many relationships with the call to build a culture of encounter across differences will be explored in greater detail in the next chapter.

Fourth, Jesus taught about this rightly ordered love and modeled it so that disciples could partner in practicing it in the world. This gives credence to Jon Sobrino's claim that the twin concerns for orthodoxy (right belief) and orthopraxis (right action) are incomplete without orthopathy. By this he means not only right feeling, but "the correct way of letting ourselves be affected by the reality of Christ."[71] Practicing orthopathy is eschatological: Christ is the agent of mercy, making Yahweh's compassion and covenantal renewal already partially realized through the unfolding Reign of God. The Reign of God is God's power transforming the world and confronting the forces that resist love, justice, and solidarity. To love God and one's neighbor as oneself is to be near this divine reality (Mk 12:34). This is reflected in Paul's exhortations to the first churches to practice the compassion of Jesus Christ for the sake of wider and deeper unity, since Jesus's mercy brings human beings together to share in Christ's mercy (Phil 1:8; Gal 3:28).

This dovetails with a fifth important lesson from this story: that Jesus aims to reorient disciples' vision away from lower limits and toward radical possibilities. As Eduard Lohse explains, Jesus teaches his disciples that love "knows no condition and no presupposition; it is valid for every place and every time" and that whenever and wherever people may be tempted to define or dwell on limits, the

---

incompatible with the global scope of Christian solidarity. They conclude that patriotism "is a good to be fostered by the gospel precisely because it is a locus of our experience of love for others" but warn against the idolatry of nationalism and other forms of too-narrow loyalties. See *Fullness of Faith: The Public Significance of Theology* (Mahwah, NJ: Paulist Press, 1993), 136–41.

[70]Temperance defines a limit. It moderates the drive for more and seeks fulfillment in what is sufficient. This virtue thus obviates justifying luxury or excess for those closest to us at the expense of providing more minimal goods and services to those in need. In conjunction with fidelity, temperance reminds us of our proper place in relation to others and God. This can prevent making some relationships, responsibilities, or goods quasi-idolatrous. In sum, fidelity and temperance cultivate proper attachment to people and things. Attachment is an important moral issue, as being over- or under-attached to people or things can lead to inappropriate relations. William Cavanaugh contends that a significant problem in consumer culture is not inordinate attachment to things (i.e., greed), but widespread detachment and dissatisfaction, placing people on a hedonic treadmill of never-ending consumption. See Cavanaugh, *Being Consumed: Economics and Christian Desire* (Grand Rapids, MI: Eerdmans, 2008), 34–35.

[71]Jon Sobrino, *Christ the Liberator: A View from the Victims* (Maryknoll, NY: Orbis Books, 2001), 210.

Samaritan's example is a constant reminder that "love as the determining motive of every deed orients itself by the possibilities."[72] But the aim here is not to make this an impossible ideal. Instead, it is a reminder that Jesus was posed a limit question about belonging and responded with a command to act in such a way that everyone belongs. The emphasis on doing is meant to be eminently practical, a call for all to participate in mission and communion. It is part of the project of *dikaiosynē* in line with Jesus's teaching to his disciples to be peacemakers and to put love and conciliatory right relationship ahead of religious legalism (e.g., Mt 5:23–24).[73] It coheres with Matthew's lesson (25:31–46) that disciples are judged not by what they believe but on whether they meet the needs of their neediest neighbors. In the face of any temptation to restrict solidarity or responsibility, the Samaritan's example is a constant challenge to make neighborly concern and commitment ever more inclusive.[74] Luke 10:25–37 urges us to expand our imagination, reaching for new possibilities in practicing love and cultivating solidarity.

The cost of discipleship is glossed over if it is not heard afresh, if it is accepted as familiar, or reduced to voluntary benevolence or hyperbolic heroism. As it was for Jesus's original hearers, the aim of this example story is to shatter expectations and excuses. It seeks to catalyze conversion to a deeper, fuller, and freer love of God and neighbor. Just as the priest and Levite are indicted for their lack of compassionate care—whether for religious reasons, moral myopia, or ethical inertia—so the goats in the Last Judgment are denounced for refusing to help the nearby in need (Mt 25:41–46).[75] This reinforces the single command to love God and neighbor in Luke 10:25–27, sending the message that disciples are to love God *by* loving their neighbor.[76] This leads Karl Rahner to cite the example

---

[72]Lohse, *Theological Ethics of the New Testament*, 57–58.

[73]Lohse summarizes this point by saying this passage is part of the overall aim to impose "the obligation on Jesus' disciples to be peacemakers and ministers of reconciliation, to overcome the differences that separate people, to promote mutual understanding, and to commit themselves in word and deed to peaceful cooperation among the peoples in their realm of influence" (ibid., 58–59).

[74]Maureen O'Connell writes, "Samaritanism in an age of globalization demands that [privileged Christians] recognize the connection between our ability to travel comfortably, if not prosperously, on our way and others' *in*abilities to even climb out of roadside ditches. It requires that we see the connection between our privilege and the under-development of others and between our inability to perceive injustices and others' perpetual experiences of them. It also requires acknowledging that our moral imaginations have failed to understand that a seemingly endless cycle of charity only calcifies social inequalities." See O'Connell, *Compassion*, 1–2.

[75]Importantly, however, neither the sheep nor the goats thought about God when they served or failed to serve those in need. The only difference between the sheep and goats is that the sheep (those who are saved) are the ones who offered assistance.

[76]Augustine explains that since God is love (1 Jn 4:8), all love is love for God and for union with God (*in Deo* and *propter Deum*; see *Confessions* XI.xxix.39) and that God alone is to be enjoyed and the world is to be used in loving God (*De Doctrina Christiana*, I.iv.4, 10). Love of God, according to Augustine, means loving God *in* the neighbor. For Augustine, the moral life is about loving the right

of the Samaritan in Luke 10:30–37 and the Last Judgment scene in Matthew 25:31–46 to conclude that "every act of charity towards our neighbor is indeed formally, even though perhaps only implicitly, love of God" and also that "every act of explicit love of God is truly and formally . . . love of neighbor."[77]

Gustavo Gutiérrez makes a similar claim when he uses the phrase, "theology of the neighbor" in *A Theology of Liberation*. This phrase comes from a brief passage by Spanish theologian José María González Ruíz, who exhorts Christian theologians to emphasize the Samaritan's fraternity as he writes, "it is inexcusable to omit an authentic 'theology of the neighbor.'" As González Ruíz sees it, this involves taking up the example of the Samaritan who "makes himself a neighbor from the others," serving as a model for being a person "completely universal, the sworn enemy of every kind of discrimination."[78] A theology of the neighbor implies a commitment to more fully realize the inclusive bonds of human solidarity for the flourishing of all.[79]

CONVERSION TO THE SACRAMENT OF THE NEIGHBOR

Duties to our neighbors are rooted in a reverence for God present in every person. Yves Congar claims that disciples' "deepest commitment" is "a paradoxical sign of God" who is our neighbor, or better, the "sacrament of our Neighbor!"[80] Congar continues, "Our neighbor is privileged above all because God is actually present in him. It is right and it is necessary to speak of the 'mystery of our neighbor' . . . [as] something which has a meaning beyond itself and in relation to the final reality towards which the whole history of salvation moves. We never know

---

things in the right way for the right end. The proper ordering of love lies in the objects of one's love (e.g., *De Doctrina Christiana*, I.xxvii.28), with everything following one's primary focus on loving God ("Descend that you may ascend to God," *Confessions* IV.xii.19).

[77]Rahner adds, "one can love God whom one does not see only *by* loving one's visible brother lovingly." See Rahner, "Reflections on the Unity of the Love of Neighbor and the Love of God" *Theological Investigations* VI (London: Dartman, Longman and Todd, 1969), 231–49, esp. 239, 247.

[78]See José María González Ruíz, *Pobreza evangélica y promoción humana* (Málaga: Manantial-Aguaviva, [1966] 1999), 98. As this book has not yet been translated into English, translations are my own.

[79]Shortly thereafter, González Ruíz cites *Nostra Aetate*, no. 5 (the Vatican II declaration on the relation of the church to non-Christian religions), which reads, "We cannot truly call on God, the Father of all, if we refuse to treat in a brotherly way any man, created as he is in the image of God. Man's relation to God the Father and his relation to men his brothers are so linked together that Scripture says: 'He who does not love does not know God' (1 John 4:8). No foundation therefore remains for any theory or practice that leads to discrimination between man and man or people and people, so far as their human dignity and the rights flowing from it are concerned."

[80]Yves Congar, *The Wide World My Parish: Salvation and Its Problems*, trans. Donald Attwater (Baltimore: Helicon, 1961), 124.

exactly who it is we are meeting in the person of our neighbor."[81] A "theology of neighbor" recognizes that God is revealed in our neighbors and that we are responsible for receiving the other through encounter that leads to accompaniment and exchange, aspiring for mutual embrace that nurtures inclusive belonging.

A theology of neighbor involves a particular way of perceiving others with reverence and respect. It resists distraction (following Mary's example in Luke 10:38–42) and less dignified visions of humanity. Gutiérrez suggests that a commitment to this manner of seeing requires a process of openness and conversion in encountering others.[82] As in the case of the Samaritan, this process requires a movement toward others in need: recognizing the other as a neighbor and being a neighbor to those considered "other." Gutiérrez explains, the neighbor "is not the one whom I find on my path, but rather the one in whose path I place myself, the one whom I approach and actively seek."[83] Partiality for the other—particularly the one in need—is the reason Gutiérrez believes the Samaritan's merciful actions represent the preferential option for the poor.[84] The preferential option for the poor has sometimes been misunderstood to be optional or to be an exclusive preference for the poor. It is instead a commitment to inclusively extend the reach of love, justice, and solidarity by beginning with those in greatest need. It is a commitment to emulate God's preferential care and concern for the most vulnerable members of the human family, those most deprived security and status.[85]

In rhetoric and practice, caution must be exercised, as words like *the poor, the vulnerable*, or *the marginalized* risk reifying conditions and treating people as a category by homogenizing them into a group of others. It can also perpetuate dichotomous thinking between us and them, making the poor people who need something from us, rather than first being our equal sisters and brothers in Christ. Emphasizing solidarity in tandem with the preferential option for the poor reminds the nonpoor that we have much to learn and receive from those who are poor. This also helps to avoid paternalistic or instrumental views that only see the poor

---

[81]Ibid., 125. Congar connects this to Matthew 25:31–46 to conclude, "We shall be judged on what we have done, not on what we have known" (ibid., 125–26).

[82]Gutiérrez argues this is not only true for individual others, but entire groups, including the poor and suffering "masses [who] are also our neighbor," in *A Theology of Liberation*, 116.

[83]Ibid., 113.

[84]Gutiérrez explains that the preferential option for the poor "involves a commitment that implies leaving the road one is on, as the parable of the Good Samaritan teaches, and entering the world of the other, of the 'insignificant' person, of the one excluded from dominant social sectors, communities, viewpoints, and ideas . . . The priority of the other is a distinguishing mark of a gospel ethic, and nobody embodies this priority more clearly than the poor and the excluded." See Gustavo Gutiérrez, "The Option for the Poor Arises from Faith in Christ," *Theological Studies* 70 (2009): 318.

[85]This is a theme that runs through both the Hebrew and Christian Scriptures. See, for example, Ex 3:7–8; Dt 14:29, 15:7; 1 Cor 1:28; and Jas 2:5: "Has not God chosen the poor in the world to be rich in faith and to be heirs of the kingdom that he has promised to those who love him?"

through their condition of socioeconomic deprivation or treat them as objects of Christian duty. Solidarity differs from charity because it replaces unilateral doing for with the mutuality of being with; solidarity seeks mutual empowerment to receive and build up the Reign of God already initiated but not yet fully realized.[86]

A theology of the neighbor is attentive to the ways that God accompanies and suffers with the poor and others pushed to the margins because of the dehumanization and deprivation they face. It is a call to recognize these suffering brothers and sisters as one's neighbors, not only in reference to particular people but entire masses of those who are poor, hungry, sick, suffering, and rendered invisible or voiceless. Gutiérrez points out that the poor should refer to our brothers and sisters who experience material deprivation as well as other forms of exclusion, thus becoming "socially insignificant." Hence, to speak of the poor is to describe those who have been rendered "nonpersons" and subject to "premature death."[87] Solidarity with the poor does not mean that the "haves" must provide for the "have-nots," as this provides necessary aid but does not necessarily cultivate mutual respect and understanding, sharing of power and resources, or a shared commitment to transform the status quo that benefits some at the expense of others. Solidarity provides the necessary conditions for engendering the respect, safety, and trust of all, keeping us always sensitive to the poverties around us and in us.[88] It ensures that discipleship does not shirk its public or political duties, providing the much-needed "interruption" to society described by Johann Baptist Metz.[89] The interruption needed today is the recognition that even though many

---

[86]The connection between evangelization and liberation was made explicit by Pope Paul VI in his 1975 apostolic exhortation *Evangelii Nuntiandi,* wherein the pope asserts that the church "has the duty to proclaim the liberation of millions of human beings . . . the duty of assisting the birth of this liberation, of giving witness to it, of ensuring that it is complete" (no. 30). Solidarity and the preferential option for the poor gained significant attention after the Second Vatican Council, especially as the Conference of Latin American Bishops (CELAM) interpreted the documents of Vatican II while reading the "signs of the times" in their sociocultural context. Gustavo Gutiérrez was an important theological advisor to the bishops during the conferences that gathered in Medellín in 1968, Puebla in 1979, Santo Domingo in 1992, and Aparecida in 2007. Although liberation theology and the preferential option for the poor have caused controversy with the Magisterium, Pope John Paul II and Pope Benedict XVI endorsed the preferential option for the poor as a matter of Christological faith and Christian charity. For example, in his opening address to the bishops gathered at Aparecida, Benedict XVI proclaimed that "the preferential option for the poor is implicit in the Christological faith in the God who became poor for us, so as to enrich us with his poverty (cf. 2 Cor 8:9)." In his 1987 encyclical *Sollicitudo Rei Socialis,* Pope John Paul II asserts, "This is an option, or a special form of primacy in the exercise of Christian charity, to which the whole tradition of the Church bears witness" (no. 42).

[87]Gutiérrez, *A Theology of Liberation,* xxi–xxii, xxix.

[88]Jean Vanier reflects on an abiding lesson at L'Arche communities: very often, people come to help the poor only to learn that they themselves are impoverished in many ways. See Jean Vanier, *The Heart of L'Arche: A Spirituality for Everyday* (New York: Crossroad, 1995).

[89]By "interruption," Metz contends that religion provides a radical break with the banal, a witness

of the billions of people who live in or near impoverished conditions are not visible to us on a daily basis, they are indeed our neighbors and make claims on us.[90] The task at hand is twofold: first, to determine how to raise this consciousness among Christians; second, to develop a prudential response to do what we can, where we are.

For Gutiérrez, this task begins with a spirituality of solidarity with God and with all human beings. This spirituality centers on ever deeper conversion to Christ-in-the-poor and is sustained by disciples' lifelong pilgrimage in prayer, commitment, and action.[91] It is a spirituality rooted in thanksgiving for God's bestowal of life and love. Conversion is an unending process of being transformed in greater gratitude and generosity. Though it is constant, it is not necessarily gradual; Gutiérrez concedes it implies a break in personal biases, prejudices, and mental categories, as well as in social, economic, and political structures.[92] This break—like Metz's vision of religion as interruption—shifts one's point of view. As with the Samaritan, it is a movement out of one's way and into the ditch to take up the vantage point of those who are poor, vulnerable, and marginalized. Therefore, conversion requires more than a new way of seeing or believing; it demands an intentional change of place. Gutiérrez proposes that this new place should be the locus for virtuous friendships, where disciples can share life with

---

to the "dangerous memory" of the passion, death, and resurrection of Jesus Christ. This involves attunement to the memory of suffering (past, present, and future) and a process of translation between the Reign of God and a specific context. It rejects the privatization, domestication, and neutralization of faith through a political theology that stands in solidarity with those who suffer and takes responsibility for their suffering. The "dangerous memory" means more than aligning the faithful with those who suffer from poverty or oppression; it empowers believers to embrace their agency for social awareness and responsibility. It challenges Christians to be critical of the status quo and the allure of progress and bourgeois triumphalism. See Johann Baptist Metz, *Faith in History and Society: Toward a Practical Fundamental Theology*, trans. J. Matthew Ashley (New York: Crossroad, 2007), especially 58, 88, 99–107, 158.

[90]Gutiérrez draws near to this point in his call for conversion, transformation, and a "radical change in the foundation of society." Speaking of the poor as marginalized groups, Gutiérrez writes, "Our attitude towards them, or rather our commitment to them, will indicate whether or not we are directing our existence in conformity with the will of the Father. This is what Christ reveals to us by identifying himself with the poor in the text of Matthew [25:31–46]. A theology of the neighbor, which has yet to be worked out, would have to be structured on this basis" (Gutiérrez, *A Theology of Liberation*, 116). Hence, a theology of the neighbor is not just an I–Thou encounter, but rather a sense of being in relationship with (and responsible to) many neighbors precisely *as* a neighbor.

[91]Ibid., 117. Elsewhere, Gutiérrez succinctly defines spirituality as discipleship, that is, following the Holy Spirit through life lived in love. See Gutiérrez, *We Drink from Our Own Wells*, 45.

[92]Gutiérrez, *A Theology of Liberation*, 118. He adds, "Christians have not done enough in this area of conversion to the neighbor, to social justice, to history. They have not perceived clearly enough yet that to know God *is* to do justice. They still do not live *in one sole action* with both God and all humans. They still do not situate themselves in Christ without attempting to avoid concrete human history. They have yet to tread the path which will lead them to seek effectively the peace of the Lord in the heart of social struggle."

those who experience the in-breaking of the Reign of God as nonpersons.

A theology of neighbor is a call to accompany neighbors in need. It is a proactive, place-changing love for God in the poor, as part of each disciple's vocation to *koinōnia* and solidarity with God and the family of God.[93] As the Samaritan shows, it is a love that is not content to stay "on its own front porch." Instead, as Gutiérrez claims, it means defining the neighbor "as the one I must go out to look for, on the highways and byways, in the factories and slums, on the farms and in the mines," which means that "my world changes."[94] Or, to put a finer point on this, it means that my *place* in the world changes. To "go and do likewise" is to be a neighbor who courageously and compassionately goes into the ditch in order to draw near to neighbors in need.

GO AND DO LIKEWISE

Doing likewise is fundamentally an exercise in "creative fidelity."[95] This means, on the one hand, being faithful to the Samaritan's example. On the other hand, this involves creatively imagining new possibilities, especially as they may be informed by one's specific context, abilities, and needs. It means exercising one's imagination to seek similarity in difference, that is, what is shared in common in and through diversity. Doing likewise implies discernment that is simultaneously personal and communal. It invites individuals to consider how they can practice courage, mercy, generosity, humility, and fidelity just as much as it involves building communities that share these traits. The measure of neighborliness is, after all, not about individual actions as much as it is building inclusive communities that are attentive and responsive to the needs of all. Doing likewise is a matter of prudence, a process of discernment to envision the goals and strategies by which people can live up to this standard without asking too much of themselves and others.

In the American cultural context that views the Samaritan as a model for random acts of kindness or a hero in an emergency, the Samaritan's paradigmatic example needs to be more robustly connected to the everyday demands of Christian neighbor love, including duties of solidarity and the preferential option for the poor. This process develops as people and groups practice courage, mercy, generosity, humility, and fidelity in such a way that it informs their way of seeing,

---

[93]See Gutiérrez, *We Drink from Our Own Wells*, 21.

[94]See Gustavo Gutiérrez, *The Power of the Poor in History* (Maryknoll, NY: Orbis Books, 1983), 44.

[95]William Spohn appeals to "creative fidelity" as part of the analogical imagination (informed by David Tracy's work) necessary for disciples to discern how to appropriately "go and do likewise" in their own context and relationships (Spohn, *Go and Do Likewise*, 50). See also Gabriel Marcel, *Creative Fidelity* (New York: Crossroad, 1982).

thinking, feeling, and acting. Although Luke 10:25–37 does not entail a relationship between the robbers' victim and the Samaritan or long-term neighborly relations, we can infer that such ties should be marked by mutual respect, accompaniment, and shared loyalty. Christian neighbor love puts us in touch with God's love, embodying God's work to create new life and new community, to actively serve the good of the other, build community, seek justice, exercise civic duty, and withstand personal risks.[96] In light of all the causes of anxiety and insecurity discussed in the first chapter, it is helpful to remember that "do not be afraid" is among the most repeated lines in Scripture. If we are lacking in solidarity, fear is the most likely culprit. Doing likewise is a commitment to overcome deception, cynicism, ignorance, indifference, and any form of anxiety that keeps us from going into the ditch, willing to risk encounter. In the face of cultural messages trying to convince us to buy into the myth of scarcity, the biblical witness maintains that our trust should remain firmly rooted in the superabundant providence of God.[97]

Encounter is a first step toward solidarity. This involves a dynamic and complex process that moves from encounter to accompaniment over time. Showing up for others over time builds trust, creating the conditions for people to authentically share in meaningful exchange. Through sharing life together and interacting across differences, we approach the vision for friendship described by Gutiérrez. These intimate connections—especially with those who may be easily ignored or isolated—will help cultivate a greater respect for "nonpersons," sensitivity to their suffering, and commitment to work for empowered action to alleviate these dehumanizing conditions.[98] What might begin as concern or compassion can grow into real affection and accountability, the tender embrace of fidelity as yet another step toward solidarity.

In sum, a theology of neighbor implies closeness with the poor and any estranged member of God's family.[99] "Love your neighbor as yourself" does not allow

[96]See the fourteen traits of "neighbor-love as a biblical and theological norm" in Cynthia Moe-Lobeda, *Resisting Structural Evil: Love as Ecological-Economic Vocation* (Minneapolis: Fortress Press, 2013), 186–87.

[97]Walter Brueggemann reflects on this dynamic between scarcity and abundance in his essay, "The Liturgy of Abundance, the Myth of Scarcity," *Christian Century*, March 24, 1999.

[98]Gutiérrez often notes that poverty is a complex reality and that solidarity with the poor requires a closeness and accompaniment in order to understand their concrete situation and to overcome fear and misperception. These intimate encounters will help us overcome fear, the "enemy of faith," and its "offspring, despair and indifference." See Gustavo Gutiérrez, *The God of Life* (Maryknoll, NY: Orbis Books, 1991), 173–79, 187.

[99]Gutiérrez lobbied to have this emphasis on proximity with the poor made explicit at the CELAM Conference in Aparecida. In the concluding document the bishops state, "Only the closeness that makes us friends enables us to appreciate deeply the values of the poor today, their legitimate desires, and their own manner of living the faith. The option for the poor should lead us to friendship with the poor. Day by day the poor become agents of evangelization and of comprehensive human promotion" (no. 398).

for any exceptions, not by sex, gender, or sexual orientation; age, health, or ability; race, ethnicity or nationality; class, religion, or politics. A theology of neighbor provides the basis for a culture of encounter because it moves us from random acts of kindness, assistance in an emergency, or spontaneous interactions to the reliability and mutuality of meaningful, mature, and responsible relationships between equals. As Gutiérrez explains, "If there is no friendship with [the poor] and no sharing of the life of the poor, then there is no authentic commitment to liberation, because love exists only among equals. Any talk of liberation necessarily refers to a comprehensive process, one that embraces everyone."[100] Avoiding the narrowing loyalties that mark some understandings of friendship, these relationships are a practice that seek an ever-widening "comradely communion" that effects the unity it signifies: the Body of Christ.[101] This is a friendship firmly committed to restoring the bonds broken by sin.[102] It involves gratuitous love for real people, especially the alienated and exploited.[103] It is founded on respect and freedom, shared agency and accountability, and mutual empowerment. Friendship is a mode of "social charity" that promotes interpersonal solidarity and inspires a commitment to work for the just ordering of society in systems and structures.[104] This commitment is part of what it means to work toward the biblical vision of right relationships in *shalom* and *dikaiosynē*, and it also realizes the analogical application of Samaritan-like neighbor love in one's relationships by drawing near to those in need. It is how disciples concretely engage the principles of solidarity and the preferential option for the poor in their everyday lives. It is part of the mission of the church to embrace the margins and marginalized, not as an act of charity "but a fundamental repositioning of the human geography of our time . . . a real and proper restructuring of Catholicism."[105] A theology of the neighbor lays the foundation for the beliefs, actions, and relationships that can make a culture of encounter possible. It is oriented toward hope, aspiring "to be human in this

[100]Gutiérrez, *A Theology of Liberation*, xxxi.

[101]Gutiérrez, *We Drink from Our Own Wells*, 70. Gutiérrez links solidarity to the "Body of Christ" imagery found in the Pauline Epistles, as seen in 1 Corinthians 12.

[102]This requires a humble posture of pardon and mercy; see Gutiérrez, *We Drink from Our Own Wells*, 96–102.

[103]Gutiérrez sums this up well: friendship is not a matter of fulfilling a duty, but the "work of concrete, authentic love for the poor that is not possible apart from a certain integration into their world and apart from bonds of real friendship with those who suffer despoliation and injustice. The solidarity is not with 'the poor' in the abstract but with human beings of flesh and bone. Without love and affection, without—why not say it?—tenderness, there can be no true gesture of solidarity" (ibid., 104).

[104]For more on the relationship between friendship and justice, see also Paul Wadell, *Becoming Friends: Worship, Justice, and the Practice of Christian Friendship* (Grand Rapids: Brazos, 2002).

[105]Andrea Riccardi, *To the Margins: Pope Francis and the Mission of the Church*, trans. Dinah Livingstone (Maryknoll, NY: Orbis Books, 2018), 28.

most inhuman of ages, to guard the image of man for it is the image of God," as Thomas Merton wrote.[106]

But living up to the depth of the challenge to consistently "go and do likewise" is no small feat. How should disciples be the kinds of neighbors who draw near to their neighbors in need without neglecting their preexisting roles, responsibilities, and relationships? This requires a moral framework, proposed in the ethics of encounter discussed in the next chapter.

[106]Thomas Merton, *Raids on the Unspeakable* (New York: New Directions, 1966), 6.

3

Discerning the Ethics of Encounter

The command to "go and do likewise" does not mean "go and do exactly the same" or "go and do this once in a while."[1] Rather, Jesus tells his disciples they are expected to do likewise in a way that suits their abilities and needs, given their specific context.[2] In this way, the story of the Samaritan serves as a "metaphorical framework" for the Christian moral life.[3] Doing likewise relies on faithful and creative discernment for what is required to follow the Samaritan's example. This chapter works through the discernment process so that each person can exercise prudence to do likewise by practicing the ethics of encounter. In Luke 10:25–37, the Samaritan's neighbor love is a practice of solidarity marked by courage, mercy, generosity, humility, and fidelity. The ethics of encounter requires more than a commitment to these virtues by individuals; in order to overcome the personal and social sins that contribute to social separation and unjust inequalities, these virtues must be integrated into one's relationships and communities. This means that the Samaritan's example challenges the way we prioritize our attachments and commitments. To go and do likewise is to go out of our way and into the ditch, drawing near others in need, and cultivating more inclusive relationships. The ethics of encounter serves as a guideline to receive and respond to others like the Samaritan on the road to Jericho in order to build a culture of encounter. These dispositions and actions help us move from encounter to accompaniment to exchange to embrace and ultimately toward a culture of solidarity that leaves out no one.

---

[1]In the Lucan text, "likewise" is *homoiōs*, not *homo*, meaning similar, not exactly the same.

[2]Jesus taught his disciples that it is not enough to know God's will revealed through Scripture and tradition; they must also interpret its meaning according to the "signs of the times" (Mt 16:3).

[3]This story uniquely guides disciples to faithfully follow Jesus Christ, who is the "concrete universal of Christian ethics, the paradigm that normatively guides Christian living." See William C. Spohn, *Go and Do Likewise: Jesus and Ethics* (New York: Continuum, 2006), 4.

DISCERNMENT FOR DOING LIKEWISE

As noted in the previous chapter, to "do likewise" is not about being heroic in an emergency or committing to random acts of kindness, even if this is how we popularly talk of "Good Samaritans" today. Jesus's parting words, "go and do likewise," urge disciples to personally adopt the Samaritan's disposition and actions into their identity, habits, and relationships. It is not enough to know that there are no nonneighbors; one has to "behave as though [this] truth were true."[4] This means imagining what it would take to practice Christian neighbor love for solidarity like the Samaritan on the road to Jericho. Jesus's command to go and do likewise is neither univocal nor equivocal; it functions as a template for moral action without being too confining or abstract. It operates in "creative fidelity" with the Christian tradition while seeking what is suitable for each person's abilities, needs, and circumstances.[5] Doing likewise implies the exercise of the imagination to creatively and concretely realize the Samaritan's example of love as solidarity in action. This means drawing an analogical link between the Samaritan and myself. It also means being open to the "surplus of meaning" in the text, the multiple interpretations that arise from a variety of perspectives, and the mystical nature of reality that is never exhausted of meaning or significance.[6]

Discernment employs the "analogical imagination" in seeking what is fitting for particular people in specific times and places.[7] In the previous chapter, I outlined how the Samaritan's exercise of courage, mercy, generosity, humility, and fidelity represents the love in action that makes solidarity real. The virtue of prudence is the practical wisdom to know what is fitting in order to pursue right action with the right intentions in the right way for the right outcome.[8] Prudence, which provides the integrating function to order these considerations, is the practical

---

[4]Daniel Berrigan, *No Gods but One* (Grand Rapids, MI: Eerdmans, 2009), 111. Berrigan writes that grace "makes a new start possible" like a "transfusion from on high." He urges, then, "Make the impossible possible, then probable. Make it actual. Behave as though the truth were true."

[5]David Tracy, *The Analogical Imagination: Christian Theology and the Culture of Pluralism* (New York: Crossroad, 1981), 57. Tracy describes the task of theology as linked in solidarity with those in need of liberation (ibid., 70).

[6]Tracy writes, "There is no one central interpretation around which all interpretations focus. There is no longer one, single fundamental question that all ask. There are several" (Tracy, *The Analogical Imagination*, 346). On the world as mystical, see pp. 358–62. The "surplus of meaning" of a text derives from Paul Ricoeur's *Interpretation Theory: Discourse and the Surplus of Meaning* (Fort Worth: Texas Christian University Press, 1976).

[7]Spohn explains that "moral implications are drawn less by strict logic than by a sense of what is appropriate and fitting" (Spohn, *Go and Do Likewise*, 55).

[8]Aquinas states that every virtue "is a kind of prudence" (*Summa Theologiae* I-II. 58. 4 and 2) (hereinafter *ST*).

reason to discern what is good and to freely choose it. Aquinas calls it "right reason in action" that is "caused by love."[9] Prudence moves from moral knowledge of the good to moral striving for the good; it integrates the intellect and desire ("appetite") to do what is good without experiencing inner turmoil or burden.[10] Prudence yields virtuous action in the habituation of exercising practical wisdom and guides our practice of virtue—the disposition to and habits of moral excellence—that construct our character.[11] Prudence helps us to reflect on experience, to judge good from evil (or a greater good from a lesser good), and it forms one's conscience. Prudence is essential for the ethics of encounter because unlike principles or norms, it takes into account the context of one's role, responsibilities, and relationships.[12] Prudence prevents other virtues, like courage or mercy, from becoming inordinately restrictive or expansive. Prudence is essential for never-ending discernment on how we can best love God, others, and self.[13]

Prudence, like all virtues, represents personally appropriate and applied means of cultivating the dispositions and actions that order a person to the *telos* of personal and collective flourishing. Prudence aids in effectively cultivating these virtues for each person, in each place. In the case of solidarity, it can be understood as a universal vocation, a moral principle for application, and a virtue to be cultivated. Solidarity and the preferential option for the poor cannot be considered reserved for certain experts, saints, or moral heroes. Instead, solidarity and the preferential option for the poor are core components of Christian neighbor love.[14]

---

[9]*ST* II-II.47.1–2. See also *Catechism of the Catholic Church*, no. 1806 (hereinafter *CCC*), where prudence is called the "charioteer of the virtues" as it "guides the other virtues by setting rule and measure . . . [to] overcome doubts about the good to achieve and the evil to avoid."

[10]*ST* I-II.107.4.

[11]Here and elsewhere I draw on Alasdair MacIntyre's discussion of virtue and practice among individuals, communities, and institutions as he presents in *After Virtue*, 3rd ed. (Notre Dame, IN: Notre Dame University Press, 2007). See, for example, 219–22.

[12]This is not meant to discount the value of universal precepts, middle axioms, or concrete moral norms. Rather, as Aquinas observes, the more one descends to matters of detail, the right action will not be known to all, nor will it be applicable to all (*ST* II-II.94.4)—hence the need for personal prudential judgment.

[13]*ST* II-II.31.3.

[14]In his "ordering of love," Augustine gives preference to special relations with those who, "by the accidents of time, or place, or circumstance, are brought into closer connection" with us (Augustine, *On Christian Doctrine* I.xxviii.29). To this circumstantial dimension I add with emphasis the importance of intentionally *drawing near* to others (especially those in need). In other words, the solidarity of someone like Mother Teresa cannot be held as the standard for all people; it would be vicious to expect a single mother of three children or with ill parents to forsake these special relations to pursue love and justice for faraway neighbors in need. The common good is best served by her faithful care for these people who rely so heavily on her, so long as this is not her only (i.e., exclusive) concern. A moral vision for solidarity provides a constant challenge to acknowledge and compassionately, courageously, and prudentially respond to the needs one encounters by happenstance as well as by aspiring to include those presently being excluded.

Each Christian individual and community should recognize solidarity as a part of their identity and purpose, an essential practice for realizing right relationship with family, friends, and neighbors that includes going out of one's way in order to draw near to others in need.

Prudence is related closely to conscience, which is the God-given ability to order, interpret, and judge what is good in response to the moral wisdom gleaned from Scripture, tradition, reason, and experience. The *Catechism of the Catholic Church* describes the dignity and freedom of the human conscience as the "Vicar of Christ" and the "sanctuary" to hear the voice of God.[15] One can never go against one's well-informed conscience, which is not the same as "going with your gut" or trusting your instincts because it seeks wisdom inside as well as outside the self. Conscience means "to know together" and is considered less a "thing" than a capacity, an activity, and a process of seeking how to best practice prudence.[16] Prayer and discernment are important tools to help each individual—as well as groups and communities—discern what is required in order to "go and do likewise."[17]

Special attention to prudence and conscience is important in light of the many obstacles to building a culture of encounter. As mentioned earlier, not every encounter is safe, edifying, or fruitful. History points to a great many encounters between individuals and cultures that proved harmful and even deadly. War, slavery, and colonialism inflicted pain and suffering, disease and death through violent encounters. Today, many encounters continue to be exploitative and involve any number of risks to personal safety and well-being. People with less privilege and power are justified in feeling unsafe encountering certain others because of who they are or who the other is. Helplessness, fear, contempt, hatred, and deception all pose real challenges to cultivating a culture of encounter. The same is true for those who bear especially strong beliefs and feelings, as well as those who are closed off to receiving the other, perhaps in judgment that they have nothing to learn or no way to benefit from an exchange with others. Some barriers are mental and emotional while others are learned from personal experience, like encounters that left a person feeling duped, used, or betrayed. Threats to physical safety represent legitimate reasons to avoid encounter. Bullying and harassment—online and in person—exacerbate insecurity and alienation, and can cause lasting trauma. Other encounters, including among friends and family, can be harmful, as is the case with physical, emotional, and sexual abuse. One in four women and one in nine men experience some form of intimate partner violence in their lifetime, representing

[15] *CCC*, nos. 1776, 1778.

[16] Kenneth R. Overberg, *Conscience in Conflict: How to Make Moral Choices*, 3rd ed. (Cincinnati, OH: St. Anthony Messenger Press, 2006), 38.

[17] See, for example, Dean Brackley, *The Call to Discernment in Troubled Times* (New York: Crossroad, 2004).

just one example of the way that encounter can become exploitative.[18] Another example includes encounters marred by gun violence.

While a culture of encounter relies on courage, mercy, generosity, humility, and fidelity, these virtues are always held in check by the virtue of self-care, ordering justice to oneself.[19] The demands of encounter should not outweigh the "unique responsibility to care for ourselves, affectively, mentally, physically, and spiritually."[20] Self-care ensures that just as a person strives to show respect and compassion to others, these same values are applied to oneself. The most basic rule in ethics—to do good and avoid evil, or at least, do no harm—certainly applies to the self. By practicing the virtue of self-care, individuals can better fight the temptation to feel anxious, overwhelmed, depleted, or defeated. Self-care is essential for cultivating the resilience to endure difficult encounters, unexpected outcomes, and deflating setbacks. It can also help us avoid overreacting to conflict or responding to harm with retribution.[21] These risks need to be addressed in full so that building a culture of encounter does not become party to endangerment. Prudence and conscience formation play key roles in ensuring that encounters affirm the dignity and freedom of everyone taking part. This is a reason why tenderness—rather than tolerance—is instrumental for moving toward a culture of solidarity marked by mutuality and inclusive belonging in partnership together. Tenderness affords the sensitivity and strength to meet the needs of those involved.

THE MORAL DEMANDS OF ENCOUNTERING OTHERS

The Samaritan's courageous, merciful, generous, humble, and faithful actions model the kind of boundary-breaking solidarity required by Jesus's command to love all, including enemies (Lk 6:27–36). The lasting lesson of this passage is that disciples have a duty to love those in proximity who are in need and also to never allow another human being to stand outside one's moral concern. To clarify, this "duty" is a moral ideal. In reality, a person's moral vision excludes more people than it includes. Human finitude means that people have a limited amount of time, energy, and resources. Our moral vision is always incomplete and in need of correction. What is required is a virtuous midpoint between deficient concern and its excess; just as finitude cannot be invoked to justify the *antiparechomai* embodied by

[18]Statistics available at https://ncadv.org/statistics.

[19]On self-care as a cardinal virtue, see James Keenan, "Proposing Cardinal Virtues," *Theological Studies* 56, no. 4 (1995): 709–29.

[20]Ibid., 727.

[21]For an illuminating treatment of how to better handle conflict, see Sarah Schulman, *Conflict Is Not Abuse: Overstating Harm, Community Responsibility, and the Duty to Repair* (Vancouver: Arsenal Pulp Press, 2016).

the priest and the Levite that deny care to one nearby, so the Samaritan's courage, mercy, generosity, humility, and fidelity cannot be used to set an impossible moral standard.[22] Though universally valid, the command to "go and do likewise" cannot be reduced to mere abstraction. Luke 10:25–37 illustrates that to "love your neighbor as yourself" is to be practically applied toward the next person one encounters.[23] Put simply, universal neighbor love is mediated through loving actual, nearby people. But too often, expressions of Christian neighbor love are episodic and partial.

Given the expanding networks of social, economic, and political interaction, "neighbor" takes on a more complex meaning today than when Jesus first told this story. Globalization and digital connections transform how we might define the word *neighbor,* referring to the one who is "nearby" (in English, Latin, and the Romance languages, for example, *proximum, prójimo, prossimo,* and *prochain* all connote proximity with another person). The question to ask, then, is, "To whom am I near?" The present social context presents new challenges for honoring obligations to neighbors near and far who experience varying degrees of need. All of this complicates what it means to be a loving neighbor and how to carry forward the Christian tradition that aspires for human flourishing in *dikaiosynē, koinōnia,* and solidarity.

Recognizing afresh the challenge of Jesus's command to "go and do likewise," the goal of this chapter is to construct a framework for the ethics of encounter that connects Christian neighbor love to solidarity. This framework draws on the moral vision of Luke 10:25–37 in order to shape identity, interpretation, and responsibility. It seeks a virtuous mean between the traditional view that presents Christian discipleship as oriented by charity and justice without sufficiently integrating the demands of solidarity and the preferential option for the poor on the one hand, and the liberationist perspective that exhorts every Christian to a life dedicated to solidarity with the poor in proximate communion with poor peoples, regardless of preexisting relationships and responsibilities, on the other hand.

---

[22]The command to love one's neighbor as oneself is, in reality, a standard higher than can be consistently met. But the significance is in the *striving* for the standard, and how, with grace, human capacity for love increases. Bruno Schüller explains, "Both the law of Christ and the natural law command love of neighbor. But in accordance with its essence the natural law can impose as a duty only a purely human (natural) love of neighbor, whereas the law of Christ commands a love of neighbor which surpasses all human capability, a supernatural love of neighbor." See Bruno Schüller, "A Contribution to the Theological Discussion of Natural Law," in *Readings in Moral Theology No. 7: Natural Law and Theology*, ed. Charles E. Curran and Richard A. McCormick (New York: Paulist Press, 1991), 83.

[23]Victor Paul Furnish, *The Love Command in the New Testament* (Nashville: Abingdon Press, 1972), 202. Furnish emphasizes that this summons to love is a Christian duty, a lifelong vocation, and a claim placed upon believers by God. Love is more than a disposition or feeling; it is an act of the will obliged by God's command that is not contingent on personal inclinations, attractiveness, benefit, or merit (ibid., 201).

This moral vision of solidarity moves forward in three steps. First, I address how solidarity has been developed as a theological principle and moral virtue in Catholic theology. I compare this vision of human life with the cultural theory of Charles Taylor to explore possible reasons why these teachings have not been received as important.[24] Next, I aim to find middle ground between the traditional understanding of Christian duties in charity and justice for the common good and the liberationist position that calls for solidarity with the poor without adequately accounting for the social context that helps and hinders progress toward this goal. Third and finally, I present solidarity as a life pattern characterized by three traits: (1) a virtuous identity formed by practicing courage, mercy, generosity, humility, and fidelity; (2) a practice of interpreting one's social context through a lens of attentiveness and appropriate response to those nearby; and (3) an exercise of responsibility through practices, relationships, and in specific locations to promote inclusive participation for human dignity and rights, solidarity, and the common good. In contrast to abstract principles or situation ethics calibrated to specific contexts, this life pattern of neighbor love orients personal dispositions, habits, and relationships to form people in community in order to "go and do likewise" today.

The Christian tradition, informed by Scripture, operates with a theological anthropology that defines personhood in terms of God-given dignity, as inherently social, and as called to freedom and integral development for human flourishing in communal settings marked by truth, charity, and justice.[25] As noted in the previous chapter, the command to "love your neighbor as yourself" illustrated by the Samaritan in Luke 10:25–37 strikes at the core of Jesus's teaching about what it means to be a Christian disciple. This is carried forward through the social mission of the church that promotes human dignity and rights grounded in the creation of the human person in the *imago Dei* (Gn 1:28), articulated in the canon of Catholic social teaching.[26]

---

[24]Roger Bergman contends that Catholic social thought remains the church's "best-kept secret" because it is not being *received* as "valuable or important." See Roger C. Bergman, *Catholic Social Learning: Educating the Faith That Does Justice* (New York: Fordham University Press, 2011), 9.

[25]These points provide the framework for the introduction of Pope Benedict XVI's final encyclical, *Caritas in Veritate* (nos. 1–9), written to commemorate Pope Paul VI's 1967 encyclical, *Populorum Progressio* ("On the Development of Peoples"). The *CCC* directly states, "All men are called to the same end: God himself. Here is a certain resemblance between the unity of the divine people and the fraternity that men are to establish among themselves in truth and love. Love of neighbor is inseparable from love for God. The human person needs to live in society. Society is not for him an extraneous addition but a requirement of his nature. Through the exchange with others, mutual service and dialogue with his brethren, man develops his potential; he thus responds to his vocation" (nos. 1878–79).

[26] On the subject of solidarity, the Pontifical Council for Justice and Peace's *Compendium of the Social Doctrine of the Church* (hereinafter *CSDC*) states, "In the light of faith, solidarity seeks to go beyond itself, to take on the *specifically Christian* dimensions of total gratuity, forgiveness and reconciliation. One's neighbor is then not only a human being with his or her own rights and a fun-

Insofar as Luke 10:25–37 delivers the message that there are no nonneighbors, it challenges disciples to be agents who advance human solidarity. Solidarity—used here as a theological principle and moral virtue—describes the condition of interdependence and shared human filiation resulting from humanity's common source and destiny. Solidarity can be understood as the *praxis* of human rights, characterized by equality, mutuality, and reciprocity.[27] Solidarity is a form of "social charity" that seeks unity across difference and inspires action for justice. It strives for a deep sense of communion, one that does not ignore conflict but is committed to reconciling differences by promoting shared interests and joint efforts to liberate the suffering and oppressed.[28] Solidarity is oriented toward hope; it trusts in the restorative, conciliatory, liberative, creative, and ultimately transformative powers of love to make new forms of human communion possible.

The word "solidarity" does not appear in the Bible, however. It has been extrapolated from related themes of community, kinship, and universal neighbor love in the Christian Scriptures.[29] For example, Paul's letters routinely appeal to the image of the Body of Christ as a metaphor for the church (see, for example, 1 Cor 12:12–31; Eph 1:22–23; Gal 3:28), expressed through the equality and unity of its members, without distinction between them. The word *solidarity* was popularized in nineteenth-century European labor union movements to motivate workers to unite as a group around common interests.[30] Used to promote strong in-group bonding, the slogan of solidarity thus maintained an "us versus them"

---

damental equality with everyone else, but becomes the *living image* of God the Father, redeemed by the blood of Jesus Christ and placed under the permanent action of the Holy Spirit. One's neighbor must therefore be loved, even if an enemy, with the same love of which the Lord loves him or her, and for that person's sake one must be ready for sacrifice, even the ultimate one: to lay down one's life for the brethren (1 John 3:16)" (Pontifical Council for Justice and Peace, *Compendium of the Social Doctrine of the Church* [Dublin: Veritas Publications, 2005], no. 196).

[27]Meghan Clark, *The Vision of Catholic Social Thought: The Virtue of Solidarity and the Praxis of Human Rights* (Minneapolis: Fortress Press, 2014), 102.

[28]Recall that *koinōnia* implies more than "communion"—it is also in partnership with the Holy Spirit. For that reason, I use *koinōnia* to link this biblical vision for communal bonds in right relationship with cooperating in the Spirit's desire to advance human unity and flourishing.

[29]This implies close relationships and a commitment to justice for those members of the community. According to Richard B. Hays, the New Testament authors aimed to show how community life in the early church provided a credible witness of Jesus's resurrection through virtuous friendships not restricted to dyadic relations or a tight-knit circle but "now exponentially expanded into the life of a community of thousands." See Richard B. Hays, *The Moral Vision of the New Testament: Community, Cross, New Creation; A Contemporary Introduction to New Testament Ethics* (San Francisco: HarperSanFrancisco, 1996), 135.

[30]Pope John Paul II, who frequently spoke and wrote on the theme of solidarity, was influenced by witnessing the *Solidarność* labor union movement in Poland, his native country. See Gerald J. Beyer, *Recovering Solidarity: Lessons from Poland's Unfinished Revolution* (Notre Dame, IN: University of Notre Dame Press, 2010).

connotation that defined boundaries and did not avoid conflict.[31] In the twentieth century it was applied theologically to highlight humanity's intrinsic social nature and interdependence, the equality of all people in dignity and rights, and the virtuous commitment to overcome obstacles to the unity of the human family.[32] With its view of society as basically organic and cooperative, Catholic solidarism intentionally created a middle way between liberalism that exalts individual choice and views community based on social contracts and communism that subjugates the human person to the collective will of the group or nation. As part of the church's teaching on human dignity and rights, solidarity moderates individual claims and duties relative to the common good.[33]

Before moving forward into the ethical obligations of solidarity, a brief overview of its theological development as a theological principle (universal teaching) and moral virtue (for personal formation) is in order.[34] Solidarity first appeared in church teaching in Pope Pius XI's encyclical *Quadragesimo Anno*, commemorating the fortieth anniversary of Leo XIII's 1891 encyclical *Rerum Novarum* on the rights of workers (the first document in the canon of Catholic social thought). It gained notoriety through Pope John XXIII's encyclical *Pacem in Terris* (1963) and Paul VI's encyclical *Populorum Progressio* (1967), and was a particularly favored term for Pope John Paul II, who advanced it as an ontological and historical principle and moral virtue. Ontologically, solidarity is a gift from God in creating and redeeming humanity. Historically, solidarity is an ethical imperative for humans to cooperate in advancing integral human development and the global common good.[35] As a virtue, solidarity is "not a feeling of vague compassion or shallow

[31]In evolutionary biology, preference for one's own kin is promoted and passed on through strong in-group bonding in order to maximize genetic representation in future generations. This sociobiological condition should be "appreciated for alerting us to the myopia and narrow exclusivity of kin preference," and should challenge Christian ethics "to recognize that a universal human need for some kind of ordering of affections and moral responsibility has been built into human nature by millions of years of natural selection," as Stephen Pope suggests in *The Evolution of Altruism and the Ordering of Love* (Washington, DC: Georgetown University Press, 1994), 132.

[32]This was a focal theme for liberation theologians like Gutiérrez and Sobrino, and was also highlighted in the social encyclicals of Pope Paul VI and Pope John Paul II. Note that John Paul II claims in *Sollicitudo Rei Socialis* (hereinafter *SRS*), "The freedom with which Christ has set us free (cf. Gal 5:1) encourages us to become the servants of all. Thus the process of development and liberation takes concrete shape in the exercise of solidarity, that is to say in the love and service of neighbor, especially of the poorest" (no. 46).

[33]It is also defined as a social virtue by way of proposing a vision for social order and the organization of institutions (*CSDC*, no. 193).

[34]This summary is informed by Matthew L. Lamb's entry, "Solidarity," in *The New Dictionary of Catholic Social Thought*, ed. Judith A. Dwyer (Collegeville, MN: Michael Glazier, 1994), 908–12.

[35]John Paul II later applied solidarity to include ecology as part of a "new solidarity" necessary for peace with the whole of creation. See his message for the 1990 World Day of Peace, "Peace with God the Creator, Peace with All of Creation," nos. 10–11.

distress at the misfortunes of so many people, both near and far. On the contrary, it is a firm and persevering determination to commit oneself to the common good; that is to say to the good of all and of each individual, because we are all really responsible for all."[36] Solidarity is an intellectual and moral virtue cultivated in friendship and accountable to justice.

Solidarity has received special attention from liberation theologians to unite Christians to share in experiences of struggle, suffering, inequality, and oppression as well as aspirations for collective action to overcome cycles of violence, oppression, and other experiences of injustice.[37] Liberation theologians point to the solidarity shared between God and humanity through the Incarnation and Jesus's triumph over sin and death through his passion and resurrection in order to argue that wider solidarity—especially with and among poor people—is possible as part of the unfolding reality of the "new creation" in the communion of the Body of Christ (see, for example, 2 Cor 5:17; Gal 6:15; Rv 21:5). This, in turn, makes possible a "new humanity."[38]

A theological view of solidarity provides a divine perspective on the integral human family as ontologically related creatures sharing the same source and destiny. This shared nature is the grounds for solidarity that promotes equality, friendship, social charity, and justice. Solidarity thus operates on interpersonal and systemic levels, as a fruit of shared love and as part of a commitment to the just distribution of goods and reform of vicious social, economic, and political structures.[39] Pope John Paul II recognized that the increasing interdependence resulting from globalization would need to be met by a moral solidarity to ensure that these interlocking relationships and systems would promote the global common good.[40]

---

[36] *SRS*, no. 38.

[37] Jon Sobrino describes solidarity as a fruit of a spirituality of liberation, a kinship with God and with others, and a spiritual exercise to more fully realize our "kinship with God in incarnation among the crucified of history." By drawing close to the poor and journeying with them in the struggle for liberation, we draw nearer to God. In this way, "God draws us godward" to vertical and horizontal right relationship and ever deeper and more integral flourishing." See Jon Sobrino, *A Spirituality of Liberation: Toward Political Holiness* (Maryknoll, NY: Orbis Books, 1988), 40–41.

[38] This is an important concept for Gutiérrez, who envisions liberation as essential to the vocation of "new humanity" (see, for example, Gustavo Gutiérrez, *A Theology of Liberation: History, Politics, and Salvation*, Eng. trans. [Maryknoll, NY: Orbis Books, 1988], 81, 106). Gutiérrez cites *Gaudium et Spes*, which claims, "We are witnesses of the birth of a new humanism, one in which man is defined first of all by his responsibility toward his brothers and toward history" (no. 55).

[39] The *CCC* states, "Socio-economic problems can be resolved only with the help of all forms of solidarity: solidarity of the poor among themselves, between rich and poor, of workers among themselves, between employers and employees in a business, solidarity among nations and peoples. International solidarity is a requirement of the moral order; world peace depends in part upon this" (no. 1941).

[40] *SRS*, no. 26.

However, these theological visions of solidarity do not consult social theory or social analysis in order to address how solidarity functions as an organizing principle, moral norm, or virtue.[41] Operating in a "top-down" fashion, church teaching begins with an anthropological premise of organic unity and harmony that does not sufficiently address the realities of individual self-interest, anxiety, and social conflict.[42] This approach of deductively following key principles differs from a sociological view of the organization of society. It speaks *to* rather than *from* human experience and addresses human identity and interaction in the abstract, removed from contextual setting. As a result, church teaching on solidarity still requires a more grounded development of its possibilities and limits.

The church could begin with the lived experience of its own one billion members, exploring how identity, interpretation, and responsibility function to create new possibilities and define real limits to solidarity. The simultaneously local and global reach of the church could be better recognized as a latent strategic and normative framework to spread a "Catholic social imagination,"[43] which represents a "social opportunity structure" for disciples to image culture

[41]Globalization and interdependence are not synonymous with solidarity. Though interdependence is often touted as an asset to solidarity, there are also experiences of fragmentation, alienation, and growing asymmetries in shared goods that cannot be overlooked. This is briefly acknowledged in *SRS* (no. 17). The *CSDC* also accounts for the "stark inequalities" between developed and developing countries that must be countered with the institutionalization of solidarity in structural form (see nos. 192–93). David Hollenbach suggests that "unequal interdependence" is a more appropriate description of the asymmetries of power reflected in today's globalized systems. See David Hollenbach, *The Common Good and Christian Ethics* (Cambridge: Cambridge University Press, 2002), 184.

[42]For example, Reinhold Niebuhr argues that Catholic social thought fails the test of realism by minimizing humanity's sinfulness. Human rejection of finitude and misuse of freedom leads to what Niebuhr describes as a constant state of anxiety and insecurity. To compensate, humans pridefully overstep their limits and are tempted to conflate their own interests with the divine will. In Niebuhr's view, Catholic ethicists tend to inadequately account for these sins of pretension and overestimate human capacity despite finitude and sin. See Reinhold Niebuhr, *The Nature and Destiny of Man: A Christian Interpretation, Volume I: Human Nature* (Louisville, KY: Westminster John Knox Press, 1996), 137, 178–86.

In addition to being a universal human condition, fear, anxiety, and even anger about scarcity, the threat of violence, and the unknown "other" seem to be especially pervasive in American culture. Gregory Baum asserts that these must be addressed as specific cultural traits (and vices) before solidarity can be pursued in *Compassion and Solidarity: The Church for Others* (New York: Paulist Press, 1990), 90–94.

[43]Joseph M. Palacios, *The Catholic Social Imagination: Activism and the Just Society in Mexico and the United States* (Chicago: University of Chicago Press, 2007), 17, 57–62. Palacios develops the concept of a "Catholic social imagination" as an "ideal-type" borrowed from C. Wright Mills (*The Sociological Imagination*, 1959) and informed by Ann Swidler's work on culture in action (see Ann Swidler, "Culture in Action: Symbols and Strategies," *American Sociological Review* 51, no. 2 [April 1986]: 273–86). Palacios's thesis is that Catholics possess "distinctive ways of understanding, developing, organizing, and analyzing public issues of social justice based on their social doctrine" that are sociologically relevant for understanding and practicing solidarity (Palacios, *The Catholic Social Imagination*, 58).

as oriented toward unity and harmony, to articulate strategies for action, and to rely on resources, rituals, and local, regional, and national networks to cultivate mutuality, interdependence, inclusive belonging, and collaboration for the common good. It provides an alternative vision to instances of inordinate social disengagement, self-interest, and conflict. It invites its members to cultivate habits and virtuous relationships that could more widely promote human dignity, rights, and responsibilities, and lead to integral development and flourishing. In particular, this opportunity structure can and should be used to promote knowledge and practice of the principles of Catholic social thought, as many US lay Catholics demonstrate little familiarity with tenets like solidarity and are unable to articulate it as part of their social justice principles.[44] The potential of a "Catholic social imagination" remains more latent than realized, especially in light of the significant gap between the teaching of the US Catholic Church and the convictions and practices of Catholic laity.[45]

One could point to any number of examples of this disconnection, but on the subject of solidarity, a relevant one is US Catholics' views on immigration. In 2003, the US Catholic Bishops issued a pastoral letter on immigration, "Strangers No Longer: Together on the Journey of Hope," cowritten with the Catholic Bishops of Mexico. Echoing the call to conversion, communion, and solidarity raised in John Paul II's 1999 apostolic exhortation, *Ecclesia in America,* the bishops emphasize the universal experience of migration in human history and Scripture (nos. 13–27), the rights of migrants according to human dignity and other tenets of Catholic social teaching (nos. 28–39), and the urgent need for Christians to work together in pastoral response and policy reform (nos. 40–55). To establish the framework for making this call, the bishops highlight that the bonds of human interdependence transcend the US–Mexico border. After drawing from and applying themes like conversion, communion, and solidarity, midway through the document, the content shifts from theological principles to addressing the crucial challenges of the immigration policies and practices between the United States and Mexico. The document is well informed about the related issues of enforcement, detention, employment, and legalization; it offers a clear-eyed view of the effects on individuals, families, and communities; and it brings together human and divine perspectives on immigration to call Catholics to stand in solidarity

[44]Palacios summarizes the findings of his ethnographic studies of US Catholics by stating, "U.S. Catholics do not appropriate solidarity as a principle and do not know how to incorporate it into their normative sense of social Catholicity—even though they use more pragmatic discourses of collaboration, networking, partnering, and the like. Certainly the idea of solidarity as a virtue does not emerge" (Palacios, *The Catholic Social Imagination,* 77).

[45]This does not imply there was once a golden age where church teaching was met by popular practice. A historical view indicates this gap has long persisted—see A. M. Crofts, *Catholic Social Action: Principles, Purpose, and Practice* (St. Louis, MO: B. Herder Book Co., 1936), 23.

with their migrant brothers and sisters, and, out of this conviction and vantage point, advocate for and participate in immigration reform.

Although this document was praised by many in the United States and Mexico, it also received backlash from those who rejected the bishops' authority to speak on immigration policies and practices.[46] One poll showed significant differences in opinion between Catholic Church leaders and the laity, with 64 percent of Catholics supporting greater enforcement to encourage "illegal immigrants" to return to their place of origin.[47] A Pew Research Center report found that 56 percent of non-Hispanic white Catholics agreed with the statement that immigrants are "a burden because they take our jobs, housing, and health care."[48] Despite the bishops' efforts to encourage compassion and solidarity for people beyond the US border, many Catholics view this issue more in terms of national citizenship than border-transcending discipleship. Xenophobia among Christians—despite repeated commands to welcome the stranger in Scripture—continues today. More than two-thirds of white evangelicals and nearly one in two Catholics say America has no responsibility to house refugees.[49]

This example illustrates a major drawback in the dominant "top-down" approach of Catholic social teaching, employing a method of moving from church teaching to popular reception. As philosopher Charles Taylor suggests, this is due in part to the present "social imaginary," or "the generally shared background understandings of society, which make it possible for it to function as it does."[50] The "social imaginary" has important implications for shared moral imagination, as it shapes what people believe is socially valued, the scope of obligation, and

[46]Michael Budde recounts popular response to bishops' teaching on immigration, citing newspaper editorials and online comment sections filled with opinions like the following: "If the bishops want to get involved in politics, they should lose their tax-exempt status"; "Bishops who do not comply with the law—and encourage others to resist immigration laws—should be locked up"; "Bishops are motivated by the collection basket, since so many illegals are Catholic"; and even an extreme view that the Roman Catholic Church is "aiding and abetting" the "reconquista" of the United States by Mexico and the Vatican. See Michael Budde, *The Borders of Baptism: Identities, Allegiances, and the Church* (Eugene, OR: Cascade Books, 2011), 85. See also Peggy Levitt, *God Needs No Passport: Immigrants and the Changing American Religious Landscape* (New York: New Press, 2007).

[47]Full report available at the Center for Immigration Studies, http://cis.org/ReligionAndImmigrationPoll. These statistics should be compared with considerably more favorable views of immigrants and immigration policies reported by a June 2012 Knights of Columbus–Marist poll. See "Poll Finds Americans Respect Immigrants, Want 'Non-Partisan' Solution," Catholic News Agency, June 12, 2012.

[48]Gregory A. Smith, "Attitudes toward Immigration: In the Pulpit and the Pew," Pew Research Center, April 26, 2006.

[49]Hannah Hartig, "Republicans Turn More Negative toward Refugees as Number Admitted to U.S. Plummets," Pew Research Center, May 24, 2018.

[50]Charles Taylor, *Modern Social Imaginaries* (Durham, NC: Duke University Press, 2004).

what can reasonably be expected from social participation. On the one hand, Taylor understands some features of the contemporary Western social imaginaries to foster shared values for connection and kinship. On the other, experiences of violence, chaos, and disorder can generate feelings of fear, vulnerability, and despair. Living in an age of the "buffered self" means being influenced by this social imaginary of expressive individualism. The chief values are freedom, invulnerability, self-possession, and personal achievement. Taylor warns that this social imaginary also contributes to blindness and insensitivity, moral malaise and mutual fragilization.[51] Those who maintain their religious belief tend to express what Taylor calls "minimal religion," which is confined mostly to one's immediate circle of family and friends.[52] When faith or morals are socially applied in this context, they risk being lost in abstractions like "systems" or "markets" or privatized concepts like "individual rights" or "solidarity" that are marked by clear insiders and outsiders (which is not in fact solidarity).

Returning to Taylor's discussion of the "immanent frame" and "closed world structures" (see Chapter 1), the domestication of Christianity sends the message that God only desires individual human well-being accomplished through therapeutic care and augmented through God's love. Sacrifices to exercise social responsibility for the common good are rendered superfluous. Optional altruism threatens to replace obligations of justice and bonds of solidarity.[53] What is the cause of this impoverished social imaginary? Taylor points to the fact that, for all the connection and promise touted in our globalized and technological age, the persistence of poverty, violence, and injustice contributes to a growing sense of futility, despair, and disappointment. This, in turn, contributes to the "closed world structures" of the immanent frame and the retreat back into the safety of the "buffered self." In stark contrast, Christianity calls believers to conversion, to a new way of seeing and acting as participating with God who is at work in

---

[51]Charles Taylor, *A Secular Age* (Cambridge, MA: Belknap Press, 2007), 300–304. This is not itself a negative quality of social life; indeed, "weak ties" can strengthen overall social cohesion and efficiency. A classic articulation of this position is made by Mark S. Granovetter, "The Strength of Weak Ties," *American Journal of Sociology* 78, no. 6 (May 1973): 1360–80. Nonetheless, Taylor argues that these weak ties are replacing strong ties in some instances, thus diffusing the quality of social life and making social relations and commitments more fragile.

[52]This phrase is borrowed from Mikhaïl Epstein in his description of Russian Christianity in a post-Soviet context (Taylor, *A Secular Age*, 533–34).

[53]Taylor contends this is already the case: "our philanthropy [is] vulnerable to the shifting fashion of media attention, and the various modes of feel-good hype. We throw ourselves into the cause of the month, raise funds for this famine, petition the government to intervene in that grisly civil war; and then forget all about it next month, when it drops off the CNN screen. A solidarity ultimately driven by the giver's own sense of moral superiority is a whimsical and fickle thing. We are far in fact from the universality and unconditionality which our moral outlook prescribes." Taylor, *A Secular Age*, 696.

the world. Courageously and publicly working toward a sacramental vision and transcendent cosmic order could lead to a transformation of the frame away from the buffered self and closed world structures. This could shift the impetus away from unencumbered autonomy and optional altruism toward the possibilities of grace-empowered participation in community life. This would produce a more life-giving social imaginary.

In a fitting move for a culture of encounter, Taylor describes the transformation of the frame as pivoting on the example of the Samaritan who acts in response to a wounded person, evoked through a corporeal encounter. This inaugurates new bonds of "we," which, due to the Incarnation, binds God to humanity and extends outward into a network of solidarity.[54] This implies not a new set of rules, but rather another way of being: specifically, a way of belonging together that strives to transcend boundaries.

The Samaritan's example points to the need for fidelity to an ever-more-inclusive network of relations. But as these relations are categorized and duties articulated, divided, and institutionalized, it can generate the counterproductive effect of a "bureaucratic hardening" of people, their relationships, and systems of belonging. Taylor identifies this as part of the excarnation of Christianity, wherein bowel-wrenching *splanchnizomai* (i.e., compassion) is delegated and diffused through abstract networks of agape.[55] Christian ethics only exacerbates the problem when it is distorted by a "fetishism of rules and norms" that dwells more on rhetoric than praxis.[56]

These insights identify a reason why theologizing and moralizing about solidarity fail to be effectively received: because of their dramatic incompatibility with the immanent frame and present social imaginary. The feedback loop between the buffered self and the social imaginary only reinforces the ideas, values, and practices that permit moral obtuseness, moral diffusion, moral incompetence, and moral impotence to persist. This feedback loop creates a closed world structure

[54]Taylor describes this as a "skein of relations which link particular, unique, enfleshed people to each other, rather than a grouping of people together on the grounds of their sharing some important property" or interest. Ibid., 739.

[55]In Taylor's view, the bureaucratic hardening of these networks is both unintentional (simply the result of trying to institutionalize agape) and also the effect of the unavoidable desire for power, wherein the "monstrous comes from a corruption of the highest, the agape-network." This only drives people further into the problems of objectification and disenchantment, two main culprits of secularity. Ibid., 740–41.

[56]Ibid., 742. From Taylor's analysis of the Samaritan story, we can surmise that a "theology of neighbor" is less about definitions and norms and more about a consistent life pattern that is attentive to others, draws near to the "other," and acts in love, justice, and solidarity with others. It must make an effort to avoid the "idolatrous traps" of even the best codes and avoid the temptation to identify temporal order and progress with Christian faith and one of its chief objects, the Reign of God (ibid., 743).

that marginalizes alternative social imaginaries, making it more difficult to resist and reform the status quo.

And yet, Taylor does not despair at this situation—instead, he recognizes it as all the more reason for Christians to respond to the call to conversion and participate in shared efforts to transform the immanent frame into a broader, more communal account of reality. Hope is found in being led by "God's pedagogy" of solidarity with humanity, revealed in Scripture and tradition, toward a new way of being, seeing, acting, and belonging to each other. To cultivate solidarity is to move beyond concepts, categories, and rules, breaking through the feedback loop between the buffered self and closed world structure of the present social imaginary. It requires the incarnation of solidarity as a principle and virtue exercised in relationships and practices of mutual respect and responsibility, interdependence, and inclusive belonging.

Turning to Taylor is important for proposing the ethics of encounter for several reasons. First, his analysis confirms the present need for neighbor love as a practice of solidarity for the common good. Second, it sheds light on the difficulties of proposing as solutions theological principles and moral virtues like agape, justice, and solidarity in two ways: (1) they need to be translated and applied to be effective within the present socio-cultural reality; and (2) the potential for bureaucratization can obstruct the integration of these principles and virtues into social relations and macrolevel systems. And third, Taylor's work provides a crucial reminder (both for Luke's passage and the corresponding theology of neighbor) to avoid the idolatrous trap of overemphasizing codes and categories. The ethics of encounter must heed these features of the present social context. The ethics of encounter should rely on the resources within a Catholic social imagination to transform the immanent frame and actively cultivate the creative fidelity that will inspire and sustain disciples to "go and do likewise" today.

THE PROPHETIC IMAGINATION

The present social context makes it difficult to imagine how Christian disciples should adopt the moral and social obligations imparted by Jesus in Luke 10:25–37. To begin to follow the Samaritan's example first requires seeing that this way of living is possible. It points to the need for what Walter Brueggemann describes as "prophetic imagination."[57] This promotes a vision that is both critical and en-

[57]Brueggemann identifies several ways for this prophetic imagination to be cultivated and sustained. The key, as he sees it, lies in small group participation characterized by the following traits: (1) long and available memory that immerses the present community into the tradition's past, (2) a sense of pain that is adopted and recounted as social reality and publicly honored, (3) an active

ergizing, denouncing present injustices and infidelities as well as presenting an alternate vision of "faithfulness and vitality."[58] This, linked to the Catholic social imagination described by Palacios, provides disciples with access to ways of seeing, thinking, feeling, speaking, and acting in order to transform the immanent frame into one that more fully captures the gospel-informed vision of the good life and more deeply embraces the responsibilities required by the "signs of the times" (Mt 16:3).

This prophetic vision does not turn a blind eye to the realities of finitude and sin; it looks through these natural limits and moral failures to the potential of graced human nature in cooperation with God's will. A Catholic social imagination is necessarily Christocentric, modeled on the incarnate, kenotic teaching and healing ministry of Jesus Christ. In this mode of *kenosis* (Phil 2:5–11), a Catholic social imagination focuses not only on human goods like flourishing and fulfillment but on the vulnerability, sacrifice, and courageous and compassionate actions necessary to more fully realize them. It attends to others' needs and inspires a contextually appropriate response. It operates on the personal and communal level, guiding "the way" of discipleship from the personal to the structural.[59]

A prophetic imagination complements a Catholic social imagination that envisions discipleship as public and prophetic. A public and prophetic imagination inspires disciples to participate in articulating and working cooperatively to advance the public good rather than private interests or parochial benefit.[60] It is motivated by an "intellectual solidarity" in pursuit of the common good.[61] It searches for public spaces to converse, debate, and organize how to promote

---

practice of hope in the promises of God that judge the present facts, and (4) an effective mode of discourse that involves people across generations. See Walter Brueggemann, *The Prophetic Imagination*, 2nd ed. (Minneapolis: Fortress Press, 2001), xvi.

[58]Ibid., 59. Brueggemann writes, "The riddle and insight of biblical faith is the awareness that only anguish leads to life, only grieving leads to joy, and only embraced endings permit new beginnings" (ibid., 56).

[59]Examples of effective action in this regard may be found in John Hogan's *Credible Signs of Christ Alive: Case Studies from the Catholic Campaign for Human Development* (Lanham, MD: Sheed & Ward, 2003). The Catholic Campaign for Human Development is the official antipoverty agency of the US Catholic Bishops, although its good and important work is underfunded and struggles to receive the widespread attention it deserves. Valuable resources for joining these efforts may be found at http://www.usccb.org/about/catholic-campaign-for-human-development/.

[60]This means that instead of people focusing on "I want x," participants reflect and converse on the idea that "x would be good for the community to which we belong." See Hollenbach, *The Common Good and Christian Ethics*, 143; Benjamin Barber, *Strong Democracy: Participatory Politics for a New Age* (Berkeley: University of California Press, 1984), 171.

[61]This virtue is promoted for the way it cultivates a desire to take other people seriously and engage them in fruitful conversation about the good life and its implications for the *polis*. Like tolerance, it recognizes and respects differences and avoids coercion; unlike tolerance, it eschews avoiding conflict in favor of humble and earnest engagement with the other in a spirit of genuine freedom and civility. See Hollenbach, *The Common Good and Christian Ethics*, 137–52.

shared goods. It appeals to religious symbols and other shared expressions of value and meaning to add depth and breadth to what is meant by the "public."[62] It raises a critique against vicious excess, deprivation, and other abuses of power. It can speak for those who may be left out of the conversation, whose concerns and needs might go otherwise unheard. It aims to sustain a commitment to the common good and justice for all in the face of enduring social, political, and economic difficulties.[63] It relies on the resources of Scripture and tradition, especially in word and sacrament, offering continual renewal and recommissioning to its people through communal ritual and support.[64]

A Catholic social imagination presents a distinctive sense of identity, a particular way of practicing interpretation, and a commitment to exercise responsibility in response to encountered needs. As public and prophetic, it reorients disciples' vision away from unfettered freedom and self-interest to the benefits, indebtedness, and duties of living interdependently as part of the covenanted community.[65] It cultivates inventiveness based on the memories and hopes of the Christian tradition.[66] Bringing together the shared responsibilities of neighbors as disciples and citizens, a Catholic social imagination can help foster social capital and build on networks of relations to expand spheres of justice and solidarity. In this way, a Catholic social imagination helps disciples faithfully witness to the "fullness of faith."[67]

---

[62]See Martin Marty, *The Public Church* (New York: Crossroad, 1981). "Public" refers to what is available to and shared by members of a society.

[63]For a well-informed analysis of the resources and responsibilities of public theology, especially in the Catholic tradition, see Kristin Heyer, *Prophetic & Public: The Social Witness of U.S. Catholicism* (Washington, DC: Georgetown University Press, 2006).

[64]Eucharist, for example, is a sacrament full of reminders of the shared identity and mission of the faithful in the world. As Pope Benedict XVI (then Joseph Cardinal Ratzinger) writes, "we cannot have communion with the Lord if we are not in communion with each other . . . when we go to meet him in the Mass, we necessarily go to meet each other, to be at one with each other." See Joseph Cardinal Ratzinger, *God Is Near Us: The Eucharist, the Heart of Life*, trans. Henry Taylor (San Francisco: Ignatius Press, 2003), 52–53. The *Catechism of the Catholic Church* states that the "Eucharist commits us to the poor" (no. 1397).

[65]The *CSDC* includes as part of the work of solidarity that it "requires that men and women of our day cultivate a greater awareness that they are debtors of the society of which they have become part. They are debtors because of those conditions that make human existence livable, and because of the indivisible and indispensable legacy constituted by culture, scientific and technical knowledge, material and immaterial goods and by all that the human condition has produced" (no. 195, emphasis removed).

[66]I use inventiveness here to refer to the work of bringing about something new and envision this as a constructive feature of the "interruption" J. B. Metz describes in his work on political theology based on the "dangerous memory" of the passion, death, and resurrection of Jesus Christ (see Metz, *Faith in History and Society*, 105–7).

[67]This phrase is drawn from Michael J. Himes and Kenneth R. Himes, *Fullness of Faith: The Public Significance of Theology* (New York: Paulist Press, 1993). They write, "Public theology makes the linkage between the faith we profess and how we live in society . . . Only an interpretation of the

A Catholic social imagination flows from a sacramental vision that recognizes the manifestation of grace in every time, place, and person. Rather than being diffused in abstraction, this recognizes the concrete as sacred, holding together the particular and universal, the local and global. This is especially significant for a "theology of the neighbor" that calls disciples to reverence every other person as neighbor and to be a loving neighbor to each and to all.[68]

THE ORDERING OF LOVE

Returning to the subject of a "theology of neighbor," we consider Gutiérrez's claim that "neighbor" applies not only to each, but to all in the sense that the poor and suffering "masses are also our neighbor."[69] This raises the question of how to love these neighbors.[70] This leads to additional questions, like how to love these neighbors relative to nearer neighbors and how to make a moral judgment between competing claims based on proximity and need. In short order, we can identify several important moral concerns: (1) the difficulty of loving distant neighbors, (2) deliberating to whom and how to respond when faced with competing claims between neighbors (what may be good for one may not be good for another), (3) negotiating between competing claims based on proximity and need, (4) prudently discerning care for neighbors relative to one's preexisting relationships with family and friends, and (5) discerning how to love in these proximate relations while also taking into account the moral claims of solidarity and the preferential option for the poor.

Jesus's teaching in the story of the Samaritan in Luke 10:30–37 establishes the standard that every human person is to be recognized as a neighbor. Gutiérrez is right to state that this solidaristic view of the human family means that masses of suffering people cannot be written off as nonneighbors.[71] Although the Samaritan's

---

Christian tradition which accords a central place to public theology can provide an account of the tradition that embraces the fullness of faith" (ibid., 25).

[68]As Himes and Himes succinctly state, "the movement to the universal occurs only in the embrace of the particular" (ibid., 135).

[69]Gutiérrez, *A Theology of Liberation*, 116.

[70]By "love" I mean the effective willing of the good of another, which can be traced back to Aquinas's presentation of love as an operation of the will (*ST* I.20.1).

[71]David Hollenbach contends that one essential way to institutionalize solidarity is to defend and promote human rights worldwide, that is, to honor "the moral claims of all persons [for how they are] to be treated, by virtue of their humanity, as participants in the shared life of the human community." He continues, "These moral claims will be practically guaranteed when respect for them is built into the basic structures of society, i.e., into the main political, social, and economic institutions that set the overall terms of social cooperation. When understood this way, the protection of human rights is part of the common good . . . [and] is required by a Christian commitment to solidarity." See Hollenbach, *The Common Good and Christian Ethics*, 159.

movement into the ditch should rightly be praised in contrast to the *antiparechomai* embodied by the priest and Levite who avoid helping the man beaten, stripped, robbed, and left for dead, there is a difference between seeking neighbors in need and nearing neighbors in need. The latter—that is to say, recognizing another person in need and moving nearer to them—is the example set forward by the Samaritan. To expect Christians to abandon their path in seeking others in need is not only unrealistic, it also unjustly diminishes the importance of their current path and the needs to be encountered therein. This is not an argument against changing one's social location in order to better serve others in need. Too much suffering and injustice persist because people confine themselves to their own "front porch" or "backyard."[72] Moving closer in response to a neighbor in need is different than uprooting oneself to seek out neighbors in need.

Gutiérrez fails to account for the unique roles, relationships, and settings of people's lives. He exhorts disciples to a conversion that implies a "break" with their previous lives[73] and to "go out to look for, on the highways and byways, in the factories and slums, on the farms and in the mines"[74] neighbors in need, without attending to their preexisting relationships and responsibilities. In moral discernment between competing claims based on proximity versus need, Gutiérrez tips the scales to favor need. This departs from the traditional ordering of love that gives priority to those who are nearest, including family and friends more than neighbors.[75]

A moral vision of solidarity aims for a virtuous midpoint between these two positions. It sets its sights on inclusive solidarity—especially with the neediest among us—without ignoring what is owed to one's family and friends. In constructing this position, I propose that the ethics of encounter prudently fits each person's social context. I cite a number of voices from the field of Christian ethics to indicate various "signposts" for consideration to guide this process of personal and communal discernment. Disciples should apply this moral vision of solidarity to inform their sense of identity, practice of interpretation, and exercise of responsibility for the global common good.

[72]On the other hand, the Samaritan's movement into the ditch should challenge the "not in my backyard" views that protect self-interest and try to contain social ills "elsewhere." The social isolation of the poor is widespread in American social life. It is especially pernicious in the case of inner-city African Americans, who typically face a "lack of contact or of sustained interaction with individuals and institutions that represent mainstream society." See William Julius Wilson, *The Truly Disadvantaged: The Inner City, the Underclass, and Public Policy* (Chicago: University of Chicago Press, 1987), 60.

[73]Gutiérrez, *A Theology of Liberation*, 118.

[74]Gutiérrez, *The Power of the Poor in History* (Maryknoll, NY: Orbis Books, 1983), 44.

[75]Aquinas affirms, "We love in more ways those who are more closely related to us" (see *ST* II-II.26.7).

To "do likewise" is to prudently exercise neighbor love for solidarity while doing justice to one's responsibilities to family and friends, as well as oneself. Analogically applying the Samaritan's standard for neighbor love must be done by each person according to what is fitting for their time and place, resources and limits, roles and responsibilities. The call to solidarity is a universal vocation. Although it applies to everyone, it does not demand the same from everyone. Instead, the vocation to solidarity invites prudent discernment from each person, held accountable by family, friends, neighbors, and other members of their communities of belonging. In responding to this call, disciples embark on a lifelong journey to integrate solidarity into their dispositions, habits, and relationships. There is no single rule or norm applicable for all people in all places.[76]

Striving for *dikaiosynē* and *koinōnia* combines the duties of love, justice, and solidarity. But what this requires varies by person, relationship, and circumstance. That is not to ignore the validity of universal principles or standards, like defending human dignity and the rights of all people.[77] It does mean, however, differentiating between various kinds of relationships, like those that are conditioned by mutual consent (i.e., friendships) and those that are not chosen (i.e., a parent or child).[78] To be partial to a parent, child, or spouse is not a whim of personal preference; this partiality is justified by the duties imposed by those who rely most heavily upon us.

It is sometimes assumed that preferential love—that is, showing partiality to a person or group instead of impartiality toward all—is incompatible with universal obligations, like those of neighbor love.[79] This question arises with regard to the preferential option for the poor. As noted above, this principle should not be

---

[76]Given that gifts and tasks are shared among community members, duties should be assigned in light of these abilities and obligations. As a requirement of justice, members of a community should be on guard against communal obligations (or "encumbrances") becoming overwhelming or oppressive for any person or subgroup. See Michael Sandel, *Justice: What's the Right Thing to Do?* (New York: Farrar, Straus and Giroux, 2009), 221.

[77]See David Hollenbach on institutionalizing solidarity through human rights, as noted above. Himes and Himes share this view in *Fullness of Faith,* as they write, "While love for the distant neighbor is quite unlike love for those with whom we have closer relations, it does not necessarily follow that love for all persons is a purely critical principle devoid of all substance. A commitment to human rights theory as articulated in modern Catholic social teaching is a useful way of expressing universal-regarding love . . . [and] illustrates how love of a particular nation can be reconciled with a global ethic that pushes us toward a universal love" (149).

[78]See Sandel, *Justice,* 225.

[79]Himes and Himes clarify that a "preferential love of some should not be seen as antithetical to universal regard to all" because "by loving the particular we can love the universal" (Himes and Himes, *Fullness of Faith,* 151). This is a helpful reminder in light of Gutiérrez's emphasis on the poor "masses" being our neighbor (which he interestingly keeps in the singular "neighbor," not plural "neighbors"). Gutiérrez's position might be strengthened if he acknowledged, as Himes and Himes do, that one way to exercise neighbor love for solidarity is to love poor people on an individual basis, which can at least partially mediate love-in-solidarity for "marginal groups" (Gutiérrez, *A Theology of Liberation,* 116).

understood as an exclusive concern for one group or a zero-sum calculation that weighs benefits for one person or group at the expense of others. The "preference" in opting for the poor is best understood under the rubric of justice. It seeks to compensate for inequalities in access, resources, or participation and is thus part of the work of distributive, contributive, commutative, and restorative justice.[80] It should be understood as inclusive rather than exclusive, expansive in terms of love and justice, and proportionate to need.[81] In contrast to in-group bonding or collective selfishness, neighborly solidarity strives to navigate across multiple groups and contexts and virtuously honor the "differential pull" of the various claims made within the whole web of one's relationships.

Defining solidarity as a virtue follows the tradition put forward by Aristotle that understands moral virtue as a habit practiced to achieve the right end. It is the "middle position between two vices," one of excess and the other of deficiency.[82] Understanding and practicing solidarity as a virtue means finding the right balance between competing interests and loyalties; it is the mean between excessive and deficient commitment to others. Solidarity cannot be reduced to platitudinous inclusion because it is not mutually inclusive across all contexts; the interests of some are incompatible with others. Negotiating between conflicting interests requires an orientation to the common good, rather than the benefit to a single person or group, especially if that person or group is not deprived of status or security. Although proximate relations justify stronger commitments, they become vicious when friends and family monopolize one's moral concern: excessive concern for proximate relations translates into deficient attention to distant neighbors, which is increasingly problematic in proportion to the needs of neighbors. Each person is tasked with finding the "mean between extremes" so that love, justice, and solidarity chastely respond to others' need, near and far. This discernment also applies to communities. Communal discernment is necessary for groups to achieve a more inclusive solidarity and corporately opt for the global common good.

This discernment, sometimes referred to as the "ordering of love," strives to

---

[80]This is similar to John Rawls's "difference principle," which he describes in two parts: "Social and economic inequalities are to be arranged so that they are both: (a) to the greatest benefit of the least advantaged . . . and (b) attached to offices and positions open to all under conditions of fair equality of opportunity." See John Rawls, *A Theory of Justice* (Cambridge, MA: Belknap, 1971), 302.

[81]Stephen Pope explains that this preference should be harmonized with justice as fairness such that "Both must be held together in a complementary and mutually-correcting account of the preferential option." See Stephen Pope, "Proper and Improper Partiality and the Preferential Option for the Poor," *Theological Studies* 54 (1993): 242–71, at 267.

[82]Aristotle taught that moral virtue needed to be discerned for every time and place through a concerted effort to do the right thing "to the right person, to the right extent, at the right time, with the right motive, and in the right way" (see *Nicomachean Ethics* Book II, chap. 9, 1109a).

find and practice a virtuous kind of love that rightly prefers some over others. The issue of preference, however, is a long-standing moral debate. Augustine wrestled with how to live up to the duty that "all people should be loved equally" while acknowledging that "you cannot do good to all people equally, so you should take particular thought for those who, as if by lot, happen to be particularly close to you in terms of place, time, or any other circumstance." He concludes, "Since you cannot take thought for all men, you must settle in favor of the one who happens to be more closely associated with you in temporal matters."[83] Danish philosopher Søren Kierkegaard adopted this position, and, informed by Martin Luther's understanding of love as Christ-empowered,[84] denounced forms of preferential love as idolatrous. According to Kierkegaard, in love of neighbor "God is the middle term," whereas in friendship love (*philia*), the middle term is preference, which is a form of idolatry.[85] He concluded that reciprocal loves—including friendship—are reducible to self-love and ultimately incompatible with Christian love, the "essential form" of which is "self-renunciation."[86]

Kierkegaard's understanding of selfless universal neighbor love suggests that we should actually ignore the unique qualities of the neighbor. He insists, "One sees his neighbor only with closed eyes or by *looking away* from all distinctions."[87] The duty of Christian neighbor love is not to see in the neighbor a lovable object, but rather to love the object (the beloved) no matter who he or she is. This means that love of neighbor does not change, even if the particular object or recipient does. Kierkegaard argued for this blanket and static concern because it avoids the temptation to judge the neighbor as worthy or unworthy, a moment when love could be expressed, but is lost. One problem with this view, however, is that it fails to be attentive to what kind of love, care, or other assistance the particular neighbor needs.[88]

---

[83]See Augustine, *On Christian Doctrine*, trans. R. P. H. Green (Oxford: Oxford University Press, 1999), I.xxviii.29. For Augustine, the entirety of the moral life is loving the right things in the right way for the right end. The proper ordering of love lies in the *objects* of our love, with everything following our primary focus on loving God ("Descend that you may ascend to God," *Confessions* IV.xii.19), including the ordering of love of neighbor and self (*On Christian Doctrine* I.xxvi.27).

[84]Luther writes, "as Christians we do not live in ourselves but in Christ and the neighbor . . . As Christians we live in Christ through faith and in the neighbor through love. Through faith we are caught up beyond ourselves into God. Likewise, through love we descend beneath ourselves through love to serve our neighbor" and especially the weak. Martin Luther, *The Freedom of a Christian*, trans. Mark D. Tranvik (Minneapolis: Fortress Press, 2008), 88, 92. Luther's point is that Christian love is unlike secular or worldly love.

[85]Søren Kierkegaard, *Works of Love*, trans. H. V. Hong and E. H. Hong (Princeton, NJ: Princeton University Press, 1995), 70. Kierkegaard describes the love of a friend as corrupted by love of likeness with oneself; friendship love is "I intoxicated in the-other-I" (ibid., 68).

[86]Ibid., 59, 65–68. In fact, Kierkegaard contends that the most Christian of all loves is love for the dead, since they cannot reciprocate (ibid., 317–29).

[87]Ibid., 79.

[88]There is some tension in *Works of Love* on this point, since at the start Kierkegaard states that

In this school of thought, neighbor love is best understood as "equal-regard."[89] For *agape* to be truly Godlike, it must be universally stable and impartial, requiring nothing less than justice. It should be impartial not in the sense of ignoring personal qualities and different abilities and needs but in not allowing potential benefit or risk to derail the selfless quality of this love.[90] To clarify, there is still room for mutual benefit or enjoyment in *agape*; importantly, what one receives from such relationships should not be the motive for entering into them. But friendship love—that is, love shared by those with similar interests, abilities, and goals—can be in tension with more expansive *agapic* relations, since the former requires so much time and effort to cultivate and maintain. In light of the contingencies, complications, and mixed motives involved in friendships, they might seem less morally ideal.

However, as Aquinas points out, a cause of love is similitude and it is impossible—and in fact morally undesirable—to avoid loving some more than others, especially when we share more in common with some than others.[91] Instead of viewing friendships as a threat to a proper ordering of love, a Thomistic approach understands them as essential for right relationship and loving union with God and neighbor.[92] Love of God orders all our loves; we even love ourselves and others in friendship for God's sake as part of the overall goal to promote the good of every person.[93]

Aquinas offers a more nuanced take on how to promote the good of every person while honoring the duties of one's special relations. First priority is given to parents, children, and one's spouse, followed by friends and near neighbors.[94] Attention to these proximate relations is moderated through an evaluation of their moral claims on a person relative to the needs of more distant (and perhaps

---

what matters for the "work of love" is "*how* the deed is done" (ibid., 30) and later, that the very power of mercifulness is "*how* it is given" (ibid., 302). On both points, Kierkegaard writes in terms of the agent's (formal) *intention* rather than how one (materially) responds to the unique *need* of the beloved.

[89]The most representative text remains Gene Outka's *Agape: An Ethical Analysis* (New Haven, CT: Yale University Press, 1972).

[90]The problem of preference and personal differences "gives particular trouble for agape," Outka admits (ibid., 270). The difficulty lies in ordering love to "equalitarian justice" without condensing love into justice (ibid., 309). Further, the challenge for a moral agent to provide "equal regard" is held in tension with the need to identify with the neighbor's point of view (ibid., 260–63).

[91]*ST* II-II.27.3.

[92]*ST* II-II.25.1. For Thomas, the cause of love is the good (*ST* II-II.27.1), and the effect of love is union expressed in mutual indwelling, ecstasy, zeal, preservation and perfection, and all the person does (*ST* II-II.28.1–6). The fact that the effect of love is unity is an important reason to make this Thomistic position a "signpost" in the moral vision for solidarity. To draw near neighbors in need and virtuously love them is a crucial part of the process of cultivating more inclusive solidarity.

[93]*ST* II-II.25.4; 27.3, 7; II-II.25.2.

[94]*ST* II-II.26.6–12; 31.3; 32.9.

needier) neighbors. In Aquinas's view, love for distant and needy neighbors can rightly be expressed through mercifully giving alms.[95] Though it can be a gesture of solidarity, almsgiving pales in comparison with Gutiérrez's vision of seeking out neighbors in need and befriending people experiencing poverty.

Here we recognize the need for a moral vision of solidarity as a virtuous midpoint between (1) the excess of Gutiérrez's emphasis on friendships in proximity to masses of poor neighbors without acknowledging preexisting roles and relationships and (2) the deficiency of the standard that one's duty to the poor can be met by almsgiving from a distance. One way to make progress toward this middle way is to integrate solidarity into one's friendships and family life. This does not mean that Christian neighbor love should be conflated with friendship and familial love relationships. Neither does it leave the matter of solidarity to virtuous friendships, despite the fact that this is a central lens through which to view the entire moral life.[96]

In seeking this midpoint position, it is important to acknowledge a departure from the biblical text describing the Samaritan's exemplary actions. Though it represents neighbor love oriented by courage, compassion, generosity, humility, and fidelity, by itself, the story of the Samaritan cannot fully depict the demands of solidarity. Yet the Samaritan's movement into the ditch to draw near the neighbor in need still serves as a template to analogically apply solidarity through proximity to those in need. In these instances of proximity, it is possible to cultivate solidarity through friendship.[97] In this social location and through these interactions, friendships with those who are marginalized can forge fidelity over time with people who experience deprivation. Being exposed to their suffering can become an oc-

---

[95]*ST* II-II.32.5. While Thomas exhibits concern and pity for the poor, his focus is more on the duties of the privileged than the rights of the poor. For example, in *ST* II-II.66.7 (on the question of justice), Aquinas concludes (with Ambrose), that if someone has a "superabundance" of goods, these rightly belong to the poor, who would not be guilty of stealing if they (out of need) took some of these goods for their own sustenance. Still, Aquinas makes no mention whether or how this might be enforced by law or require a redistribution of goods in any organized or systematic fashion. This thus falls short of contemporary standards for social and economic justice (note that for Thomas, justice is a personal habit of the will to render to each person what is due to them (*ST* II-II.58.1)).

[96]For more on the link between friendship and the Christian moral life, see Paul Wadell's treatment, which begins by describing friendship as the "crucible for the moral life." He explains that "The Christian moral life is what happens to us when we grant God, and others, the freedom to be our friends." See Paul Wadell, *Friendship and the Moral Life* (Notre Dame, IN: University of Notre Dame, 1989), xiii, 167.

[97]See, for example, Christopher L. Heuertz and Christine D. Pohl, *Friendship at the Margins: Discovering Mutuality in Service and Mission* (Downers Grove, IL: InterVarsity Press, 2010). In addition to being the work of love and justice for solidarity, friendships on the margins can also be virtuously affirming and nourishing for our own well-being. Heuertz and Pohl cite Henri Nouwen's line, "we will never believe we have anything to give unless there is someone who is able to receive. Indeed, we discover our gifts in the eyes of the receiver" (ibid., 80).

casion to consider the link between one's personal lifestyle choices and structural injustices. Witnessing a friend be deprived of their dignity or rights can prevent moral callousness to the injustices they experience.[98] In opposition to popular views of "friendship" in terms of self-interest or utility, virtuous friendships with those on the margins require vulnerability and transparency; they have the potential to challenge self-deception and the temptation to rationalize luxury, excess, and overindulgence.[99] Family life—to be examined in greater detail in the final chapter—deserves moral priority because family members present their vulnerabilities most consistently to fellow family members who are, in turn, often well suited to provide for them.[100] The Christian vision of the family "involves dual callings to serve one's own as well as the broader communities in and outside the home."[101] This implies a moral concern that extends outside the family in the form of "compassionate accountability for the well-being of their neighbors."[102] Children learn empathy and altruism, social awareness and responsibility from their parents' example. They observe who counts, who belongs (and who does not), as well as what it means to participate in social life.[103] In households lacking

[98]This would be in contrast to a generous donor who may be oblivious to the causes and effects of the injustices the donor's recipients face. Heuertz and Pohl cite several examples of the way in which friendships with those who are marginalized and oppressed can help to make privileged Christians more conscious of their participation in social sin. For example, they highlight the connection between buying products that degrade or exploit sexuality and the impact that such hypersexualized or desensitized cultures may have in making sexual abuse (even of children) less objectionable (ibid., 47–50).

[99]It would be naïve not to also acknowledge how these friendships can be fraught with difficulty. These ties can lead to complex situations in negotiating asymmetries in wealth, status, and power. Friendships on the margins and in the midst of injustice require integrity, humility, and ongoing, prayerful moral discernment among friends, and can be sustained when people are held accountable to faith, hope, and love. Heuertz and Pohl reflect, "the ones who will be able to resist evil and offer hope are those who are morally and spiritually tender, deeply committed to holiness and integrity, and aware of their own frailty and dependence on Christ. If purity of heart and openness to the wisdom of others shapes every aspect of their lives, they are more likely to do well in complicated situations" (ibid., 99).

[100]See Robert Goodin, *Protecting the Vulnerable: A Reanalysis of Our Social Responsibilities* (Chicago: University of Chicago Press, 1985), 33–34. As Goodin sees it, the ultimate criterion for the ordering of love is in response to vulnerability.

[101]Julie Hanlon Rubio, *Family Ethics: Practices for Christians* (Washington, DC: Georgetown University Press, 2010), 81.

[102]Lisa Sowle Cahill, *Family: A Christian Social Perspective* (Minneapolis: Fortress Press, 2000), 110. Cahill develops the Christian vision of the family based on three main premises: (1) families structure their internal relations according to Christian ideals of spirituality and reciprocity; (2) families serve others in society to build up the common good by transforming society itself; and (3) families struggle, survive, and thrive together, despite economic, racial, and ethnic differences or differences in family structure (ibid., 84).

[103]Cahill suggests that part of the breakdown of social capital and commitment to the common good is the habituated learning of "shifting and narrowing of what were once public allegiances and communal identities" (ibid., 103).

these virtuous attitudes and practices, it is harder for children to imagine what they look like and how they are to be incorporated into one's life as an adult.

Family bonds are to be valued relative to a more inclusive solidarity and orientation to the common good. As a subunit of social order, the family has a special role to play in promoting the common good.[104] It does so by putting into practice the tenet of Catholic social teaching called "subsidiarity," carrying out social responsibilities at the lowest effective level.[105] The family effectively bridges the personal and the public; it uniquely mediates the human community.[106] It is the first opportunity to realize the vocation of every person to participate according to one's "position and role, in promoting the common good."[107]

These observations lead to three concluding remarks. First, with respect to the unique influences of friendships and the family unit, these proximate ties need not be considered in competition with neighbor love for solidarity and a preferential option for the poor. This proves true when these relationships maintain an inclusive orientation and sense of obligation. When attentiveness to the needs of others is shared among family members and friends, and includes a healthy sense of finitude, fidelity, and self-care, practicing neighbor love can be more readily recognized as an essential—rather than supererogatory—duty.[108]

---

[104]This is a central claim in Cahill's text. She writes, "The Christian family defines *family values* as care for others, especially the poor; it appreciates that truly Christian families are not always the most socially acceptable or prestigious ones; it values and encourages all families who strive earnestly to meet the standard of compassionate action; and it encourages both personal commitment to and the social structuring of mercy and justice" (ibid., 135). For Cahill's constructive recommendations for Christian family life, see ibid., 135–37.

[105]Subsidiarity is a principle that protects against the dangers of collectivism or bureaucratic intervention that can viciously encroach on human freedoms and undermine personal initiative. See *CCC*, no. 1883.

[106]Roberto Goizueta attests, "The Jesus of the gospels relativizes the nuclear family in order to insist that the most intimate, most particular, and most personal of relationships, our family relationships, must extend beyond the nuclear family and characterize *all* our relationships. The authentic community is inclusive not exclusive; it is, of its essence, open to 'the other' as a unique human person. The family is not merely a collection of self-sufficient, autonomous individuals, but the birthplace of our very personhood; the person is not the 'building block' of the family but its unique mediation. Likewise, the larger human community is not merely a collection of self-sufficient, autonomous families, but the network of social relationships which gives birth to our families; the family is not the 'building block' of the human community but its unique mediation." Roberto Goizueta, *Caminemos con Jesús: Toward a Hispanic/Latino Theology of Accompaniment* (Maryknoll, NY: Orbis Books, 1995), 201–2.

[107]*CCC*, no. 1913. See also *CCC*, nos. 1914–17 on the responsibility of all to participate in public life for the common good.

[108]The lack of emphasis in Scripture to love one's family and friends (and self, for that matter) is not because these loves are unimportant, but because the biblical authors took them for granted. Repeated attention to care for those we are not predisposed to or benefitted by loving is a challenge to expand our circles of concern and commitment. Augustine writes, "since there was no need for a precept that anyone love himself and his own body, because we love that which we are and that

Second, the responsibilities to cultivate social inclusion and responsibility, courage and compassion, cooperation and accountability should not fall to groups of friends or families alone; local governments, churches, groups, clubs, and neighborhood associations need to share in this work. Local leaders should bring people together from across all sectors of society to persevere through conflicting interests and priorities to increase the visibility of cooperative commitment between the private and public spheres in promoting the common good as inclusively as possible. This multilevel approach has the potential to institutionalize neighbor love and solidarity in overlapping communities from the personal to the structural.[109]

Third, the ordering of love for solidarity is a public project to more fully realize the inclusive bonds and commitments of the "family of faith" (Gal 6:10). Like faith, morality is personal but never private. The moral life is a matter of both personal and collective discernment. This means pushing back against the temptation to identify whatever is "public" with only the state or market. Moral agency includes a social dimension, specifically a "moral obligation as a socially constructed practice negotiated between learning agents capable of growth on the one hand and change on the other."[110]

By failing to address preexisting friendships and family obligations, Gutiérrez misses how solidarity can be integrated into disciples' social context without the dramatic "break" of conversion and far-off pursuit of the poor or "nonpersons" in the world. Alternatively, traditional views of friendship and family need to be more consistently and forcefully oriented toward solidarity and the common good. Taken together, these efforts to prudently order relationships and responsibilities are part of the moral formation of people, groups, and the just ordering of society. Additionally, one key component of a moral vision for solidarity remains: the cultivation of specific dispositions, actions, and practices in everyday life.

SOLIDARITY IN EVERYDAY LIFE

To this point, the downsides of solidarity have been largely set aside. But it should be noted that solidarity can also take on certain vicious forms: those com-

---

which is below us . . . there remained a necessity only that we receive precepts concerning that which is equal to us and that which is above us" (Augustine, *On Christian Doctrine*, I.xxvi.27).

[109]However, it should also avoid the "bureaucratic hardening" that Taylor warns against (Taylor *A Secular Age*, 740–41). Peter Berger and Richard John Neuhaus propose "mediating structures" to link the personal to the structural and the private to the public. See Peter Berger and Richard John Neuhaus, *To Empower People: The Role of Mediating Structures in Public Policy* (Washington, DC: American Enterprise Institute, 1977), 2.

[110]Alan Wolfe, *Whose Keeper? Social Science and Moral Obligation* (Berkeley: University of California Press, 1989), 220.

mitted to a certain cause can become so overconfident in its value that they use it to marginalize other features of the common good; the in-group can become elitist, sectarian, and divided against those who are less committed to the same interests; power can become coercive and abusive; weakness, vulnerability, and ignorance can be manipulated; and the goal of unity or liberation might be used to justify vicious habits or interpersonal relationships and thereby abandon the necessary means for solidarity in love and justice.[111] Despite its great value, solidarity could be distorted as an urgent, never-ending moral obligation that might result in the neglect of one's own self-care and the gifts and tasks of family and friend relations.

To avoid these temptations and to develop a realistic[112] and effective ethics of encounter, I propose that solidarity be understood as a practice of neighbor love in the following ways: (1) solidarity as expressed through a virtuous identity constructed by practicing courage, mercy, generosity, humility, and fidelity; (2) the interpretation of one's social context through a lens of attentiveness and appropriate response to those nearby; and (3) an exercise of responsibility through practices, relationships, and in specific locations to promote inclusive participation and liberation.

The ethics of encounter is framed by the five virtues illustrated by the Samaritan, as discussed in the previous chapter: courage, mercy, generosity, humility, and fidelity.[113] To avoid repeating material, my present aim is to demonstrate how solidarity is habituated by specific people through intentional dispositions and actions. What makes solidarity distinct from Christian neighbor love is its orientation to mutuality. Whereas love—especially *agapic* love—can be viewed as unilateral, mutuality is "the sharing of 'power-with' by and among all parties in a relationship in a way that recognizes the wholeness and particular experience of each participant toward the end of optimum flourishing for all."[114] Solidarity

[111]Jean Vanier, founder of the L'Arche community for the mentally handicapped and their aids, has written extensively on community and solidarity, and the unexpected obstacles (see, for example, Jean Vanier, *Community and Growth* [New York: Paulist Press, 1989], 17–18, 34–35). He suggests that solidarity comes from sharing weakness, vulnerability, and suffering, but that we must first overcome our various fears, such as of exclusion, difference, failure, loss, and change. See also Jean Vanier, *Becoming Human* (New York: Paulist Press, 1998), 73–103.

[112]Owen Flanagan cautions, "Make sure when constructing a moral theory or projecting a moral ideal that the character, decision processing, and behavior prescribed are possible, or are perceived to be possible, for creatures like us," in Owen Flanagan, *Varieties of Moral Personality: Ethics and Psychological Realism* (Cambridge, MA: Harvard University Press, 1991), 32.

[113]Solidarity as related to these five virtues is inspired in part by Christopher Vogt's essay proposing three "interdependent virtues" (solidarity, compassion, and hospitality), and "heavily influenced by justice operating as a general virtue" to promote the common good. See Christopher Vogt, "Fostering a Catholic Commitment to the Common Good: An Approach Rooted in Virtue Ethics," *Theological Studies* 68 (2007): 394–417, at 400.

[114]Dawn Nothwehr, *Mutuality: A Formal Norm for Christian Social Ethics* (San Francisco: Catholic Scholars Press, 1998), 96.

is equality and mutuality expressed in an inclusive community of belonging in partnership for just social, economic, and political structures.[115] Solidarity is realized through neighbor love and the virtues of courage, mercy, generosity, humility, and fidelity. Virtues aspire for the perfection of thought, emotion, and action.[116] These five virtues are part of a discipline to achieve the "mean between extremes" in right relationships between God, neighbor, and self. As seen in the story of the Samaritan, these virtuous attitudes and actions generate compassion for those who suffer.[117] Courage motivates a person to persist in the face of adversity, apathy, and fatigue. Virtues keep individuals and communities from settling for something less than what is good, right, true, or just.

Virtues also enhance perception and interpretation of one's social context. In the face of widespread fear and anxiety, insecurity and alienation, these virtues help people cultivate *eusebeia*, or the virtue of "piety."[118] Piety is a form of trust in God and gratitude for one's blessings. Interpreting one's social context through appreciation can evoke a deep generosity, providing a striking contrast to the more normative attitudes of self-interest and concerns about security. This interpretive posture inspires reverence for the other in respect and reception, akin to hospitality. But it is unlike hospitality that welcomes guests to the home of the host; it is a "welcoming on the way," just as the Samaritan receives the man lying in the ditch in Luke 10:25–37 and the disciples receive the Risen Christ on the road to Emmaus in Luke 24:13–35.[119] This welcome cuts across differences and is responsive

---

[115]David Hollenbach summarizes, "Solidarity is not only a virtue to be enacted by persons one at a time. It must also be expressed in the economic, cultural, political, and religious institutions that shape society. Solidarity is a virtue of communities as well as individuals" (Hollenbach, *The Common Good and Christian Ethics*, 189).

[116]Jean Porter defines virtue as "a stable quality of the intellect, will, or passions through which an individual can do what morality demands in a particular instance, and do it in the right way." See Jean Porter, "Virtue," in *The HarperCollins Encyclopedia of Catholicism*, ed. Richard P. McBrien (New York: HarperCollins, 1995), 1316–17, at 1316.

[117]Maureen O'Connell writes, "Compassion takes seriously the suffering of others and in so doing uncovers the conscious and unconscious values that we rely on in order to perceive and to evaluate accurately what is going on in our reality. When viewed from the perspective of those who suffer, we realize that the social beliefs and values that shape our lifestyle choices, our interactions in a variety of public spheres, and our understandings of human flourishing are not all valid or morally viable" (Maureen O'Connell, *Compassion: Loving Our Neighbor in an Age of Globalization*[Maryknoll, NY: Orbis Books, 2009], 12).

[118]*Eusebeia* may be translated as "godliness," "piety," "devotion," or "worship." It shares with *dikaiosynē* a desire for holiness, fidelity, and right relationship with God. *Eusebeia* connotes reverence for God and God's people, and interestingly, was exhorted in the Pastoral Letters in conjunction with contentment (e.g., 1 Tm 6:6). The call to piety and contentment is not to placate disciples with a naïveté of faith or benign acceptance of the status quo. See Daniel Harrington and James Keenan, *Paul and Virtue Ethics: Building Bridges between New Testament Studies and Moral Theology* (Lanham, MD: Rowman & Littlefield, 2010), 118–19.

[119]Hospitality—even "on the way"—is a recurrent theme in Luke's Gospel (e.g., Jesus and Zac-

to people's needs.[120] It offers security for those who are vulnerable, reprieve for those who face deprivation, and the invitation to belong to and participate in a community for those who may be alienated and isolated.[121]

This interpretive lens best receives and appropriately responds to others by drawing near to them. It can be corrected through encounters and exchanges that widen, deepen, and improve focus for accurately seeing others. Just as the Samaritan could only know how to help the robbers' victim by going to his side, this approach to interpreting one's specific context is especially sensitive to marginalization and injustice; it operates from a locus of deprivation. Its hallmarks are proximity and accompaniment with others, those considered "other," and those most in need.[122] Drawing near to others in need is an exercise of responsibility for solidarity. The ethics of encounter hinges upon an identity, interpretation, and shared practices that normalize mutual respect and responsibility. An ethics of encounter aims to construct social imaginaries that promote human dignity, rights and duties, and liberation for the global common good. In a globalized, digital age, "neighbor" is not confined to physical proximity; neighbor love can and should be expressed between those who are near and far, online and offline. To make progress toward that end, physical and digital communities should be evaluated for the kinds of values and meaning being learned and whether and how they are forming members to "go and do likewise" in their social context.

---

chaeus in Luke 19:1–10 and Jesus, Mary, and Martha in Luke 10:38–42). See, for example, Brendan Byrne, *The Hospitality of God: A Reading of Luke's Gospel* (Collegeville, MN: Liturgical, 2000).

[120]Hospitality was a defining characteristic in the early church, as it helped bring the first followers together across social, ethnic, and geographical differences. On the "sociology of food" for the early church, see Graydon Snyder, *Inculturation of the Jesus Tradition: The Impact of Jesus on Jewish and Roman Cultures* (Harrisburg, PA: Trinity Press International, 1999), 129–74. Snyder contends, "Despite the importance of theology, the death and resurrection of Jesus, and an ethic of caring, the real alteration in Judaism occurred (and Christianity clearly emerged) when table fellowship was not blocked by dietary obligations or the rejection of food dedicated to idols" (ibid., 155). These practices followed the example Christ set himself in abolishing the exclusion of sinners or others considered unworthy or impure (see Mt 9:10–13; Lk 5:30) and the challenge to share food and fellowship with the poor (Lk 14:12–14; see also Jas 2:15–16).

[121]Wayne Meeks cites the coordinated efforts of hospitality and humility as one of the factors in the early church growing and becoming institutionalized so quickly. See Wayne Meeks, *The Origins of Christian Morality: The First Two Centuries* (New Haven, CT: Yale University Press, 1993), 105–8.

[122]This proximity and accompaniment can be described as a "walking with the poor." Roberto Goizueta suggests that when we "walk where poor persons walk" we become "*compañeros* and *compañeras*" with the poor, companions who share their desire for dignity, rights, and flourishing. Goizueta explains, "Unless social transformation is rooted in an everyday accompaniment of the poor, that is, in the everyday act of walking with, living with, breaking bread with particular poor persons in the concreteness of the poor persons' everyday struggle for survival, the transformation of social structures will, in the long run, simply perpetuate the oppression of the poor" (Goizueta, *Caminemos con Jesús*, 207).

NEIGHBOR 2.0

Jesus's contemporaries could never have imagined the possibilities of "loving your neighbor as yourself" in an age of globalization, digital technology, and the internet.[123] Taken together, these trends and tools put us in touch with people across great distances. Globalization—the complex network of interdependent cultural, economic, and political systems—produces a variety of effects. On the one hand, it serves an integrating function through trade, transportation, and communication. On the other hand, forces that unite and homogenize can also create friction and become oppressive. For example, in light of the way that time and space are compressed through these exchanges, globalization reconfigures the meaning of place, seemingly minimizing the importance of territoriality: it is now possible to be "near" someone despite great geographical distance. This can make it possible to forge connections with some, while also feeling more threatened by others. Globalization is marked by considerable insecurity and instability, especially in competition between the local and global.[124] "Culture," understood as the locally shared values, rituals, symbols, and other expressions of meaning, is now shaped by vastly larger and more complex influences. Globalization can spread cultures across continents, but it can also do so in a way that is unpredictable, unstable, and disjointed from local contexts. In sum, globalization contributes to a rather porous sense of place and to more "translocal" cultures, linked to diverse webs of peoples and places with their intermingling narratives and practices.[125] It also produces an effect described as "deterritorialization," wherein human interaction is unmoored from geography, missing the territorial significance of its particular physical space.[126] This poses detrimental ramifications for personal and collective identities as much as it does shared cultural expressions of history, values, ideas, and hopes. In the face of such flux—and as some would say, chaos—there are a variety of reactions from hope for new unity in diversity to fear, distrust, and fundamentalism. Suffice it to say, the possibilities for connection inherent in glo-

---

[123]The impact of digital technologies, the internet, and social media will be examined in the final chapter, as part of the proposal for a culture of encounter mediated through a screen.

[124]Anthony Giddens describes the "upward pulls" that centralize power at the transnational level away from the local, the "downward pressures" on local market economies to cut costs and raise revenues, and the "sideways squeezes" as more and more people are brought into competition with each other. See Anthony Giddens, *Runaway World: How Globalization Is Reshaping Our Lives* (New York: Routledge, 2000), 6–19.

[125]Gerald A. Arbuckle, *Culture, Inculturation, & Theologians: A Postmodern Critique* (Collegeville, MN: Michael Glazier, 2010), 13.

[126]On globalization's homogenizing, heterogenizing, and deterritorializing effects, see Vincent J. Miller, "Where Is the Church? Globalization and Catholicity," in *Theological Studies* 69 (2008): 412–32.

balization do not always facilitate mutually respectful and responsible encounters, accompaniment, exchanges, embraces, or experiences of belonging.

Globalization presents real dangers to people and the planet. Increasing interdependence means that it is hard for any part of the world to avoid the effects of market failures, debt crises, and other instances of economic distress, climate change, ecological degradation and resource sustainability, terrorism and war, migrants and refugees. The prominent—and widely unchecked—growth of transnational corporations has led some to conclude that corporations may soon become more powerful than states at both the global and local levels.[127] If the goal of such companies is to maximize profits above all else, this could conflict with the fundamental role of the state to protect and provide for its people and resources. Radical inequalities in wealth distribution and economic development have generated severe—and still growing—conditions of marginalization and deprivation, especially in developing countries lacking enforceable labor standards.[128] As more and more people suffer the disadvantages of globalized politics and economies, there is concern that too many folks around the globe are growing insensitive to dehumanizing suffering. This has led some to denounce globalization as a new kind of "apartheid," with those who benefit from the system touting global integration while those on the other side of these stark asymmetries lament the cultural, political, and economic imperialism.[129]

Despite the gravity of these trends, this is not the full story of globalization. The world's emerging interdependence implies greater resources and networks that can be leveraged to advance the common good.[130] Economic neoliberalism

---

[127]One classic example of this view is David C. Korten's *When Corporations Rule the World* (San Francisco: Berrett-Koehler Publishers, 2001). Korten unmasks the attempt by transnational corporations "to integrate the world's national economies into a single borderless global economy in which the world's mega-corporations are free to move goods and money anywhere in the world that affords an opportunity for profit, without governmental interference" (ibid., 3).

[128]In opinion polls, Americans generally express laissez-faire viewpoints on global economics; sweatshops, child slavery, and other forms of poverty and injustice are sometimes viewed as inevitable undersides of capitalism. See, for example, Ann E. Tenbrunsel, Kristina A. Diekmann, Kimberly A. Wade-Benzoni, and Max H. Bazerman, "The Ethical Mirage: A Temporal Explanation as to Why We Aren't as Ethical as We Think We Are" (forthcoming in *Research in Organizational Behavior*; http://www.hbs.edu/research/pdf/08-012.pdf). On the issue of international policy, most Americans believe the United States does more than enough to help the rest of the world. See http://www.cfr.org/content/publications/attachments/PublicOpinionProject.pdf.

[129]In May 2013, Pope Francis made headlines for his criticism of "savage capitalism" that has put profit ahead of all other goods. See, for example, "Pope Criticizes 'Savage Capitalism' on Visit to Food Kitchen," Reuters, May 21, 2013.

[130]See Lisa Sowle Cahill, "Globalization and the Common Good," in *Globalization and Catholic Social Thought: Present Crisis, Future Hope*, ed. John A. Coleman and William F. Ryan (Maryknoll, NY: Orbis Books, 2005), 42–54. Cahill looks at four features: substance (human goods), procedures (government and participation), dispositions (solidarity and hope), and efficacy (effective action with other traditions and movements) to redefine and implement social change for the common good (ibid., 45).

insists that global capitalism will be an overall net gain by extending the influence of developed countries, creating the potential for higher levels of prosperity, health care, education, and other potentially liberating effects.[131] There is hope that increasing interaction across borders will lead to greater understanding, respect, and cooperation among the world's peoples, ushering in a new age of multicultural appreciation or, perhaps even better, a global cosmopolitanism.[132] It also makes the world more compressed, leading to a new kind of unity and friction, as proximity is no longer conditioned by geography.

In light of the classic definition of neighbor (one who is "nearby"), this shift in proximity changes how one can love the neighbor in a globalized context. Although, as discussed in the previous chapter, Jesus's teaching in Luke 10:25–37 expanded the definition of neighbor to include all people, this ethical challenge is made both more difficult and perhaps more tenable in light of this age of interconnection and interdependence. As Maureen O'Connell argues,

> Unlike the priest and the Levite, who had no direct culpability in this physical assault, we fail to minister to people *we directly and indirectly assault* through our participation in unjust systems, structures, and institutions. We wound these others with our everyday choices about what to wear, what to eat, what to do with our waste, how to heat our homes, how to spend our leisure time, and how to invest our savings. And unlike the priest and the Levite, who did not have the resources to address the structural injustices of the road to Jericho even if they had considered them, *we have the material and human resources to end extreme poverty*. We tragically fail to use them. Finally, unlike the priest and the Levite, who failed to see that the man in the ditch depended on their compassion in order to flourish, we fail to see that our *own flourishing depends on the compassion* we extend to those who suffer. We fail to realize that those to whom we minister can minister to us in return. Their vulnerability can penetrate our defensive invulnerability; their fundamental dependence on others can break through our isolating

[131]See John Sniegocki's essay, "Neoliberal Globalization: Critiques and Alternatives," *Theological Studies* 69 (2008): 321–39. Sniegocki points out that while neoliberals tout a net benefit to globalized systems, most assets go to those at the top while, by and large, there is little measurable improvement for local laborers, either by design or corruption. Women, children, and indigenous people are consistently left out of this alleged "net gain" (ibid., 325–26).

[132]See Kwame Anthony Appiah, *Cosmopolitanism: Ethics in a World of Strangers* (New York: W. W. Norton, 2006). Appiah claims that global diversity is to be protected at the local level, while finding important areas of overlap across cultures to make progress in recognizing that all people matter, and moreover, that no one matters any less than another. To "accept the cosmopolitan challenge" is to require more from developed countries to better protect the dignity and rights of those in developing countries, especially because they are better equipped to do so (ibid., 174).

> autonomy; their imagination can interrupt our market-driven logic; and their vision of the future can push us beyond our self-obsession with the present.[133]

O'Connell cites several social trends in the United States that hinder Samaritan-like neighbor love: individualism, autonomy, self-sufficiency, consumerism, and American *bourgeois* Christianity.[134] In particular, she addresses the "white privilege" that most American Christians enjoy without being fully aware of their unearned privilege, power, access to resources, comfort, and security.[135] Compassion and solidarity require that disciples cultivate a critical consciousness attentive to the widespread suffering experienced by billions of neighbors today. Stepping beyond awareness, it also demands a willingness to confront realities of sin—both personal and social—that dehumanize, exclude, and otherwise undermine bonds of human filiation and solidarity. According to O'Connell, this willingness involves "neighbor-oriented values" including "vulnerability and relationality, self-reflective social responsibility, and an appreciation for nonmaterial aspects of human flourishing."[136] Her proposal differs from traditional understandings of neighbor love because it necessitates more than charity. Recalling Gutiérrez's emphasis on changing one's social location, Christian neighbor love ought to include analyzing globalized structures and systems from the vantage point of the marginalized and dispossessed as well as an active commitment to foster a more inclusive solidarity through new relationships, networks, and communities of practice that promote human dignity, rights, and responsibilities for the global common good.

Charles Taylor sees this as a profoundly countercultural task in the current secular age. As noted in Chapter 1, his understanding of "secularism" does not only signify the declining public prominence of religion but also the separation of church and state, exclusive humanism (excluding any reference to transcendence), and a tolerant plurality of diverse beliefs and practices.[137] Secular social imaginaries have shifted our understanding of the "good" in a way that has altered how we view ourselves and the entire universe. This involves a turn inward, part of the condition Taylor describes as the "buffered self." This gives Taylor reason to lament "the world we have lost, one in which spiritual forces impinge on porous agents, in which the social was grounded in the sacred and secular time in higher times."[138] The corresponding losses include convictions of belief, belonging, and shared responsibilities.

---

[133] O'Connell, *Compassion*, 15–16.
[134] Ibid., 20–28.
[135] See ibid., 19.
[136] Ibid., 28.
[137] Taylor, *A Secular Age*, 2–3.
[138] Ibid., 61.

Taylor is not wholly rejecting secular ethics; in fact, he recognizes the need for tolerance and openness in secular aims to civilize the world order. But he proposes that something important has been lost in the age of the buffered self. Specifically, in replacing the "bounded self" and the "porous self" of the earlier age of faith and enchantment, present social imaginaries have constructed an image of human flourishing via individual self-interest, autonomy, and invulnerability as the highest goods.[139] Present social imaginaries have created a set of rules for personal flourishing that include the ability to opt out of social obligations.[140] The buffered self comes out of an awareness of the possibility for social disengagement. This flies in the face of the purpose of the Christian life, which is meant to incarnate an agapic way of being in the world, replacing disengagement with dedication to solidarity.

Taylor acknowledges the demands of solidarity in this current "secular" age. He writes, "Our age makes higher demands of solidarity and benevolence on people today than ever before. Never before have people been asked to stretch out so far, and so consistently, so systematically, so as a matter of course, to the stranger outside the gates."[141] To this he adds a word of caution about a "lofty humanism" that drives philanthropy and solidarity with a Janus face: on the one side, endless inspiration to act; on the other, an almost inevitable sense of futility and disappointment.[142] The pinnacle moral achievement in this set of rules is heroically gratuitous generosity. But, Taylor warns, this "unilateral heroism is self-enclosed," that is, it leaves no room for reciprocity.[143] The ethics of encounter seeks mutual respect and responsibility, meaning that it is wholly incompatible with unilateral heroism. This is why the story of the Samaritan needs to be corrected from its popular understanding of endorsing random acts of kindness, unilateral aid, or

---

[139]Taylor succinctly puts it in a "one-line description of the difference between earlier times and the secular age: a secular age is one in which the eclipse of all goals beyond human flourishing becomes conceivable; or better, it falls within the range of an imaginable life for masses of people" (ibid., 19–20). He later describes this vision of flourishing as being without "reference to something higher which humans should reverence or love or acknowledge" (ibid., 245). Taylor identifies the biggest difference in the age of the buffered self as the possibility of "taking a distance from, disengaging from everything outside the mind." He explains, "My ultimate purposes are those which arise within me, the crucial meanings of things are those defined in my responses to them" that allows the "buffered self" to "avoid distressing or tempting experiences." The buffered self is a master of one's own meanings, in that they are not necessarily guided by religious or social bonds (ibid., 38).

[140]This is in direct contrast to the previous age of the bounded self or the porous self who was always vulnerable to the influence and causal power of one's relationships and surrounding environment (ibid., 35). In these earlier ages, "disengagement" was not a possibility, either from society or religion (ibid., 41).

[141]Ibid., 695.

[142]Ibid., 697.

[143]Ibid., 702. Taylor juxtaposes this set of rules with Christian faith, which "proposes a quite different view," one that beckons people into "relationship where giving and receiving merge."

heroism in an emergency. Solidarity is not measured by individual selflessness, but rather in inclusive relationships that foster coresponsibility for the common good.[144]

One of the classic problems with solidarity is the way it can be misunderstood or misapplied to undermine human freedom. In his review of the bounded self and the porous self, Taylor understates how these previous states of being marked by vulnerability were also susceptible to coercion. He later clarifies that one of the advantages of the buffered self is a freer personhood.[145] But he also recognizes in the Samaritan the paradigm of the totally free person: the one who acts not by principle or rule, neither from incentive nor coercion. In contrast to the buffered self who can exercise freedom from encroachment, vulnerability, or obligation (i.e., disengagement), Taylor presents a case for using that freedom for right relationship in coresponsibility for the common good—not an avoidance of contingency, but the embrace of it as part of the incarnational reality of agape. He writes,

> A world ordered by this system of rules, disciplines, organizations can only see contingency as an obstacle, even an enemy and threat. The ideal is to master it, to extend the web of control so that contingency is reduced to a minimum. By contrast, contingency is an essential feature of the story [of the Samaritan] as an answer to the question that prompted it. Who is my neighbor? The one you happen across, stumble across, who is wounded there in the road. Sheer accident also has a hand in shaping the proportionate, the appropriate response. It is telling us something, answering our deepest questions: *this* is your neighbor.[146]

The ethics of encounter aims to shift the understanding of freedom more toward the exercise of agency that draws near the other, that replaces the safe distance of tolerance with the caress of tenderness, and supplants autonomy with a shared commitment to solidarity. Solidarity is the mean between the vicious extremes of excessive individualism and coercive collectivism. It seeks harmony in human

---

[144]Ibid., 706, 710. Taylor clarifies that "Christian faith can never be decanted into a fixed code" since "it always places our actions in two dimensions, one of right action, and also an eschatological dimension. This is also a dimension of reconciliation and trust" that is both horizontal and vertical (ibid., 706). The eschatological dimension "involves a kind of motivational conversion" and "people bonding in a new way," knowing that "transfiguring [the world] in the name of a new kind of common world" will be only partially realized until the eschaton (ibid., 707, 710).

[145]Taylor does not identify with those who might wish to return to an earlier way of life; he sees the rise of personal agency and "the practical primacy of life" to be a "great gain for human kind, and that there is some truth in the self-narrative of the Enlightenment . . . we might even be tempted to say that modern unbelief is providential, but that might be too provocative a way of putting it" (ibid., 637).

[146]Ibid., 742.

freedom that celebrates both rights and duties. In our American context, we much prefer to claim rights without also delivering on their corresponding duties. This contributes to the social divisions and unjust inequalities that separate and subjugate. The ethics of encounter rooted in equality, mutuality, and interdependence aims to restore these responsibilities by delivering justice and peace on the personal, social, and institutional levels. There is no other way to mend our broken relationships and communities. While this sounds fair enough in theory, it is meaningless unless and until it is put into practice. The next chapter focuses on what it will take to practice the ethics of encounter as described here.

4

Practicing the Ethics of Encounter

Pope Francis's call to build a culture of encounter aims to bring people together across differences, to celebrate diversity rather than fear it, to share life together in solidarity, and to promote the global common good. But interpersonal encounters are not always marked by respect, equality, and mutuality; neither do they automatically produce strong bonds of coresponsibility, clear and effective communication, and collaboration for comprehensive flourishing. For a culture of encounter to be possible, more people need to practice the kind of lifestyle that initiates and sustains personal and social transformation. To "go and do likewise" (Lk 10:37) is to practice Christian neighbor love for solidarity by drawing near others, especially across differences. It means cultivating a lifestyle oriented by the ethics of encounter, via a five-stage matrix of virtues that embody solidarity: courage, mercy, generosity, humility, and fidelity. This chapter explores what is required to practice the ethics of encounter in order to create conditions conducive for a culture of encounter. This process moves forward in five steps that parallel the dynamic process of moving from encounter to accompaniment to exchange to embrace to the end goal: a culture of inclusive belonging.

The first step centers around courage, acknowledging that social change has to begin on the personal level. Personal transformation is proposed through five spiritual practices: mindfulness, contemplation, prayer, sacraments, and imagination. The second step enacts mercy by tenderly acknowledging the pervasive and pernicious effects of implicit bias in the world, as well as what it takes to virtuously respond to these culturally informed unconscious attitudes and associations. The third step proposes that generosity be applied to communication in order to more graciously engage in conversations across differences, especially through a commitment to "deep listening." In the fourth step, humility is applied to the sociological concept of *habitus*, recognizing the weight of formation that happens through our local environment, interactions, and shared practices. Finally, fidelity is illustrated by the example of Fr. Greg Boyle, SJ, founder of Homeboy Industries, whose work with gang members provides a compelling blueprint for a *habitus* of healing. This interpersonal, bottom-up approach helps to fill in the gaps left by the top-down approach of Catholic social teaching. The goal is to illuminate what is possible when people are empowered to create more inclusive, equitable, and mutually respectful and responsible relationships, which are necessary ingredients for neighbor love and solidarity to advance peace, reconciliation, and justice.

CHANGE STARTS WITH ME

It would be easy to say that social separation and unjust inequalities are problems too big to solve, or that I am powerless to effect change as only one person out of billions on the planet. Change is possible when people decide to live their way into a new approach to self and society. Change begins with the courageous commitment to adjust my perceptions, words, and actions. This includes lamenting, repenting, and atoning for sinful thoughts and actions that keep me from loving God, self, and others as they deserve. Growth and change are possible for every person, and it is also important to acknowledge that people have a unique capacity to effect change in their lives. This is based on many personal factors, including their mental, emotional, and physical health and ability. It is also contingent on social factors, like their social status, range of choice, and exercise of agency. Not everyone shares the same access to freedom and power. This is important for a culture of encounter because we cannot expect everyone to be willing to encounter others when some face much greater hurdles than others. This is not just a matter of the difference between people who tend to be more extroverted than introverted; it also means taking seriously the mental, emotional, and physical well-being of the people involved as well as the resources and opportunities (or lack thereof) at their disposal. In the first step of moving from encounter toward a culture of belonging, we have to acknowledge the courage required to receive and be received by others.

Courage plays a role in the cognitive, affective, and physical factors that play into encounter. For example, while mental illness continues to receive a good deal of stigma among some and silence among others, it affects approximately one in five Americans.[1] Mental illness might be considered as a spectrum of both severity and longevity; some experience debilitating bouts of mental illness for a specific amount of time while many others encounter better or worse mental health over

[1]For data on mental illness, see https://www.nami.org/learn-more/mental-health-by-the-numbers.

a lifetime. In the United States, diagnoses of anxiety and depression are on the rise. There has been a particularly acute surge in anxiety in recent years, with the sharpest increases among women and people of color.[2] Social anxiety disorder has never been higher, affecting more than fifteen million American adults and a growing number of children and teens. A disproportionate number of people dealing with homelessness, under- or unemployment, and incarceration also live with mental illness. Mental illness can make it more difficult for someone to be inclined to encounter others, and in some cases, it can also lead to a negative encounter with others.

In a similar way, a person's emotional well-being has to be considered for building a culture of encounter. People who have endured neglect, abuse, and various forms of trauma may not feel safe being put in a position to encounter others. The same is true for those who have experienced discrimination, degradation, or danger, perhaps being ridiculed, silenced, or threatened. Some of us have been hurt at the hands of another person who is suffering from a mental health disorder while others of us have been betrayed by a friend or family member. Many have been judged or isolated because of physical appearance, skin color, the outward expression of their identities (the way they dress or style their hair, their piercings or tattoos), or their body's size, shape, and ability. When people are deemed "less than," they are isolated, sometimes rendered untouchable or invisible. Physical illness, injury, and disability can present visible challenges for encounter—however, some estimates suggest that close to 90 percent of disabilities are invisible (like chronic illness or a physical limitation), and these experiences can create less obvious barriers for a culture of encounter.

Many people do not feel socially valued or welcome. The young are not always taken seriously, the elderly are often ignored, and minority groups typically feel pushed to the margins of security, status, and power. All of this generates a widespread questioning of worthiness, both of the self and the other. If we want to do something to change the social separation and unjust inequalities that exist in our world, we have to choose to change how we think and feel, what we want and need, especially in how we understand our worthiness and the worthiness of others. Shame casts doubt on my worthiness while pride can make me question the worthiness of others. In both cases, we are given reasons to avoid a culture of encounter. It is hard to imagine progress being possible if we continue to question the worthiness of each and every person, including ourselves.

Brené Brown has studied shame extensively and concludes that worthiness grows by practicing courage, compassion, and connection. She notes that courage

---

[2]Jacek Debiec, "39% of Americans More Anxious Today Than This Time Last Year," University of Michigan Health Lab, May 10, 2018.

originally meant "To speak one's mind by telling all one's heart." Yet Brown sees courage differently today: now courage is more about "putting our vulnerability on the line."[3] Vulnerability is something most people try to hide or ignore. Vulnerability opens us to harm, but it is also the only way to give and receive love. God meets us in our vulnerability, offering resilience, resistance, and healing in the face of harm.[4] There is no culture of encounter without the courage to be vulnerable.

People learn virtues through habituation: we become more compassionate by practicing compassion just as we become more courageous by making a habit of acting with courage. For those petrified at the prospect of exercising social courage, it is worth noting that courage starts with small, manageable words and deeds. An individual needs to practice being honest (even if it might not be convenient or comfortable) with their own self, with family and friends, and then also with colleagues and neighbors, and eventually strangers before they can be expected to prophetically speak truth to power in a social, economic, or political setting. Like a muscle, courage needs to be trained and strengthened; as a person sees courage taking root in their life and making an impact on others, he or she can endeavor to embrace more courageous words and actions. Courage builds resilience through expanding the strength of one's inner core, the heart, the etymological root of the word "courage." When other people see courage in action, it inspires them to be more vulnerable by helping others, too. When people live by the "I do me, you do you" credo, this is a false claim of invulnerability, pretending that I cannot be negatively impacted by others' decisions. It is also a failure of courage to hold people accountable to shared moral norms. It is a form of betrayal that refuses to call out discrimination or deception, fear or hatred, abuse or violence. A culture of encounter is impossible without more individuals and groups dedicating themselves to cultivating greater social courage to defend and promote innate and equal human dignity, rights, and duties.

Courage is related to compassion because compassion is daring to move "toward what scares us," whether that is pain or brokenness, confusion or fear, mourning or misery. Compassion is a whole-hearted, full-blown immersion into the human condition. It means to "suffer with" (as the Latin roots suggest), by opening oneself to hurt rather than protection.[5] Compassion requires perception sensitive enough to feel the suffering of other people, enough concern to care about their suffering, and enough commitment to act in a way that tries to alleviate their suffering. Compassion fights denial and fatalism; it is the opposite of a

---

[3]Brené Brown, *The Gifts of Imperfection* (Center City, MN: Hazelden, 2010), 12–13 (emphasis removed).

[4]On this topic, see Elizabeth O'Donnell Gandolfo, *The Vulnerability of Love: A Theological Anthropology* (Minneapolis: Fortress Press, 2015).

[5]Brown, *The Gifts of Imperfection*, 15–16.

cold cynicism that tempts us to think, "Why bother?" Compassion takes risks; it is a bold gesture of vulnerability and tenderness that is radically countercultural in a social context that is more inclined to feign invulnerability and foment blame and rage. Compassion draws near the other as equals; this recognition of equality is essential for solidarity that can heal personal wounds and social breaches. Compassion must also include proper boundaries as well as accountability to keep people from being manipulated, exploited, or abused. Without appropriate boundaries and accountability, a person risks falling prey to "compassion fatigue," which can leave them feeling depleted and ineffective.

Courage and compassion make connection possible. Brown defines connection as "the energy that exists between people when they feel seen, heard, and valued; when they can give and receive without judgment; and when they derive sustenance and strength from the relationship."[6] Humans are social beings who crave connection with others, but these connections are only life giving when they are moderated by mutual respect, trust, freedom, and responsibility. Connection is most meaningful when it reaches beyond a single encounter and becomes the copresence of accompaniment, the reciprocity and mutuality of exchange, the movement toward embrace and belonging. Love is a fundamental human need that is vital for human flourishing. We make a grave mistake when we think that anyone—including ourself—deserves anything less than encounter, accompaniment, exchange, embrace, and belonging.

For Brown, experiencing love and sharing one's story are key factors in feeling worthy of this path toward belonging. Love is affirming and empowering. Telling my story helps me better understand why I am who I am, and how my story is caught up in the stories of others. When I share my story and hear the stories of others, I more easily recognize how my story belongs in the grand narrative of human experience. Narrative is crucial for empathy and perspective changing, since it offers a glimpse of the world through another person's eyes; it is a way to imagine what it is like to be human in another way than being me. Put simply, sharing our stories helps us stitch together a sense of solidarity. These affirming connections help us overcome shame, fear, and vulnerability, the "swampland of the soul."[7] Even when we face our flaws, this should not make us feel unworthy or unlovable, because we cannot be reduced to the worst thing we have done or failed to do. Instead, when we feel guilt for something we have done wrong or failed to do something we should have, the message ought to be "Let's avoid repeating that mistake again in the future," not "I am bad" or "I am unlovable" or "I am beyond redemption." Part of humility is embracing our innate goodness and knowing

---

[6]Ibid., 19 (emphasis removed).

[7]Ibid., 36.

the truth about our strengths and limits. This acknowledgment is also part of the "audacity of authenticity," being honest with ourselves and letting "our true selves be seen" by others.[8] Authenticity means prizing integrity ahead of social status or the approval of others. It means letting go of unrealistic expectations for myself and others, recognizing that having limits is liberating because we cannot be all things to all people. (If someone disapproves of something I've said or done, I remind myself, even Jesus Christ didn't get all twelve disciples.) In the face of widespread shame and cynicism we need to practice resilience, gratitude, joy, and playfulness—all traits that make worthiness sustainable through the highs and lows that life brings.

All people wrestle with questions of worthiness. However, Christians have ample theological resources that verify the inherent and unconditional goodness of every human person. In the Book of Genesis, which begins with the story of creation, everything that exists is described as "good." This does not mean that everything is useful or valuable for some other purpose or profit, but rather that everything is good simply because it exists. When God looks at everything God has created, God delights in it as "very good" (Gn 1:31). This includes the human person, who is created in the "image and likeness" of God (Gn 1:26). This means that humans are internally related to God and externally represent God; we make God present in the world.[9] As C. S. Lewis wrote, "Next to the Blessed Sacrament itself, your neighbor is the holiest object presented to your senses."[10] To encounter another person is to encounter God in our midst—and to manifest God's presence for the other we encounter as well. This means that every encounter has the potential of being holy. It is one thing to believe this, and it is yet another to be fully awake to this reality, to pay attention to the latent depth of every encounter. Insofar as everyone bears this divine "image and likeness," it reinforces our interrelationship and interdependence as co-equal members of God's family. To be human is to be capable of a personal relationship with God and made for community. The culture of encounter beckons us to be attentive and responsive to this vision of what it means to be human, aspiring to heal whatever wounds divide the human family.

Christian faith, then, is more than a creed to be professed. It is a relationship to be nurtured, a relationship that seeks union with God and neighbor. While many might imagine God to look something like Dumbledore or Zeus, God should be

---

[8]Ibid., 51, 49.

[9]John R. Sachs writes, "Human beings are radically different from God but uniquely and intimately related to God, capable of personal relationship with God." See John R. Sachs, *The Christian Vision of Humanity: Basic Christian Anthropology* (Collegeville, MN: Michael Glazier, 1991), 16.

[10]C. S. Lewis, *The Weight of Glory: And Other Addresses* (New York: HarperOne, 1949), 46.

thought of less as a person than as a relationship. The Trinity communicates God's relational nature: a communion of love that is offered, received, and returned. Or as Augustine describes the Trinity, the Lover, the Beloved, and the Love that bonds them together. In this way, God is more *being* than *a* being, "closer to being a verb than a noun."[11] God is not some elderly man far removed from human experience, not a stern judge who is constantly evaluating human activity, or some strange union of two men and a bird.[12] God is revealed in Scripture as *hesed* and *eleos,* terms that signify mercy (Ex 34:6–7; Lk 6:36). Over and again, Scripture describes who God is and what God wants in terms of steadfast love and loyalty, tenderness and forgiveness, gratuity and solidarity.[13] Pope Francis emphasized mercy as central to God's character and purpose in declaring the Jubilee of Mercy from 2015 to 2016 and in his book, *The Name of God Is Mercy*. Francis explains that mercy "means opening one's heart to wretchedness. And immediately we go to the Lord: mercy is the divine attitude which embraces, it is God's giving himself to us, accepting us, and bowing to forgive . . . we can say that mercy is God's identity card."[14] Francis adds that it is better to think of God in terms of the gerund "mercifying"; God is mercy in action.[15]

To be in relationship with God-who-is-mercifying implies becoming people of boundless mercy. This begins by encountering God, a chance to "learn tenderness directly from God." Even though to be "touched by God can be profoundly disconcerting," it "teaches us what it is to be real. It brings an intimate awareness of a tenderness within ourselves, a godly tenderness that we might not ordinarily understand that we possess."[16] Pope Francis reminds us that tenderness is not weakness but fortitude.[17] It takes real strength to be tender in the face of anxiety

---

[11]Michael J. Himes, *Doing the Truth in Love* (Mahwah, NJ: Paulist Press, 1995), 18.

[12]Sandra Schneiders, quoted in Elizabeth Johnson, *Quest for the Living God: Mapping Frontiers in the Theology of God* (New York: Continuum, 2007), 208. Johnson continues, writing, "The subversive trinitarian notion that God is not an absolute monad but one whose very nature is communion, relation-to-another-who-is-equal, became submerged in waves of theory that justified the domination of some over others."

[13]The biblical words for mercy (*hesed* and *eleos*) appear nearly three hundred times; see, for example: Ex 20:6; Lv 19:2; Dt 5:2, 7:7–9, 15:4, 7; Nm 14:18; Josh 2:12; 1 Sm 20:14–17; 2 Sm 7:11–16; Ru 1:8, 2:20, 3:10; Ps 13:6, 25:6, 33:5, 111:4, 136:1, 145:9; Is 54:8–10, 55:3; Mi 7:19; Hos 2:16–21, 6:6; Dn 7:9–14; Jer 42:12, as well as Mt 5:7, 9:13, 12:7, 18:21–35, 23:23; Mk 5:19; Lk 1:58, 6:36, 10:25–42; 2 Cor 1:3, 4:1; Rom 12:1–2; Eph 2:4; 1 Pt 2:10; Jas 2:13.

[14]Pope Francis, *The Name of God Is Mercy*, trans. Oonagh Stransky (New York: Random House, 2016), 8–9.

[15]Ibid., 12.

[16]Gillian T. W. Ahlgren, *The Tenderness of God: Reclaiming Our Humanity* (Minneapolis: Fortress Press, 2017), 35.

[17]Pope Francis, "Why the Only Future Worth Building Includes Everyone" [Video file] [illegible] 2017), https://www.ted.com.

or fear, shame or anger. It requires great stamina to maintain tenderness when we doubt others' intentions, our abilities, or effectiveness. Tenderness means connecting at the same level as the other, it seeks an intimacy for authentic understanding and affirmation. We exemplify courage when we make tenderness a defining trait, when it mediates the way we encounter others. In the face of so many temptations to give up, so many examples of sin, evil, and other ways we fall short, Christian disciples need to invest in spiritual practices that will help make tenderness an intentional posture and overall lifestyle. There are many spiritual practices to help people stay in touch with their deepest desires, to stay connected with God, and to initiate and maintain healthy relationships with others. In the pages that follow, I highlight five practices to help map out some possibilities for a spiritual discipline of worthiness and belonging: mindfulness, contemplation, prayer, sacraments, and imagination.

Mindfulness is being awake to the present moment. It strives to cultivate a "peaceful heart" for "interbeing" in communion with others.[18] Mindfulness helps to integrate body, speech, and mind. It exercises compassion, showing tenderness to what we think and feel rather than judging our thoughts and feelings as "good" or "bad." The Buddhist monk Thich Nhat Hanh suggests that whatever we feel—whether sadness or anger, fear or hurt—we look at it tenderly, as if to say, "My darling, I see you, and I feel compassion for you." This practice brings understanding, crucial for harmony within and beyond the self. Thich Nhat Hanh writes, "By cultivating peace within, we bring about peace in society. It depends on us. To practice peace in ourselves is to minimize the numbers of wars between this and that feeling, or this and that perception, and we can then have real peace with others as well, including the members of our own family."[19]

Contemplation can be defined as a practice of "taking a long loving look at the real."[20] Contemplation means immersing oneself in reality, not to analyze it or argue about it, but to experience it, to recognize our unity with all existence. To see with eyes of love is to see as God sees, to appreciate and affirm the goodness in and around us. Contemplation means recognizing the nearness of God and implies a readiness to encounter God wherever we are. Mindfulness is a matter of presence while contemplation is a practice of attentiveness, using one's entire being to experience what is real. Taking a long look means not rushing the process, savoring the goodness in and around us. Contemplation generates wonder and awe; it means being filled with gratitude instead of disappointment, resentment, or comparison with others. Through contemplation, delighting in creation leads to

---

[18]Thich Nhat Hanh, *Love in Action* (Berkeley, CA: Parallax, 1993), 73, 66.

[19]Ibid., 70.

[20]Walter Burghardt, SJ, "Contemplation: A Long Loving Look at the Real," *Church* (1989): 89–98.

feeling love for the rest of creation, even when it is not always pleasant. In the face of sin, contemplation produces compassion, an expression of love for those who suffer and a desire to ease their burdens. Ultimately, contemplation orients us to commune with one another. A busy lifestyle is not conducive to contemplation; some might not even know where to start. It often helps to change our routines or take a break to withdraw from our daily responsibilities. It could mean we try to adopt a sober perspective free from distraction or deception. Other times renewal might come from being playful. Contemplation can be aided by poetry, music, or artwork that helps us to look at the world with fresh eyes. This practice "is not a luxury" but a distinguishing "mark of a Christian" and a person who loves.[21]

Thomas Merton offers an oft-cited illustration of an experience of contemplation, which took him by surprise one day in March 1958:

> In Louisville, at the corner of Fourth and Walnut, in the center of the shopping district, I was suddenly overwhelmed with the realization that I loved all those people, that they were mine and I theirs, that we could not be alien to one another even though we were total strangers. It was like waking from a dream of separateness, of spurious self-isolation in a special world, the world of renunciation and supposed holiness . . . This sense of liberation from an illusory difference was such a relief and such a joy to me that I almost laughed out loud . . . I have the immense joy of being man, a member of a race in which God Himself became incarnate. As if the sorrows and stupidities of the human condition could overwhelm me, now I realize what we all are. And if only everybody could realize this! But it cannot be explained. There is no way of telling people that they are all walking around shining like the sun.[22]

It is unrealistic to walk around in anticipation of mystical experiences like Merton describes. But his reflection on this epiphany in downtown Louisville reminds us that every moment and every place is an opportunity to participate in the culture of encounter that seeks union with God and others. To prepare ourselves spiritually to encounter God and others, we should aim to become "contemplatives in action," people who integrate reflection and discernment as well as other spiritual practices like prayer into our daily habits.

Prayer is the intention to be in union with God. Prayer can take many forms—like petition or praise, for example—as a way to encounter God. Whether we pray for ourselves or for others, our hope is to become more like Jesus. Prayer puts us

---

[21]Ibid., 98.

[22]Thomas Merton, *Conjectures of a Guilty Bystander* (New York: Image, 1965), 153–55.

in touch with Jesus's heart so that we can be his body in the world, as Saint Teresa of Avila described more than four hundred years ago:

> Christ has no body but yours,
> No hands, no feet on earth but yours,
> Yours are the eyes with which he looks
> Compassion on this world,
> Yours are the feet with which he walks to do good,
> Yours are the hands with which he blesses all the world.
> Yours are the hands, yours are the feet,
> Yours are the eyes, you are his body.
> Christ has no body now but yours,
> No hands, no feet on earth but yours,
> Yours are the eyes with which he looks
> compassion on this world.
> Christ has no body now on earth but yours.

Prayer can be spontaneous, it can be informed by Scripture, or it can can be inspired by our experience. In any case, prayer is interior work that must find expression in our exteriority; it is a process of growing in awareness, attitude, and action for interconnectedness.[23] Prayer refocuses our attention on the question, What am I living for? It requires patience for spiritual growth, as God's love works in and through us, just as God's love works in and through others we encounter. There is a long and strong tradition of spiritual practices that remain relevant for developing prayer, care for others, and spiritual growth.[24] Prayer seems personal and perhaps private, but of course prayer is strengthened when it is shared in communal settings.

The *sacraments* are another important spiritual practice for developing worthiness and belonging. The sacramental life of the Catholic Church represents unique opportunities to encounter Christ. The sacraments also provide spiritual sustenance for discipleship, as these rich symbols and rituals remind us who we are and whose we are. Sacraments like baptism, reconciliation, and the Eucharist mediate grace as God shares God's life with us. The sacrament of reconciliation is a singular ritual for building a culture of encounter, since it walks us through steps to acknowledge our sins, make amends, and work to heal whatever separates us from loving God, others, and ourselves. Three-quarters of American Catholics do not participate in this sacrament even once a year, and this is a lost opportunity

---

[23]Joyce Rupp, *Boundless Compassion: Creating a Way of Life* (Notre Dame, IN: Sorin, 2018), 15.

[24]See, for example, Colleen M. Griffith and Thomas Groome, eds., *Catholic Spiritual Practices: A Treasury of Old and New* (Brewster, MA: Paraclete Press, 2012).

to experience forgiveness, wisdom, and encouragement.[25] The Eucharist, a daily celebration in the life of the church, is also a preeminent ritual for building a culture of encounter. A majority of Catholics do not receive Eucharist on a weekly basis, but for those who do, it should never become banal or stale. The Eucharist "is not simply *a* way of worshipping God, it is *the* privileged means of experiencing the presence of Jesus Christ and participating in his work of redeeming the world."[26] It intentionally re-creates Jesus's boundary-breaking table fellowship (Mk 2:13–17; Lk 7:36–50), so disruptive to Jesus's contemporaries that some of them wanted him dead.[27] Today, some people are reluctant to approach the table of the Lord's Supper, but Pope Francis insists, the "Eucharist, although it is the fullness of sacramental life, is not a prize for the perfect but a powerful medicine and nourishment for the weak."[28] No one should be made to feel unworthy of this encounter with Christ. This is especially true because the Eucharist is not only something to receive, but it is something to participate in and become. The Eucharist provides access to God's presence and power for the church to cooperate with God in the world. It can be understood as human-and-divine power sharing, a "synergy for solidarity," the food that nourishes an encounter with God and one another.[29]

The church is to be a beacon, the most reliable culture of encounter on the planet, by advancing its mission and communion. This is not to suggest that the church is sinless, for even while it is guided by the Holy Spirit, it is a human institution comprised of members who sin regularly. When the church is divided or fails in witnessing to the gospel, this is all the more reason why the people of God need to dedicate themselves to fidelity and forgiveness, hospitality and reconciliation, compassion and solidarity. And when the church is the *cause* of pain, its members should raise a cry of lament—to rage with compassion in protest of evil[30]—and strategize practices and policies to better promote inclusive welcome, the healing of wounds, and restorative justice for those who have been wronged, as well as empowerment and coresponsibility of all members of the Body of Christ. In the wake of clergy sex abuse and its cover-up, the church can only be a safe place for a culture of encounter when there is adequate remorse and atonement for sin,

---

[25]Doris K. Donnelly, "Penance and Justice," in *Sacraments in Justice* (Collegeville, MN: Michael Glazier, 2014), 57.

[26]John F. Baldovin, SJ, *Bread of Life, Cup of Salvation* (Lanham, MD: Sheed & Ward, 2003), 3.

[27]Robert Karris puts it bluntly: "Jesus was crucified because of how he ate." See Robert Karris, *Luke: Artist & Theologian: Luke's Passion Account as Literature* (Eugene, OR: Wipf and Stock, 1985), 47.

[28]*Evangelii Gaudium*, no. 47.

[29]Marcus Mescher, "Liturgy as Power-Sharing: Synergy for Solidarity," in *Liturgy + Power*, ed. Brian P. Flanagan and Johann M. Vento (Maryknoll, NY: Orbis Books, 2017), 46–62.

[30]John Swinton, *Raging with Compassion: Pastoral Responses to the Problem of Evil* (Grand Rapids, MI: Eerdmans, 2007), 104–5.

transparency and accountability for those in leadership, and effective plans in place to prevent future abuse. At this point, the Catholic Church has lost a great deal of credibility. Everything is on the line unless and until meaningful and effective institutional reforms are put into place.

The fifth and final spiritual practice is *imagination*. The imagination is essential for looking to the future with hope, tenderness, and solidarity. Instead of viewing imagination as fantasy or illusion, it is better understood as a "vehicle for liberation."[31] Imagination is the fruit of one's deepest desires, illuminating what one hopes for oneself and the world.[32] It does not disdain or reject the world, but rather embraces the world in its complex, fallen state.[33] In the face of sin, suffering, and injustice, the imagination is an exercise of resistance to evil as well as resilience in promoting the good. It is an invitation "into a different wavelength," an energizing "transformed consciousness" in alert wonder at what is and awe at what more is possible.[34] The imagination is "the capacity to imagine something rooted in the challenges of the real world yet capable of giving birth to that which does not yet exist."[35] Imagination is a practice of hope and love, affirming the goodness in every member of creation, and inspiring collaboration. Imagination is at its fullest and freest when it is a shared exercise, marked by mutuality and equality among people.[36]

Pope Francis has urged more emphasis on imagination. Along with restlessness (the refusal to accept mediocrity and the commitment to be audacious in seeking

---

[31]So argues Johann Baptist Metz, who envisions the restoration of memory—especially the "dangerous memory" of the Paschal Mystery—as precipitating the restoration of imagination that resists the acceptance of suffering as complacent with the status quo. See Johann Baptist Metz, *Faith in History and Society: Toward a Practical Fundamental Theology*, trans. J. Matthew Ashley (New York: Herder & Herder, 2007), 177–78.

[32]William Lynch insists that hope is impossible without imagination. He posits, "Hope is, in its most general terms, a sense of *the possible*, that what we really need is possible, though difficult, while hopelessness means to be ruled by the sense of the impossible. Hope therefore involves three basic ideas that could not be simpler: what I hope for I do not yet have or see; it may be difficult; but I *can* have it—it is possible." See William F. Lynch, *Images of Hope: Imagination as Healer of the Hopeless* (Notre Dame, IN: University of Notre Dame Press, 1974), 32.

[33]Lynch explains, "We must *go through* the finite, the limited, the definite, omitting none of it lest we omit some of the potencies of being-in-the-flesh . . . We waste our time if we try to go around or above or under the definite; we must literally go through it." See William F. Lynch, *Christ and Apollo: The Dimension of the Literary Imagination* (New York: Sheed and Ward, 1960), 7.

[34]Michael Paul Gallagher, "Theology and Imagination: From Theory to Practice," *Christian Higher Education* 5 (2006): 83–96 (at 87).

[35]John Paul Lederach, *The Moral Imagination: The Art and Soul of Building Peace* (Oxford: Oxford University Press, 2005), 29.

[36]Lynch states, "In mutuality, each of the parties helps the other to become himself . . . such a unity is creative . . . Real mutuality also communicates freedom . . . [and] includes a profound wishing together" (Lynch, *Images of Hope*, 171).

to change the world) as well as incompleteness (always being open to the God of surprises), Francis envisions imagination as crucial for being available to the new work of the Holy Spirit in the world today. He explains,

> This is the time of discernment in the Church and in the world. Discernment is always realized in the presence of the Lord, looking at the signs, listening to things that happen, the feelings of people who know the humble way of the daily stubbornness, and especially of the poor. But we need to penetrate ambiguity, we need to enter in there, as the Lord Jesus did assuming our flesh. Rigid thought is not divine because Jesus has assumed our flesh, which is not rigid except after death. This is why I like poetry so much and, when it is possible for me, I continue to read it. Poetry is full of metaphors. Understanding metaphors helps to make thought agile, intuitive, flexible, acute. Whoever has imagination does not become rigid, has a sense of humor, always enjoys the sweetness of mercy and inner freedom.[37]

Imagination speaks to and from one's deepest desires, overcoming the banality that strips the potency of the gospel. Imagination functions on a cognitive level just as much as it does a spiritual and religious level: it dismantles limitations placed on God, one another, and oneself. Imagination is prophetic, finding a healthy balance between an overaffirmation and overrejection of the world. Imagination is creative, opening access to the spiritual and moral resources necessary for building the Reign of God and resisting the anti-Reign of God (i.e., forces that dehumanize, deprive, and divide). This raises the moral question of how imagination is exercised: which values are embraced, which are rejected, and who benefits or suffers from these choices? As a "key battleground for meaning, values, and in particular for religious faith," the imagination is "where the quality of our lives is shaped and where we shape our vision of everything. Imagination is the location both of our crisis and of our potential healing. It is vital for the quality of our seeing, because it can save us from superficiality and torpor and awaken us to larger hopes and possibilities."[38] When social divisions seem insurmountable, the imagination makes it possible to discover what we share in common with others through empathy and perspective changing, sharing narratives that help us relate to each other on a human level.[39] When we fail to connect across differences or

[37]Pope Francis, "Discourse to the Community of *La Civiltà Cattolica*," *La Civiltà Cattolica*, February 9, 2017.

[38]Michael Paul Gallagher, "Culture and Imagination as Battlegrounds," Shaping the Future: Networking Jesuit Higher Education for a Globalizing World, Mexico City (April 21–25, 2010), 3, 7.

[39]This can also take place through sharing music, poetry, and artwork: not in an unrealistic "Kumbaya" mentality, but in a way that is open to receiving the complicated, honest, and unique

fail to find solutions to problems, this is a failure of imagination. Moral, social, and spiritual growth develop in direct proportion to developing the capacities of one's imagination.

Opposed to abstraction or hypothetical daydreaming, imagination activates a curiosity that evaluates how power is exercised in systems and structures. When imagination is paired with social analysis, it is possible to better understand "social realities with an abiding respect for complexity" as well as to maintain "a refusal to fall prey to the pressures of forced dualistic categories of truth, and an inquisitiveness about what may hold together seemingly contradictory social energies in a greater whole."[40] In this way, the imagination functions with clear-eyed realism, or even what might be described as a "pessimism" that "is a terrain-based understanding of the social setting. What it seeks to engage is a deep understanding of human affairs, the true nature of how change happens, and the necessity of integrity as a condition for surviving manipulation and mendacity."[41] Imagination serves as the bridge between personal and social change. The imagination trains us to explore what it would take to create conditions for a culture of encounter that affirms human dignity, fosters right relationships, and produces inclusive solidarity for the common good. If we do not test the limits of what is possible, the status quo will remain unchanged. After all, nothing happens in history unless it first happens in our imagination.[42]

OVERCOMING BIAS

These spiritual practices can help individuals make the conscious choice to overcome bitterness and fear, shame and anger. Christian faith maintains the worthiness of every individual and the duty to build right relationship in the spirit of love and justice. However, a culture of encounter cannot be accomplished by exhortations to empathy, kindness, and compassion alone. Persistent inequalities in power and access pose serious obstacles to building a culture of encounter, as does the ubiquity of prejudice. If we fail to address the root causes of bias—contributing to sexism and heterosexism, racism and xenophobia, etc.—we will be

---

experience of what it is like to be someone other than me. This is an act of hospitality just as much as it is imagination. See Christopher Pramuk, *Hope Sings, So Beautiful: Graced Encounters across the Color Line* (Collegeville, MN: Michael Glazier, 2013), 143–58.

[40]Lederach, *The Moral Imagination*, 36. Lederach observes that the root of curiosity has to do with both "cure" and "care."

[41]Ibid., 55.

[42]This line is inspired by Gloria Anzaldúa: "Nothing happens in the 'real' world unless it first happens in the images in our heads," in her book *Borderlands/La Frontera: The New Mestiza* (San Francisco: Aunt Lute Books, 1987), 87.

unable to change the personal perceptions and cultural norms that distort some encounters and prevent others from happening. This is what mercy demands: accompanying others; learning from them; and attending to and dismantling the beliefs, practices, and structures that separate and subjugate.

One of the main obstacles to building a culture of encounter is the baggage we bring to encounters with others. When we are hurt by someone, it makes it harder to open ourselves to others because we may be anxious about getting hurt again. Or we might come from a context that normalized prejudice against a marginalized group. For example, although it is wholly incompatible with the gospel, racism stains American Christianity. Racism—as historical, cultural, and institutional—functions like "America's original sin."[43] It is a universal, unavoidable "soul sickness," as Martin Luther King Jr. described. Racism functions through symbols that deform Christian identity. Racism assumes whiteness is superior and standard, the default setting, so that people of color become "otherized" and "less than." Through the personal and social sins of racism, "unconscious racism" becomes internalized and influences our attitudes and actions. Racism distorts how we see ourselves and others, like "spiritual cataracts" as well as an overall "ethos—as a pervasive symbol system of meaning, identity, and significance—much more than as a set of discrete, consciously motivated acts."[44] Everyone should agree that it is wrong to judge someone by the color of their skin, to deny their dignity and rights, or limit their freedom because of their race or ethnicity. But if we do not pay attention to the kinds of bias reflected in conscious and unconscious racism, then we miss the ways in which cultural images, messages, and systems impact everyone, resulting in reflexive aversion to individuals and groups with less status, privilege, and power.

Everyone operates with implicit (meaning unarticulated, unconscious, and automatic) biases that "are evaluative thoughts and feelings about social groups that can contribute to discriminatory behavior even in the absence of explicitly prejudiced motivations."[45] These biases react to a variety of traits—gender, skin color, body size and shape, disability, age, etc.—and shape how we perceive reality. Implicit bias keeps us from clearly seeing others and the damage done by bias on the personal, social, and structural levels. Researchers measure these biases through indirect means, typically through sorting attitudes associated with various identity markers and concepts like good or bad, safe or violent. People who take

---

[43]Jim Wallis, *America's Original Sin: Racism, White Privilege, and the Bridge to a New America* (Grand Rapids, MI: Brazos, 2016), xx.

[44]Bryan Massingale, *Racial Justice and the Catholic Church* (Maryknoll, NY: Orbis Books, 2010), 33.

[45]Michael Brownstein, *The Implicit Mind: Cognitive Architecture, the Self, and Ethics* (Oxford: Oxford University Press, 2018), 2, 15–16.

an "Implicit Association Test" are asked to rapidly answer questions that evaluate links between social identity and values, which reveal common stereotypes.[46] For example, in the test that measures attitudes related to race, more than 70 percent of white people exhibit negative implicit biases against blacks, as do roughly 40 percent of African Americans.[47] Other tests show widespread preference for men over women, able-bodied people over those with a disability, and thin more than overweight people, as well as pervasive negative attitudes toward LGBTQ individuals and members of other socially marginalized groups. These tests are helpful for predicting discriminatory behavior on both the personal and social levels. Some examples include bias among physicians and police officers, affecting how they treat those they serve.[48] In light of the fact that everyone possesses these implicit attitudes that correspond to unconscious positive and negative associations, we have to recognize and respond to the way bias impacts our encounters.

Human behavior is shaped by our brains, biology, social context, cultural norms, and a variety of other factors, including economic and political beliefs and systems. All of these factors have to be taken into consideration when discussing the possibilities and limits of Christian neighbor love and solidarity, because they illuminate how humans are—internally and externally—influenced to prefer some people over others. For example, sociobiology helps us to understand how humans have evolved to be more inclined to help people who look like them. This makes empathy and altruism far easier for family members than for strangers and for people of our own race as compared to those with a different skin color. These preferential attitudes are "not fully conscious and usually not deliberate," illustrating that free will does not operate from a blank slate; human choice is conditioned by these idiosyncrasies and random (and sometimes not-so-random) stimuli.[49] This raises important psychological, philosophical, and ethical questions about whether we should trust our instincts or "go with your gut." Sometimes our instincts are virtuous, and other times they are vicious. It is not always the case that when we feel unsettled or fearful, there is good reason to be suspicious of others. This is especially true when we consider how we are shaped by normative

---

[46]For a variety of tests, see https://implicit.harvard.edu/implicit/.

[47]Brian A. Nosek et al., "Pervasiveness and Correlates of Implicit Attitudes and Stereotypes," *European Review of Social Psychology* 18, no. 1 (2007): 36–88.

[48]See, for example, William J. Hall et al., "Implicit Racial/Ethnic Bias among Health Care Professionals and Its Influence on Health Care Outcomes: A Systematic Review," *American Journal of Public Health* 105, no. 12 (2015): 60–76; Lois James, "The Stability of Implicit Racial Bias in Police Officers," *Police Quarterly* 21, no. 1 (2018): 30–52.

[49]"Evolutionary theory points to certain basic motivations, often not fully conscious and usually not deliberative, underlying widespread forms of behavior that were originally shaped over the course of millions of years." Stephen J. Pope, *The Evolution of Altruism and the Ordering of Love* (Washington, DC: Georgetown University Press, 1994), 11.

cultural images and messages that sometimes degrade people based on their age or ability, sex, gender, or sexual orientation, ethnicity, race, or nationality, class or religion, etc. Of course, belonging to a racist or sexist culture does not excuse the racist or sexist beliefs or actions of the members. But understanding how our environment, sociocultural context, and brain processes work together helps us to better grasp what it would take to be more amenable to encountering others who are different.

Bias plays out in a variety of ways; it can mean being positively or negatively inclined toward others. Bias can move us to give others the benefit of the doubt because they seem more similar than strange to us. Social homophily draws us toward others who share similar characteristics, just as social structuring places us in social settings with those who are more similar than different. Friends share more genetic similarities than are seen among strangers.[50] That seems harmless enough, but when hiring employees, we are more likely to choose candidates who are like us—rather than the most qualified—a process known as "cultural matching."[51] In some cases, bias closes us off to the other or motivates a change in behavior because we see the other as a threat. Sometimes bias inspires hateful actions or condescending words with full knowledge that others will find them offensive. But implicit bias is prereflexive: in this case, people do not edit their mental associations to avoid offense. As the example of microaggressions shows, people may not intend to offend, but their verbal slights (whether a comment or question) nonetheless exacerbate the feeling of alienation in others.[52] While some might question whether a person should be held accountable for an unconscious reaction, greater moral concern should focus on the impact—rather than the intention—of a person's words or actions.

Spontaneous cognitive inclinations are the result of dynamic interaction between the brain and its environment, or stimuli. Given the complex, interrelated categories that construct identity (sometimes referred to as "intersectionality," to signify the convergence of age and ability, sex, gender, and sexual orientation, ethnicity, race, and nationality, class and religion, etc.[53]), implicit bias cannot be explained simply as an involuntary reflex in response to another person's appearance. Implicit bias responds to a particular feature of one's surroundings, senses a

---

[50]Benjamin W. Domingue, "The Social Genome of Friends and Schoolmates in the National Longitudinal Study of Adolescent to Adult Health," *Proceedings of the National Academy of Sciences* 115, no. 4 (January 2018): 702–7.

[51]Lauren A. Rivera, "Hiring as Cultural Matching: The Case of Elite Professional Service Firms," *American Sociological Review* 77, no. 6 (December 2012): 999–1022.

[52]Simba Runyowa, "Microaggressions Matter," *The Atlantic*, September 18, 2015.

[53]Kimberlé Crenshaw, "The Urgency of Intersectionality" [Video file] (October 2016), https://www.ted.com.

degree of tension, and, through an affective response, spurs a behavioral reaction that tries to alleviate that tension.[54] Context matters for understanding why some people respond to certain stimuli but not others, or what makes some individuals sensitive to some tensions but ignorant of others. A person's emotional state also contributes to one's implicit attitudes, just as decision-making is more challenging when a person is tired, hungry, distracted, or stressed. People are also shaped by the views and voices of those around them, with negative associations capable of spreading like a "bias contagion."[55] In any encounter, these biases shape the interaction between people by influencing their thoughts, feelings, speech, body language, and actions. Positive associations build chemistry, whereas negative associations make it much easier for exchanges to escalate or spiral out of control. It is easy to recognize how this plays out on the institutional level, whether in business or the criminal justice system. The ethics of encounter demands that we work to reform the sinful systems and structures that "are still influenced by primitive racial narratives and imagery" that can sometimes be the difference between getting a job offer, receiving a second chance after a mistake, or, in some cases, life and death.[56] Bias also impacts the way we judge spaces and the people who come from those spaces. Immigrants frequently endure place-based prejudice and descriptions that suggest they are "dirty," "filthy," or "diseased," just as ethnic ghettos and their residents are associated with pollution, squalor, and crime.[57] Over a lifetime, people internalize the associations others make based on their appearance, a process that begins at a very young age. It is easy to put people into boxes and then feel resentment, anger, or fear when they resist being confined by such expectations. It is also true that people often act how they are treated by others, which means that our buried biases can become seeds for self-fulfilling prophecies.

People are not captive to implicit biases, which are in fact malleable. Awareness of bias is not enough to overcome the influence of these implicit attitudes and assumptions, however.[58] Because they involve a variety of fluid feedback—the response to stimuli, sensing tension, aiming to resolve tension, and assessing whether

---

[54] Brownstein, *The Implicit Mind*, 31.

[55] Jennifer L. Eberhardt, *Biased: Uncovering the Hidden Prejudice That Shapes What We See, Think, and Do* (New York: Viking, 2019), 42.

[56] Ibid., 130. Eberhardt provides substantial evidence of how race factors into traffic stops, criminal cases, and the death penalty, where "more than 57 percent of the 'highly stereotypical' black defendants were sentenced to die for their crimes. Looking 'more black' more than doubled their chances of being sentenced to death," even when researchers controlled for other factors.

[57] Ibid., 162–63.

[58] One study found that even those who identify as "liberal" did not show signs of greater empathy after learning about white privilege. See Erin Cooley et al., "Complex Intersections of Race and Class: Among Social Liberals, Learning about White Privilege Reduces Sympathy, Increases Blame, and Decreases External Attributions for White People Struggling with Poverty," *Journal of Experimental Psychology* (April 2019), http://dx.doi.org/10.1037/xge0000605.

that has been effective, for example—there is room to shift one's impulse. These real-time adjustments should not be categorized as cognitive learning, as that takes place after the fact, when reflecting on the experience. This is more accurately viewed as an "integrated and ongoing process" than "a series of one-and-done reflexive reactions."[59] Insofar as the biases are implicit, this is better understood as a posture or orientation than a deliberative process.[60] Being intentional about mitigating bias and reconciling inequities are important steps for facilitating a culture of encounter. This means slowing down and catching ourselves in snap judgments, which are seldom virtuous. Everyone can benefit from becoming more intentional about how we perceive stimuli, interpret others, and respond.

To virtuously respond to the reality of bias, we should consider our *telos*: What kind of person am I becoming? What kind of community am I building? What is the end goal that I desire for encounters with others? When we have the end goal in mind, it can help us be more attentive to how we accompany others. Changing implicit bias relies on practicing positive associations with stigmatized groups. It is aided by a precommitment to respond to stimuli (and tension) in a particular way by setting goals ("When I see this person, I will think about ____"). It also helps to regulate context, by managing the space to make it conducive for a more positive perception of others.[61] Evaluating progress and failure is important to better understand how or why these implicit associations help or hurt. Implicit bias is mitigated even more organically when we forge close attachments between people of different groups; our friendships with others can "puncture holes in stereotypic beliefs and negative attitudes," helping us overlook the "otherness" that we instinctively perceive.[62] This dovetails with Gutiérrez's call to foster friendships with and among the poor, those rendered socially insignificant as well as those we consider strangers and outsiders. Relationships and rapport can replace judgment with tenderness, distance with fidelity, and fear with love. Friendships deepen and broaden a process of becoming more self-aware and others-centered, part of a maturity that gleans wisdom from experiences, applies wisdom to future interactions, and shares wisdom with others in order to improve the way that we—collectively—think and feel about others. Being intentional about recognizing and responding to implicit bias helps make it possible for our internal and external processing to communicate respect and support for others as well as accountability to moral norms like freedom, equality, and mutuality.

---

[59]Brownstein, *The Implicit Mind*, 68.

[60]Brownstein describes this as the "habit stance." He cautions that "in endeavoring to improve the virtuousness of our implicit attitudes, we should not treat them as rational states to be reasoned with" (ibid., 178).

[61]Ibid., 184–86, 190–91, and 193–94.

[62]Eberhardt, *Biased*, 288.

Our habits reveal our character: we are what we repeatedly do. If we do nothing to resist bias (whether or not it is conscious), we become complacent and complicit with the sins of prejudice and discrimination. If we aim to build a culture of encounter, then we have to reflect on and discern the way we encounter and accompany others, the cognitive and affective responses they spur, how we receive and react to the other. This includes being sensitive to the tensions that exist between people and committed to address the reasons why the tensions exist. We need to think more intentionally about who belongs to and is excluded from our relationships and what we can do to draw near those who look, think, and live differently than we do. It is important to construct the kinds of spaces that will facilitate inclusive encounters mediated by honesty and freedom, safety and trust, mutual respect and responsibility. We also have to consider the aesthetics and designs, symbols and rituals that would be conducive to such encounters. And we have to be attentive and responsive to the beliefs, attitudes, and intentions—shaped by shame and cynicism, pride and presumption, hurts and fears, for example—that will impact these encounters as well.

FROM CONFLICT TO COMMUNICATION

Maybe the Samaritan had it easy. Even though he showed courage by going into the ditch—risking ambush—and then taking the robbers' victim to an inn—where the Samaritan would have been treated to hostile stares and suspicion, as a despised outcast—at least he did not have to talk to the man he helped, as he would have considered him an enemy. In these divided and polarized times, it is hard to find many examples of the grace and courtesy required for meaningful conversations across difference. Cable news and social media are more likely to host shouting matches of rehearsed, tired talking points, with people speaking past each other. This is a nerve-wracking time to discuss touchy subjects: some fear saying something ignorant, intolerant, or offensive, while others complain they are being muzzled by concerns about remaining "politically correct." Some could care less about offending others, while others feel anxiety at the prospect of triggering an emotional response that might quickly get out of hand. Still others are marginalized, minimized, and degraded by the rhetoric used by others. And no one wants to risk being wrong about any subject. In the face of all these challenges, if we do not participate in honest and vulnerable conversations across differences, there is no hope that anything will change. Democracy—like any robust community—depends on truthful dialogue. The virtue of generosity requires that we put some "skin in the game" in moving from accompaniment to meaningful exchanges marked by being willing to listen to the other; to respect their freedom, honor their dignity; and, when it is our turn to speak, to show love by being a "leavening presence" in a domineering and degrading social context and media landscape.[63]

In a pluralistic society, we cannot take agreement for granted. That is not to say that everything becomes a free-for-all or that pluralism is tantamount to relativism. However, the variety of views and values makes it more challenging to encounter others, much less to understand one another across and through these distinct positions. There may be times when partial understanding is the best one can hope for. If we are to move beyond the culture wars that debate more than discuss in order to bridge social separation, we have to remain in conversation with one another. In some ways, this is not a new phenomenon, even if social tension seems unprecedented. Almost forty years ago, David Tracy observed, "We understand one another, if at all, only through analogies . . . Conflict is our actuality. Conversation is our hope."[64] Each person carries unique perspectives and experiences, some so singular, in fact, that others might not be able to understand except by analogy to something familiar in his or her own life history.[65]

A culture of encounter depends on an ability to communicate honestly and effectively. If we have any hope to overcome indifference, distrust, or conflict, we will have to revise how we approach communication. The Buddhist monk Thich Nhat Hanh envisions conversation as a "source of nourishment," unless it is toxic, in which case it then becomes food for suffering.[66] This observation points to the need to be mindful of what we consume and produce, aiming for the kinds of words that empower rather than enervate. Hanh explains,

> Nourishing and healing communication is the food of our relationships. Sometimes one cruel utterance can make the other person suffer for many years, and will suffer for many years too. In a state of anger or fear, we may say something that can be poisonous and destructive. If we swallow poison, it can stay within us for a long time, slowly killing our relationship. We may not even know what we said or did that started to poison the relationship. But we have the antidote: mindful compassion and loving communication.[67]

---

[63]Pramuk, *Hope Sings, So Beautiful*, 139.

[64]David Tracy, *The Analogical Imagination: Christian Theology and the Culture of Pluralism* (New York: Crossroad, 1981), 363.

[65]Tracy explains, "We understand one another, if at all, only through analogy. Who you are I know only by knowing what event, what focal meaning, you actually live by. And that I know only if I too have sensed some analogous guide in my own life. If we converse, it is likely we will both be changed as we focus upon the subject matter itself—the fundamental questions and the classical responses in our traditions" (ibid., 454–55).

[66]Thich Nhat Hanh, *The Art of Communicating* (New York: HarperOne, 2013), 5.

[67]Ibid., 8–9.

Mindful compassion and loving communication start within the self. Making time to communicate with your own thoughts and feelings "is a revolutionary act" in a social context marked by so much busyness and constant connectivity.[68] This is how we come home to ourselves, finding the security and stability that will help us more intentionally and effectively communicate with others. Even when we experience suffering, this is possible; to see the suffering in our self is to better understand our thoughts and feelings, and it also enables us to see the suffering in others.[69]

To encounter and really engage another person means adopting a posture of dialogue. This implies not just an exchange between perspectives but a willingness to listen and learn. The grace of self-doubt can help us remain open to growth; there is more truth in the world than I know. Conversation fails even before it begins if a person is feeling defensive or defeated, anxious or angry, irritable or judgmental, suspicious or self-righteous. Whereas blame shuts down conversations, curiosity opens them up. A culture of encounter that incorporates conversation requires a posture that is flexible and patient, insightful and creative, grateful and hopeful. It relies on habits of honesty, humility, and respect. The point of the conversation is to be understood and to better understand, which can generate greater trust and safety, and perhaps even lead to a shared sense of connection and purpose. This relies on paying attention to how we speak and listen to others. We have to be mindful of what we say; for example, it is always better to use "I" statements to share one's viewpoint honestly than to use "you" statements that may put others on the defensive. Even more, we have to be intentional about how we say it; for example, there is a difference between speaking like I'm right and speaking like everyone else is wrong. Paying attention to volume and tone of voice is essential for making conversation partners feel safe, valued, and like they belong to this exchange of experiences, perspectives, and ideas.

Effective communication requires that we make an honest attempt to understand others. This requires "deep listening," which is a matter of being attentive and also, as Hanh describes, it aspires to "listen to someone with the intention of helping that person suffer less."[70] The other person may say things that are wrong, accusatory, or antagonistic. We may lose our patience in waiting to share our counterpoints. But no progress is made if we become irascible, annoyed, or enraged. That does not mean that it is never right to point out when someone says something that is inaccurate. But listening has to come first, a listening that makes the other person feel safe, valued, and heard. Listening with compassion implies a willingness to receive what the other person has to share. It means asking

[68]Ibid., 15.
[69]Ibid., 33.
[70]Ibid., 42.

myself, "How can I understand this person better, before I seek to be understood?" When the other person feels understood, when they can feel compassion from their conversation partner, then there is potential to discuss disagreements in a calm and collegial manner. This lessens the burdens we carry. If a person jumps in to explain why the other person is wrong, that will bring only more suffering and separation.

This is not meant to put an idyllic gloss on interpersonal communication. There will be misunderstanding and disagreement. Ego can make us blind to the validity in another perspective. Loyalty to an idea or position can make us resistant to seeing its weaknesses. Comfort with our customary worldview can make us uneasy with other viewpoints that differ. And in an era of widespread "fake news" and deception, there is a real chance of being unwittingly misinformed about an issue.[71] These and other challenges can test anyone's resolve to maintain loving words or show compassion. But a culture of encounter requires keeping a focus on helping people feel safe and valued as well as a shared commitment to seek understanding, which means using effective and accurate language. Thich Nhat Hanh recommends four guidelines for "right speech":

1. Tell the truth. Don't lie or turn the truth upside down.
2. Don't exaggerate.
3. Be consistent. This means no double-talk: speaking about something in one way to one person and in an opposite way to another for selfish or manipulative reasons.
4. Use peaceful language. Don't use insulting language or violent words, cruel speech, verbal abuse, or condemnation.[72]

These are not rules that we can take for granted, especially in a cultural context where so many experience stigma and shame, and there is so much vitriol spewed in media and online. If a conversation seems to be going awry, it is helpful to focus on the facts or what you both share in common. People still need to feel heard, even when they disagree. Sometimes this is as simple as reflecting back to the speaker what you heard ("I heard you say . . ."). If something is unclear, point that out. You might say, "It seems to me that . . . do I have that right?" Or ask, "Do you think I understand you enough?" If someone says, "Please help me understand," Hanh describes this as "the language of love."[73] If there is disagreement between

[71]Senior citizens are most likely to share "fake news" on social media, according to Andy Guess, Jonathan Nagler, and Joshua Tucker, "Who Was the Most Likely to Share Fake News in 2016? Seniors," *Washington Post*, January 9, 2019.

[72]Hanh, *The Art of Communicating*, 53.

[73]Ibid., 48.

you, seek common ground ("Can we agree that . . . ?"). If you are at an impasse, find a mediator who can facilitate a conversation through difficult topics. In some cases, it is helpful to change the structure of speaking and listening, or reframe the paradigm: there need not be only two ways of seeing an issue or problem. Could there be a third alternative that hasn't yet been considered?

Everyone thinks that they are right and we all feel an impulse to persuade others to see things as we do. When someone resists our viewpoint, it can be frustrating. When strong emotions arise, when it is difficult to receive the other person, or communicate what one thinks or feels, it is important to return to compassion and the goal to ease suffering. Thich Nhat Hanh suggests the mantra, "I am here for you."[74] Communication and community share the same Latin root: to share, to make common. A culture of encounter should be an opportunity to connect, to take a step toward reconciliation, without expecting everything to be solved in a single encounter or conversation. Mindful speech and deep listening can be first steps to reduce conflict, build trust, and cultivate greater respect and understanding.[75] These are ways to practice courage, mercy, generosity, humility, and fidelity.

Communication is challenging within families and among co-workers. It is all the more daunting to imagine effective communication across political divides. Some people say they want to avoid "getting political," but such a position is mythical. Nothing is apolitical: everything ultimately supports, resists, or upends the status quo. To profess a desire to "stay out of politics" is to abdicate one's civic duty, to cede one's voice and surrender one's power to ensure representation at the local, state, and federal level. This betrays your own interests, just as it betrays those of others who would benefit from your advocacy. Only people of considerable status, privilege, and power can think that an apolitical stance or neutrality is feasible. For those facing discrimination or oppression, there is no false pretense about what apathy, silence, or inaction will bring. Their suffering at the hands of the political system exacerbates their perception of being alienated from structures of power, which is reflected in the trend of politics becoming "less representative of Americans' interests and values," due to special interests and lobbying by the elite.[76] Archbishop Desmond Tutu asserts that neutrality is a failure of justice, for "if you are neutral in situations of injustice, you have chosen the side of the oppressor."[77] He explains, if an elephant is stepping on the tail of a mouse, your neutrality does nothing to help the mouse. Certainly, it is hard to

[74]Thich Nhat Hanh shares six mantras to help guide "loving speech." They are as follows: "I am here for you." "I know you are there, and I am very happy." "I know you suffer, and that is why I am here for you." "I suffer, please help." "This is a happy moment." "You are partly right" (ibid., 73–86).

[75]Ibid., 129.

[76]Robert Putnam, *Our Kids: The American Dream in Crisis* (New York: Simon & Schuster, 2016), 238.

[77]Gary Younge, "The Secrets of a Peacemaker," *The Guardian*, May 22, 2009.

identify virtues like courage, mercy, generosity, humility, and fidelity by refusing to use one's voice or agency in the face of such widespread suffering and sin. We may not be able to always agree, but we should be able to agree that we can do better than the status quo.

A culture of encounter means engaging politics and other difficult subjects, rather than avoiding them to keep the peace. In order to do this in a meaningful, virtuous, and effective fashion, we must move past talking points or positions (e.g., pro versus con) and make room for nuance that takes seriously the complexity of the issues we face. If we can anticipate a challenging encounter, it helps to prepare for it ahead of time. A "strategic dialogue" trains for an exchange that avoids an "us-versus-them" mindset; listens attentively, sensitively, and sincerely; uses storytelling to connect on a human level (rather than loyalty to party, policies, positions, or leaders); and focuses on the facts to find common ground.[78] In an encounter with someone with different political priorities, it is important to keep in mind that arguments seldom change minds, just as evidence can sometimes backfire: Americans often double down on their positions, even in the face of evidence to the contrary.[79] Curiosity can go a long way toward better understanding what other people want, why they believe what they do, what their sources of information are, the kind of language they use, the concerns that motivate them, and what they think you want.[80] A culture of encounter seeks common ground, which means looking for shared beliefs or concerns, experiences or future hopes.

We can disagree without demonizing the other. We can listen, even if we think the other person is wrong. We can see the world differently and still belong to each other. Party allegiance or political priorities should not trump values like freedom, equality, respect, and shared duties to work for justice. When policies make us bitterly divided, we have to remember that the political system (in our town, state, or in our nation's capital) is not the center of the universe. Perspective can help us to avoid feeling like our value is tied to the fate of a piece of legislation or that winning is everything. The key to ending us-versus-them thinking is to end either/or thinking. The world cannot be categorized cleanly into categories of worthy versus unworthy, pure versus corrupt, good versus evil, innocent versus guilty, heroes versus villains, right versus wrong. A winner-take-all mentality convinces us there are winners and losers, and no one wants to belong to the latter group. But these are false binaries. When we think the only solution lies in choosing between Republican or Democrat, we ignore a more complex reality, like the 42 percent of

---

[78]Justin Lee, *Talking across the Divide: How to Communicate with People You Disagree with and Maybe Even Change the World* (New York: TarcherPerigee, 2018), 36.

[79]Joe Keohane, "How Facts Backfire," *Boston Globe*, July 11, 2010.

[80]Lee, *Talking across the Divide*, 52–53.

Americans who identify as Independents.[81] It might be easier to think in terms of either/or, but this is too simple to do justice to a reality that cannot be confined to only two ways of seeing or thinking. Jesus turned this way of thinking on its head, choosing instead to embrace paradox and a both/and worldview: saint *and* sinner, rich *and* poor, finding *and* losing, joy *and* suffering.[82] A culture of encounter means becoming comfortable with being uncomfortable, and exercising imagination by seeking more both/and approaches than simplistic either/or dualism.

In a digital age, our impulse is to connect, but this does not always reach the level of substance to really converse. A growing number of people would rather text than talk, even while screens leave people feeling more anxious, insecure, and isolated.[83] The more people rely on screens, the harder it is to detect social cues and read emotions (including one's own). This is especially noticeable in young people, the so-called digital natives who grew up with smartphones. The more time one spends on social media, the higher the likelihood for depression and loneliness.[84] Psychologist Sherry Turkle proposes an alternative: face-to-face conversation, which "leads to greater self-esteem and an improved ability to deal with others . . . *conversation cures*."[85] This means resisting the urge to be glued to a screen, which seductively promises us "first, that we will always be heard; second, that we can put our attention wherever we want it to be; and third, that we will never have to be alone."[86] The solution lies in making time for three different kinds of conversations: first, with the self, in solitude; second, with our intimate ties, like family, friends, and romantic partners; and third, in the social world, with co-workers and classmates, reaching outward toward acquaintances.[87] Different approaches will be effective for different groups. In a time of digital hyperconnectivity and access to an inexhaustible volume of content online, temptations for distraction via screens are endless. This is all the more reason we need to be intentional about making meaningful, virtuous, and effective connections through face-to-face conversation. Turkle points out that

---

[81]Sarah Stewart Holland and Beth Silvers, *I Think You're Wrong (But I'm Listening): A Guide to Grace-Filled Political Conversations* (Nashville: Nelson, 2019), 118.

[82]Richard Rohr, "Paradox: Jesus and Paul: Nondual Teachers," Center for Action and Contemplation, August 22, 2016, https://cac.org.

[83]See, for example, Steven Marchie, "Is Facebook Making Us Lonely?" *The Atlantic*, May 2012, https://www.theatlantic.com/magazine/archive/2012/05/is-facebook-making-us-lonely/308930/. See also Miller McPherson, Lynn Smith-Lovin, and Matthew E. Brashears, "Social Isolation in America: Changes in Core Discussion Networks over Two Decades," *American Sociological Review* 71 (2006): 353–75.

[84]Michelle W. Berger, "Social Media Use Increases Depression and Loneliness," *Penn Today*, November 9, 2018.

[85]Sherry Turkle, *Reclaiming Conversation: The Power of Talk in a Digital Age* (New York: Penguin, 2015), 25.

[86]Ibid., 26.

[87]Ibid., 46–50.

people would much rather return to their screen than put it down and connect with a person offline. If the Samaritan had a smartphone, he likely would have been too distracted to even notice the man who needed his help, lying in the ditch.

A culture of encounter relies on genuine interest and curiosity in others. Cynicism and conflict can be healed through people sharing their stories, deep listening, exercising empathy, and imaginatively exploring what it is like to be someone other than myself. There we can discover we have more in common than meets the eye, and perhaps even more importantly, that even when we differ, we still belong to each other. It starts with opening ourselves to receive the other, and, as the poet Judyth Hill writes, "Wage peace with your listening."[88] Listening is active, and it is demanding: it requires a posture of openness and curiosity, as well as a humility that is open to growth and even change. This reflects Pope Francis's emphasis on collegiality and synodality, to be a church that accompanies one another as a "listening church" sharing the journey together.[89] We are members of one body, as Saint Paul attests (1 Cor 12:12–31; Eph 4:1–32). A culture of encounter helps us to communicate in a spirit of generosity, like we belong to each other.

FORMED BY *HABITUS*

Listening and learning through conversations across differences are important places to begin building a culture of encounter. But in order to accomplish its ultimate aim—to create a culture of belonging—honest dialogue must flow from exchange to embrace through mutually respectful relationships and shared practices that reinforce bonds of trust, support, and accountability. Given the social, economic, and political divides that have caused the collapse of community in America, this work begins by constructing communities of healing, a task that is both personal and collective. Such a task may seem daunting if not impossible, but this kind of transformation has already taken place in communities committed to reconciliation and peace in the wake of personal trauma and violent conflicts.[90] Restorative justice aims to heal the wounds that have been left on people and communities by unjust beliefs, actions, and systems.[91] In light of sinful social fractures

[88]Judyth Hill, "Wage Peace," September 11, 2001, https://www.judythhill.com/.

[89]Pope Francis, "Pope Calls for a Listening Church," *America*, October 17, 2015.

[90]On personal trauma healing, see, for example, Bessel van der Kolk, *The Body Keeps the Score: Brain, Mind, and Body in the Healing of Trauma* (London: Penguin, 2014). On reconciliation after civil conflict, see Desmond Tutu, *No Future without Forgiveness* (New York: Image, 2000); Anna Floerke Scheid, *Just Revolution: A Christian Ethic of Political Resistance and Social Transformation* (Lanham, MD: Lexington Books, 2015).

[91]See, for example, Amy Levad, *Restorative Justice: Theories and Practices of Moral Imagination* (El Paso, TX: LFB Scholarly Publishing, 2011).

and unjust inequalities that divide and degrade, the ethics of encounter can be seen as part of this work toward social redemption through restorative justice and reconciliation. The ethics of encounter does not take place in a vacuum; this moral framework cannot find traction unless and until it accounts for the social and personal sins that have brought us to this state of animosity, indifference, and entrenched separation. A culture of encounter is possible only when people practice the ethics of encounter together in a particular context. This is related to the virtue of humility, which shares its etymological root with *humus,* a word that refers to the earth. Humility means acknowledging our place in the world, and this is represented by the *habitus* that shapes us and wherein we shape others, too. This is related to the principle of subsidiarity in Catholic social thought, which endorses participation in social responsibilities at the lowest effective levels, where movements for social change find traction.[92]

The sociological concept of *habitus*—the local environment or system of acquired beliefs, outlooks, and actions—helps us to envision how a culture of encounter can be realized, as accompaniment leads to exchange that becomes embrace in particular communities among families and schools, neighborhoods and clubs, parishes and places of work. These examples of relationships of mutual trust and support provide the security and stability required for people to be willing to be vulnerable, courageous, compassionate, and generous. Shared practices form people through repetition in the kinds of attitudes and actions that fit with "who we are" and "what we value." In their research on the effects of religion on moral formation, David Campbell and Robert Putnam find that belief matters less than belongingness.[93] People are shaped more by their relationships with friends and family, and the habits they share together in those bonds by being involved together than by the beliefs or values taught in church or school.[94] The ethics of encounter must be adopted by people in a way that integrates courage, mercy, generosity, humility, and fidelity into their relationships. These relationships should flow from and toward the intentional change in one's social location in the hope of building a more inclusive solidarity. For the ethics of encounter

[92]Marvin L. Krier Mich, *Catholic Social Teaching and Movements* (Mystic, CT: Twenty-Third Publications, 2006), 82. There is some debate about how "high up" involvement should go, between the local and national levels of the state. At the very least, there is a need for "intermediary groups" that bridge the micro- and macrolevels of society.

[93]Robert Putnam and David Campbell, *American Grace: How Religion Divides and Unites Us* (New York: Simon & Schuster, 2010), 468–75. Putnam and Campbell state, "Mobilization or exhortations by clergy seem not to be a major factor," whereas "friends in general have a powerful effect on civic involvement." They continue, "Having close friends at church, discussing religion frequently with your family and friends, and taking part in small groups at church are extremely powerful predictors of the range of generosity, good neighborliness, and civic engagement" (ibid., 471–72).

[94]Putnam, *Our Kids,* 224.

to create change at any level, it must be adopted in the beliefs, shared practices, and relationships in preexisting patterns of belongingness in a particular place.

When people intentionally share virtuous attitudes, actions, and relationships, they become a "community of character." Moral growth is shaped by the narrative the community shares to communicate meaning and purpose. Even more powerfully, moral development happens as "we learn what the moral life entails by imitating another . . . The problem lies not in knowing *what* we must do, but *how* we are to do it."[95] Children imitate parents, adults emulate those they admire, and beliefs and values get passed down. Imitation is part of the learned pattern of dispositions and actions that take place in the *habitus,* a term used by the sociologist Pierre Bourdieu to describe the structures that structure what we hold in common (i.e., what becomes "common sense"). The *habitus* regulates and reproduces unwritten rules.[96] It does not explicitly instruct how to perceive the world or think about the self and others, but it is home to the embodied learning that we take for granted: this is how I greet other people—or ignore them—because this is how I see others around me behaving, for example. In general, the *habitus* is oriented by coherence and continuity that reinforces the status quo.

Bourdieu suggests this explains the process by which the past unconsciously becomes part of ourselves in the present. Even more, the *habitus* represents the automatic process that harmonizes and homogenizes groups: it is comprised of the structures that individuals internalize together in a coordinated manner, to facilitate the group members' shared identity and meaning, with the goal of perpetuating itself into the future.[97] The *habitus* does not operate by mechanical determinism or explicit coercion, but rather through the unconscious acquisition of thoughts, perceptions, expressions, and actions conditioned by one's immediate environment.[98] When people share reproducing dispositions and actions, they establish relationships, which further strengthen the bonds they share. This is how people learn racist or sexist beliefs without questioning their veracity; even though they are repugnant, they function with authority in one's *habitus* among people who are trusted (as authorized or authorizing language, for example).[99] For this reason, the ethics of encounter has to be especially sensitive to the effects of social sin that can leave moral agents partially blind, deaf, mute, and numb to the harmful effects of discrimination and division.

The cyclic bond between reproduction and relationships generates what

---

[95]Stanley Hauerwas, *A Community of Character: Toward a Constructive Christian Social Ethic* (Notre Dame, IN: University of Notre Dame Press, 1981), 131.

[96]Pierre Bourdieu, *Outline of a Theory of Practice,* trans. Richard Nice (Cambridge: Cambridge University Press, 1977), 72.

[97]Ibid., 80–82.

[98]Ibid., 95.

[99]Ibid., 171.

Bourdieu describes as "symbolic capital," the credit or "prestige and renown" attached to those who share life together in the *habitus*.[100] This legitimates the established order that encompasses the social, economic, and political habits and bonds already in place—and it resists changing the current distribution of power among those who constitute membership in the *habitus*. Those who cooperate are rewarded with "symbolic capital" while those who do not comply are threatened with debt, a form of violence.[101] Members of the *habitus* often endure and impose "cross-censorship" in order to follow the "code of honor" and avoid the shame of moral inferiority.[102]

The *habitus* reinforces boundaries between embracing some and excluding others. On the theoretical level, this raises important questions about unity in diversity. On the practical level, it demands that Christians account for those they find unworthy of belonging. This is not to suggest that Christians should erase all boundaries, since the "absence of boundaries creates nonorder, and nonorder is not the end of exclusion but the end of life."[103] One can have differentiation without judgment, and judgment without exclusion. Exclusion does more than communicate preference; "it names an objective evil."[104] Exclusion is typically associated with sin (or at least the sinner), but do Christians ever think of the act of exclusion as a sin? In the past and present, Christian purity culture drives out or renders others inferior; and, in some extreme cases, even legitimates violence and death against the excluded. In this way, exclusion can be understood as abandonment; domination; assimilation; and, at its worst, elimination.[105] Sometimes exclusion is less overt, a kind of obfuscation that suggests the other is corrupt while claiming one's own innocence. This kind of exclusion relies on ignorance about the other, not just in terms of a lack of knowledge but a "willful misconstruction" that refuses to recognize the goodness—and our interdependence with—the other.[106] This is reflected in what Pope Francis calls the "globalization of indifference," illustrated by the priest and Levite who pass by the man who has been beaten, robbed, and left for dead on the side of the road to Jericho: they cannot be bothered to even move close enough to check on him. Francis laments, "We have become used to the suffering of others: it doesn't affect me; it doesn't concern me; it's none of my

[100]Ibid., 179.

[101]Ibid., 191.

[102]Ibid., 196.

[103]Miroslav Volf, *Exclusion and Embrace: A Theological Exploration of Identity, Otherness, and Reconciliation* (Nashville: Abingdon, 1996), 63. Volf adds that if we vilify all boundaries, we "will have aimless drifting instead of clear-sighted agency, haphazard activity instead of moral engagement and accountability and, in the long run, a torpor of death instead of a dance of freedom" (ibid., 64–65).

[104]Ibid., 68.

[105]Ibid., 75.

[106]Ibid., 76.

business!"[107] The terror of the globalization of indifference is that it convinces us that poverty and deprivation, violence and abuse are normal, if not inevitable. And it absolves us of any responsibility to resist participating in the beliefs and actions that might divide or exploit, to say nothing of working for change.

What drives this impulse to embrace some but exclude others? Perhaps it is a desire for security and stability, trying to find safety in the familiar, even if it comes at the expense of others. Or maybe it is generated by fear of our own sinfulness and weakness. For some, the primary obstacle is a sense of internalized shame, making a person feel unworthy to reach out to others or caught by fear of being rejected, manipulated, or exploited by another person. Shame is isolating, making it harder to feel capable of meaningful, mutually respectful, and empowering relationships. Exclusion might also be a form of self-protection, a way to buffer against being inundated by so many unknowns. It might be understood as a distraction from having to confront our own failures, part of a complex pattern of self-deception. The impulse to exclude could also be viewed as a combination of classic vices, whether excessive pride, hatred, or greed. Underneath these thoughts and emotions festers a deep-seated anxiety, which may well be the "internal precondition of sin," the apprehension and angst that tempts us to stray from our faith and trust in God's love.[108] Anxiety—in the face of our finitude and failure, as well as the possibilities and demands of our free will—makes it easy to question God's providence, our goodness, and the goodness of others. This fundamental insecurity can be masked by pride, a lust for power, an "inordinate ambition," and exploitative greed, which may be described as "the besetting sin of a bourgeois culture."[109] Unchecked, anxiety can lead Christians to obsess over their weaknesses. Or, to escape this insecurity, they might pridefully ignore their limits and make "virtue the vehicle of sin," by linking self-righteousness to contempt for—or even cruelty toward—the other.[110] In a group setting, anxiety is exacerbated, resulting in a social body that is "more arrogant, hypocritical, self-centered, and more ruthless in the pursuit of its ends than the individual" alone.[111] The social group "asks for the individual's unconditioned loyalty," and whether family, club, or nation, this group pride becomes a "more pregnant source of injustice and conflict than purely individual pride."[112]

---

[107]Pope Francis, "Visit to Lampedusa Homily," July 8, 2013, w2.vatican.va.

[108]Reinhold Niebuhr, *The Nature and Destiny of Man: A Christian Interpretation*, vol. 1 (Louisville, KY: Westminster John Knox Press, [1941] 1996), 182.

[109]Ibid., 191–92.

[110]Ibid., 199.

[111]Ibid., 208. Niebuhr warns of the special dangers of the state, a political idolatry that can demand obedience and abuse its considerable power (ibid., 209); "The nation pretends to be God" (ibid., 212).

[112]Ibid., 212–13. Niebuhr is not ready to condemn all groups or social projects. He is concerned with a clear-eyed grasp of the extensive influence of sin in the world. But he concludes, "Our re-

This is what makes the prominence of tribalism so problematic. Loyalty to groups can produce a sense of moral superiority and sometimes even become an idolatrous allegiance, among other sins. Unquestioned loyalty to a specific identity or group can reinforce boundaries between "us" and "them," further distancing us from solidarity. At the same time, however, in-group preferences and ethnocentrism are universal. As noted in Chapter 3, this is a feature of evolution that hardwires humans to feel empathy most easily for those nearest and most alike.[113] This results in "parochial altruism" or a moral tribalism, a preference for those closest to us.[114] Our biology makes this instinctual: "our brains are wired for tribalism. We intuitively divide the world into Us and Them, and favor Us over Them."[115] This is an extension of self-interest (if my group benefits, I benefit), unavoidable bias, and also serves as a source of conflict. When we overestimate the good we do and underestimate the harm we cause, it can lead to a sense of superiority that is allergic to compromising and sacrificing for the common good.[116]

Knowing the harm that can come from excluding others, this means that the ethics of encounter has to train the brain (through experience, deliberate thinking, and habituation) to be more open to the other, the one who is unlike me or my group. It has to exercise the imagination in order to generate empathy for the one I cannot easily relate to. It has to be open to accompaniment and to learn from others' experience by listening to their stories and finding points of connection in the diverse array of human experience. It has to practice exchanges that embrace the other in mutuality comprised of interdependence, equality, reciprocity, solidarity, and justice. The ethics of encounter means practicing the "art of gathering," which begins with purpose: What is the reason why we gather? Will it be memorable? Meaningful? Transformative? Gathering around shared purpose—rather than shared identity or interest, or simply out of habit—can make this a more diverse and inclusive ritual.[117] Jesus built community across diversity; he was not apprehensive about tension or conflict. Imagine the surprise of Peter, James, and John when Jesus

---

sponsibilities are obvious. We must seek to fashion our common life to conform more nearly to the brotherhood [*sic*] of the Kingdom of God." See Reinhold Niebuhr, *The Nature and Destiny of Man: Human Destiny*, vol. 2 (Louisville, KY: Westminster John Knox Press, [1943] 1996), 308 (fn. 10).

[113]See Pope, *The Evolution of Altruism and the Ordering of Love*, 132.

[114]Joshua Greene, *Moral Tribes: Emotion, Reason, and the Gap between Us and Them* (New York: Penguin, 2013), 50.

[115]Ibid., 54.

[116]Ibid., 101.

[117]See Priya Parker, *The Art of Gathering: How We Meet and Why It Matters* (New York: Riverhead, 2018). Parker writes that gatherings happen for a variety of reasons (to reconnect with others or address a problem), but sometimes we gather out of habit without a clear purpose and without attending to our real needs. She proposes that the purpose of gathering should be the "bouncer" that decides "what goes into your gathering and what stays out" to keep it a meaningful and effective experience (ibid., 32).

invites Matthew, a tax collector, into the group. Tax collectors would have been considered public sinners, given their collusion with the oppressive Roman Empire and acts of extortion. Jesus invites Matthew to join in, just as he invites himself to stay with Zacchaeus (another tax collector). Even while the crowd grumbles at the idea of Jesus associating himself with such a despised outsider, Zacchaeus announces that he will give half his possessions to the poor and repay fourfold anyone he extorted (Lk 19:1–10). If we pay attention and participate, encounter can make new identity, new community, and new life possible. Living in a "culture of underreaction to abuse and overreaction to conflict" that too often contributes to social separation and shame, this means that everyone has a responsibility to keep calm, avoid overstating risk or threats, refuse to use sensationalizing or shaming rhetoric, and be willing to intervene and deescalate situations that might cause harm.[118] A culture of encounter implies enduring tension and even conflict, which can be unpleasant, but also has the potential to lead to breakthroughs that help us discover that what we share is more significant than what separates us.

It is impossible to "love your neighbor as yourself" without a culture of encounter. The key is recognizing your neighbor as related to yourself. Religions like Judaism, Christianity, and Islam all share this orientation to be concerned about and related to the other. Christianity adopts a particularly strong emphasis on "others-centeredness" inspired by Philippians 2:3–4: "Do nothing out of selfishness or out of vainglory; rather, humbly regard others as more important than yourselves, each looking out not for his own interests but [also] everyone for those of others." This implies "a disposition to treat the perceived interests of each other person as more important than one's own perceived interests for purposes of deciding what to do, just because they are another's."[119] The Christian moral life involves a posture of not only openness to others but an indebtedness to others, a "debt of grace" motivated by gratitude and generosity. The aim is to move beyond unilateral aid by creating a shared "bond of indebtedness" that fosters interpersonal union.[120] In this way, courage, mercy, generosity, humility, and fidelity shift Christian neighbor love from altruistic acts to relationships rooted in mutual respect and responsibility. Cultivating inclusive empathic concern, secure attachments, and personal duty for interpersonal union with others all help reinforce prosocial behavior in a way that overcomes the typical temptations toward narrow self-interest and tribalism.[121]

---

[118]Sarah Schulman, *Conflict Is Not Abuse: Overstating Harm, Community Responsibility, and the Duty of Repair* (Vancouver, BC: Arsenal Pulp, 2016), 21.

[119]T. Ryan Byerly, *Putting Others First: The Christian Ideal of Others-Centeredness* (New York: Routledge, 2019), 5.

[120]Ibid., 65.

[121]Ibid., 174–75.

A first step in practicing the ethics of encounter is to put an end to categories of "us" and "them." This kind of thinking reinforces social separation; encourages judgment that ranks some superior to others; and naively groups people into categories of the innocent, trustworthy, or just versus the guilty, cheats, and frauds. No one is entirely blameless, just as no one is beyond redemption. The inclusive demands of Christian neighbor love—to include even enemies—aims for a solidarity that leaves no one forced to assimilate or be excluded, abandoned, dominated, or eliminated. Christians routinely fail to practice this kind of all-encompassing love, forgiveness, and reconciliation. This is why Jesus calls his followers to conversion, an opportunity to repent and atone (Mk 1:15, 2:17). Christians cannot ignore the reality of our sinfulness, our reliance on grace, and our call to work steadfastly as Christ's ambassadors for reconciliation in a fallen, fragile, and fragmented world (2 Cor 5:18–21).

WHAT A CULTURE OF BELONGING LOOKS LIKE

If our aim is to build a *habitus* conducive to encountering and accompanying others, facilitating meaningful exchange, and aspiring for transformational embrace with others, it helps to have a blueprint to see what it looks like to build a community of healing and belonging, and what it takes to put into practice this kind of inclusive fidelity on the personal, social, and institutional levels. One particularly powerful example of fidelity is Homeboy Industries in Los Angeles. Homeboy was started by Greg Boyle, a Jesuit priest assigned to Dolores Mission Church, the poorest parish in the archdiocese, shortly after his ordination in 1984. Fr. Greg, or "G" as he's affectionately called, made the church a welcoming place for gang members. Seeking peace, Boyle soon realized that gang violence is a symptom of a "lethal absence of hope" among "young people who plan their funerals and not their futures."[122] Boyle observes that every person who joins a gang "knows it will lead to death or prison . . . They just don't care that it will."[123] Having learned that "nothing stops a bullet like a job," he joined women of the parish in organizing employment opportunities through a ministry called "Jobs for a Future." Boyle made the choice to invest in gang members—rather than incarcerate them—and by 1992, Homeboy Industries was born. Boyle explains

---

[122]Gregory Boyle, *Tattoos on the Heart: The Power of Boundless Compassion* (New York: Free Press, 2010), 89.

[123]Gregory Boyle, *Barking to the Choir: The Power of Radical Kinship* (New York: Simon & Schuster, 2017), 130. Boyle explains that gang membership is less a function of belonging than total despair. He notes, "Kids join Little League because they want to belong. They join gangs because they want to die" (ibid., 131).

that Homeboy "is not for those who need help, only for those who want it."[124] His work begins by helping gang members discover that they are "clothed in God's goodness."[125] No matter what they have done, "they are exactly what God had in mind when God made them."[126] His job, as he sees it, is to show up, remind folks that we belong to each other, and let souls "feel their worth."[127]

Some might recoil in hearing a priest insist that a gang member is "exactly who God had in mind." But Boyle asserts that the "wrong idea has taken root in the world. And the idea is this: there just might be lives out there that matter less than other lives."[128] Boyle challenges the categorization of "good guys" and "bad guys." He insists, "In thirty years of walking with gang members, I've never met a bad guy." He explains, "Every homie I know who has killed somebody—everyone—has carried a load one hundred times heavier than I have had to carry, weighed down by torture, violence, abuse, neglect, abandonment, or mental illness. Most of us have never borne that weight. We are free not to like that truth, but we are not free to deny it."[129] This is reflected in Jesus's own ministry, as he touched those considered unclean, ate with those considered unworthy, and befriended the outcast. Boyle points to Jesus's encounter with the tax collector Zacchaeus (Lk 19:1–10), "the poster child of 'the bad guy,' the most despised and demonized man of the time. Above all, Jesus wants to drive out demonizing. He seems to say to the horrified, gasping crowd, 'There are no bad guys. Quit saying that there are.'" Looking at his time at Homeboy Industries and all the gang members he's met through the decades, Boyle asserts:

> There are no monsters, villains, or bad guys . . . There are only folks who carry unspeakable pain. There are among us the profoundly traumatized who deal in the currency of damage. And there are those whose minds are ill, whose sickness chases them every day. But there are no bad guys. Jesus seems to suggest that there are no exceptions to this. Yet it's hard for us to believe him.[130]

Most of us will not encounter a gang member on a daily basis like Boyle does. But we all encounter people whose dignity and rights are hard for us to recognize and affirm. And we all experience social separation and polarization. Boyle aims to reconcile the "gulf in our present age" which seems like it "could not be wider

---

[124]Boyle, *Tattoos on the Heart*, 8.
[125]Ibid., 17.
[126]Ibid., 192.
[127]Ibid., 196.
[128]Ibid., 192.
[129]Boyle, *Barking to the Choir*, 131–32.
[130]Ibid., 136.

between 'Us' and 'Them.'" He writes with an interest in the same issues that inspire the ethics of encounter: "How do we tame this status quo that lulls us into blindly accepting the things that divide us and keep us from our own holy longing for the mutuality of kinship—a sure and certain sense that we belong to each other?"[131]

The ethics of encounter must be free of coercing the other to live on our terms, or make acceptance conditional on what makes us comfortable. Insofar as every human person is created in the image and likeness of God, everyone bears innate human dignity, intrinsic value that is not earned or lost. This means that no one can ever write a person off as a thug or a threat, as lazy or a burden, and certainly not as an interruption, obstacle, or a lost cause. In the face of gunshot wounds and death—Boyle keeps track of the number of funerals he's presided over—he acknowledges that "the degree of difficulty here is exceedingly high. Kids I love killing kids I love."[132] Boyle has learned that this work begins with delighting in the goodness God has bestowed on all of us. He claims, "Delighting is what occupies God, and God's hope is that we join in."[133] Christians, then, have a duty to fight shame and disgrace, and never allow any person—no matter what they have done—to feel unworthy of God's infinite love and unconditional compassion. Boyle explains, "One of the signature marks of our God is the lifting of shame. Demons keep us from who we are. Jesus, we're told, drives out demons—or anything that's taken us over . . . Jesus wants to demote 'sinful behavior' and emphasize restoration in its place."[134] Restoration is only possible through the strength and tenderness of compassion. Healing begins with experiencing "God [who] is compassionate, loving kindness. All we're asked to do is to be in the world who God is. Certainly compassion was the wallpaper of Jesus's soul, the contour of his heart, it was who he was . . . He had room for everybody in his compassion."[135]

Christians, then, should do more than keep God at the center of their lives; they should reflect in the world who God is: a compassion so vast that no one is left out. This means, Boyle insists, replacing judgment with awe. Instead of standing in judgment at how others live, Boyle proposes that we cultivate a compassion filled with awe at what they have to carry. Boyle insists that

> Moral outrage is the opposite of God; it only divides and separates what God wants for us, which is to be united in kinship. Moral outrage doesn't lead us to solutions—it keeps us from them. It keeps us from moving

---

[131]Ibid., 9.

[132]Boyle, *Tattoos on the Heart*, 66.

[133]Ibid., 158. Elsewhere, Boyle attests, "God is just too busy loving us to have any time left for disappointment" (28).

[134]Boyle, *Barking to the Choir*, 135.

[135]Boyle, *Tattoos on the Heart*, 62–63.

> forward toward a fuller, more compassionate response to members of our community who belong to us, no matter what they've done. And this is the most difficult part for us to grasp: because what could be more terrifying than actually believing that such folks belong to us?[136]

It's so much easier to disown the "other" and to lament how they have lost their way. But this kind of moral superiority does nothing to heal the wounds of alienation and division. This is why the ethics of encounter revolves around courage, compassion, and solidarity: it means drawing near to the other instead of writing them off. Boyle reflects, "Compassion isn't just about feeling the pain of others; it's about bringing them in toward yourself. If we love what God loves, then, in compassion, margins get erased. 'Be compassionate as God is compassionate,' means the dismantling of barriers that exclude."[137]

This stands in stark contrast to our typical understanding of charity, which often takes the shape of giving from a distance. It is laudable to be compassionate and generous, but these virtues can become vices when they are motivated by paternalistic pity or to assuage guilt. While it is true that many churches, social service agencies, and nonprofits rely on people to be generous with their finances, philanthropy can backfire. It can reinforce differences between "us" and "them," and, even worse, it can train others to be dependent on others' largesse. Generosity can also be exploited by people who are corrupt; one World Bank study found that 85 percent of money allocated for aid to African countries never reached people in need and was instead used for "unproductive" if not "grotesque" purposes.[138] As Robert Lupton opines, when "relief does not transition to development in a timely way, compassion becomes toxic," and when charity comes from a place of superiority, it can create "an unhealthy culture of dependency."[139] Generosity can turn people into beggars, erode self-reliance and a diligent work ethic, and perpetuate asymmetry between the givers and receivers. Good intentions can indeed produce bad outcomes. This is part of the problem with an orientation of "doing for" rather than "being with," since "doing for" relies on and perpetuates an imbalance in power.[140]

Even before the *doing*, Boyle focuses on *being*. He suggests that we don't strategize our way out of injustice; we "solidarize, if you will, our way toward its

---

[136]Boyle, *Barking to the Choir*, 141.

[137]Boyle, *Tattoos on the Heart*, 75.

[138]Dambisa Moyo, *Dead Aid: Why Aid Is Not Working and How There Is a Better Way for Africa* (New York: Farrar Straus and Giroux, 2009), 45.

[139]Robert D. Lupton, *Toxic Charity: How Churches and Charities Hurt Those They Help (And How to Reverse It)* (New York: HarperOne, 2011), 7, 35. He concludes that compassion is "dangerous" (ibid., 39).

[140]Ibid., 29. Lupton adds, "Parity is the higher form of charity" (ibid., 37).

demise."[141] This means standing with the marginalized and the demonized—including the gang member—until the demonizing stops. He adds, "Compassion is not a relationship between the healer and the wounded. It's a covenant between equals." Compassion helps with "dissolving the myth that we are separate" from one another.[142]

Boyle admits that this work is anything but easy. And he is reluctant to take credit for the transformations that take place in the *habitus* of Homeboy Industries. Instead, he points to the courage and persistence of the homies and homegirls who open themselves to the long and difficult path toward healing. One particularly poignant story involves Sergio, a gang member who dealt with homelessness and substance abuse, and who spent a number of years in prison. When he was six years old, his mother turned to him and said, "Why don'tcha just kill yourself? You're such a burden to me." When he was nine, his mother left him at an orphanage, and it took his grandmother three months to find him and bring him home. Sergio shares what his childhood was like:

> My mom beat me every single day of my elementary school years, with things you could imagine and a lotta things you couldn't. Every day my back was bloodied and scarred. In fact, I had to wear three T-shirts to school each day. The first one cuz the blood would seep through. The second cuz you could still see it. Finally, with the third T-shirt, you couldn't see no blood. Kids at school would make fun of me. "Hey, fool . . . It's a hundred degrees . . . Why ya wearin' three T-shirts?" . . . I wore three T-shirts . . . well into my adult years, cuz I was ashamed of my wounds. I didn't want no one to see 'em . . . But now I welcome my wounds. I run my fingers over my scars. My wounds are my friends. After all . . . how can I help others to heal if I don't welcome my own wounds?[143]

Not everyone has this kind of epiphany, self-knowledge and self-acceptance, or courage as Sergio. Sometimes homies are reluctant to make peace with a former enemy. Sometimes there is more regression than progress. But if Christians are going to heal the wounds that mar the people of God, on a personal and collective level, it is going to require that we replace judgment with awe. Boyle explains,

> We are at our healthiest when we are most situated in awe, and at our least healthy when we engage in judgment. Judgment creates the distance that

---

[141]Boyle, *Tattoos on the Heart,* 173.
[142]Ibid., 77, 80.
[143]Boyle, *Barking to the Choir,* 53–54.

> moves us away from each other. Judgment keeps us in the competitive game and is always self-aggrandizing. Standing at the margins with the broken reminds us not of our own superiority but of our own brokenness. Awe is the great leveler. The embrace of our own suffering helps us to land on a spiritual intimacy with ourselves and others. For if we don't welcome our wounds, we will be tempted to despise the wounded.[144]

Boyle insightfully diagnoses the psychological barriers that help create the walls that divide us. Fear, deception, and hatred are powerful forces that contribute to "us and them" thinking. But even those of us who are not consumed by these strong emotions too easily get caught up in measuring ourselves against others and feeling less than. Theodore Roosevelt is credited with the line, "comparison is the thief of joy."[145] We compare ourselves to others or what we think God expects of us, and it is difficult not to feel down. As Boyle sees it, "When we are disappointed in each other, we least resemble God. We have a God who wonders what all the measuring is about, a God who is perplexed by our raising the bar and then raising it even higher."[146] Boyle suggests that we have to

> try and learn to drop the burden of our own judgments, reconciling that what the mind wants to separate, the heart should bring together. Dropping this enormous inner burden of judgment allows us to make of ourselves what God wants the world to ultimately be: people who stand in awe. Judgment, after all, takes up the room you need for loving.[147]

Love and compassion have to be stretched wide enough to include both the victim and the victimizer. This is where proximity comes in: Boyle's experience has taught him that "it always becomes impossible to demonize someone you know."[148] The ethics of encounter relies upon changing one's social location, interrupting social separation and polarization in order to share life with others across differences. This reflects the Samaritan's movement into the ditch—a risky and time-consuming detour—to take up a new geography. Boyle observes that this is precisely what Jesus came to teach and model in his ministry:

---

[144]Ibid., 54.

[145]Quoted in Kenneth B. Cooper, Nels Gustafson, and Joseph G. Salah, *Becoming a Great School: Harnessing the Powers of Quality Management and Collaborative Leadership* (Lanham, MD: Rowman & Littlefield, 2014), ix.

[146]Boyle, *Barking to the Choir*, 27.

[147]Ibid., 56–57.

[148]Boyle, *Tattoos on the Heart*, 142.

> Jesus was not a man *for* others. He was one *with* others. There is a world of difference in that. Jesus didn't seek the rights of lepers. He *touched* the leper even before he got around to curing him. He didn't champion the cause of the outcast. He *was* the outcast . . . The strategy of Jesus is not centered in taking the right stand on issues, but rather in standing in the right place—with the outcast and those relegated to the margins.[149]

For Christians, it means following Jesus's example in "downward mobility."[150] This means going to stand with the lost, the lowly, and the least.

Christian disciples who are called to follow Jesus's example must also resist the temptation to find security in upward mobility, to engage in the social rivalry of "keeping up with the Joneses," and to invest in the status symbols that confer honor and approval. It means choosing faith over fear, humility over pride, and cooperation instead of coercion. It means replacing concern for success with a commitment to fidelity. Boyle explains,

> If our primary concern is results, we will choose to work only with those who give us good ones . . . You stand with the least likely to succeed until success is succeeded by something more valuable: kinship. You stand with the belligerent, the surly, and the badly behaved until bad behavior is recognized for the language it is: the vocabulary of the deeply wounded and of those whose burdens are more than they can bear.[151]

This is the path to solidarity, to recognizing one another as kin. And it begins with compassion. Boyle encourages us to

> imagine, with God, this circle of compassion. Then we imagine no one standing outside the circle, moving ourselves closer to the margins so that the margins themselves will be erased. We stand there with those whose dignity has been denied. We locate ourselves with the poor and the powerless and the voiceless. At the edges, we join the easily despised and the readily left out. We stand with the demonized so that the demonizing will stop. We situate ourselves right next to the disposable so that the day will come when we stop throwing people away.[152]

---

[149]Ibid., 72.

[150]Dean Brackley, *The Call to Discernment in Troubled Times* (New York: Crossroad, 2004), 98–99. Brackley cites Philippians 2:5–11 as the basis for this "standard of Christ."

[151]Boyle, *Tattoos on the Heart*, 178–79. He adds, "Maybe success has become the new purity code. And Jesus shows us that the desire for purity (nine times out of ten) is, in fact, the enemy of the gospel" (ibid., 179).

[152]Ibid., 190.

When we emulate the Samaritan by going into the ditch to draw near those who have been left for dead, we draw near Christ who reveals himself in our neediest neighbors (Mt 25:31–46). The ethics of encounter cannot be fulfilled by attitudes or actions if it does not also include a change in social location. Boyle suggests,

> If we choose to stand in the right place, God, through us, creates a community of resistance without our even realizing it . . . Our locating ourselves with those who have been endlessly excluded becomes an act of visible protest.

He continues, the powerful will "only be moved to kinship when they observe it. Only when we can see a community where the outcast is valued and appreciated will we abandon the values that seek to exclude."[153] Boyle also clarifies that the movement to another social location is not intended to save others or benefit them; instead, "We are sent to the margins NOT to make a difference but so that the folks on the margins will make *us* different."[154] Even though service can have transformational effects—by opening our world to the complex realities others face and bringing us into relationships with those whose path we otherwise would not cross—it too often is distorted by a "white savior complex" that wants to save or at least help others by making them more like ourselves.[155] Boyle sees this differently. Instead of trying to "save the world," he suggests it's better to "savor the world." He explains, "when we seek to 'save' and 'contribute' and 'give back' and 'rescue' folks and EVEN 'make a difference,' then it is all about you . . . and the world stays stuck." Instead of trying to reach others, Boyle asks us, "Can YOU be reached by THEM?"[156]

The ethics of encounter is practiced at the intersection of spirituality and solidarity. It is where we recognize our shared humanity and how we reveal the divine in our humanity. To be present to the "sacrament of sacred presence is to be Jesus, and to see Jesus."[157] Christian neighbor love means recognizing that we belong to each other as members of the family of God. "I am the other you. You are the other me. The invitation for the Christ in me is to see the Christ in you."[158] How do we heal social separation? In the end, the solution is not as mysterious as we might think: it really is as simple as being agents of connection. In a social context marked by so much animosity and division, it also means moving closer and staying close to those who are different from us. This doesn't mean romanticizing

---

[153]Ibid., 177–78.

[154]Boyle, *Barking to the Choir*, 165.

[155]Barbara Applebaum, *Being White, Being Good: White Complicity, White Moral Responsibility, and Social Justice Pedagogy* (Lanham, MD: Lexington Books, 2010).

[156]Boyle, *Barking to the Choir*, 174–75.

[157]Ibid., 77.

[158]Ibid., 142.

the other, or adopting some Pollyannaish perspective on life in community with others who are different from us. It does mean acknowledging that our humanity is impoverished when we cut ourselves off from others, and that we cut ourselves off from the presence and power of God among those we would rather keep at arm's length. We draw lines to make us feel safe; fear keeps us from making room for everyone and making sure everyone feels like they belong. It's tempting to think, "They're not like me" or "I don't want to be associated with them." Diversity is not a threat or a burden, but rather a blessing. It reminds us that there is no single way to be human, that there is dignity in difference.[159] Boyle insists that to bridge the distance between us and them we have to stop disqualifying ourselves and others. Homeboy Industries is transformational because it focuses less on what people have done or what they need than on relationships. "Community trumps gang . . . our separation is an illusion."[160] Hope and love are stronger than fear and shame. Connection is a matter of showing up to one's own goodness and that of another. It aspires for mutuality and reciprocity, in seeking the "kinship of God [that] is where everyone matters."[161]

Critics might say, what alternative do these folks have? They have to turn their lives around, or their only other options are prison or death. And surely not everyone is a success story. But Boyle makes clear that our focus should be less on success than on healing the wounds that have made it so hard to feel like we belong to each other.[162] And to those who skeptically say he is only getting played, and that being generous or compassionate just lets people take advantage of you, Boyle responds, "We so fear being duped, yet much of that comes from being a stranger to our wounds . . . If we don't welcome our own wounds, then overconfidence in our own savviness, and fear of being taken advantage of, tempts us to despise the wounded."[163] Jesus tells his followers to love others—even their enemies—without condition. Love is the measure by which we shall be judged, St. John of the Cross once preached. How do we justify closing some people off from our love, or objecting that some folks don't belong? As the Jesuit priest Howard Gray reflects, "God has no enemies and neither should I."[164]

None of what Boyle has envisioned and enacted would have been possible if he had not started with making his space hospitable. He could have told certain

---

[159]Jonathan Sacks, *The Dignity of Difference: How to Avoid the Clash of Civilizations* (New York: Continuum, 2003).

[160]Boyle, *Barking to the Choir*, 175, 182.

[161]Ibid., 190.

[162]He states that if we have no peace, it is because we have "forgotten that we belong to each other" (*Tattoos on the Heart*, 167, 187).

[163]Boyle, *Barking to the Choir*, 86.

[164]Howard Gray, SJ, "Ignatius' Method for Letting God Shine through Life's Realities," *Company*, August 14, 1999.

members of the community they were unworthy or only worthy if they looked, believed, or acted a certain way. But by starting with belonging, he was able to help and heal the personal and communal wounds left by trauma and abuse, hatred and violence, illness and shame. He started by drawing near to the members of the community, accompanying them in love. The philosopher Martin Heidegger describes "nearness" not in terms of distance (which he asserts is disappearing in the postmodern world) but as a practice.[165] More than a perception or attitude, nearness results from the action of "nearing."[166] The ethics of encounter implies the practice of nearing; this is what it means to exercise courage, mercy, generosity, humility, and fidelity. It means putting our bodies on the line to heal the sickness of social separation and subjugation.

If men and women who were shooting bullets at each other can heal the wounds of disgrace, replace violence with compassion, and work shoulder to shoulder in kinship, then everyone has reason to hope that we can build a culture of encounter that produces a community of belonging. This is how Christians practice fidelity to their neighbors and to God. Fidelity becomes solidarity when it is inclusive, interdependent, equal, and mutual. Tenderness is the language of fidelity, reminding us that because we belong to each other, we need to be gentle with each other. Boyle insists, "Only the soul that ventilates the world with tenderness has any chance of changing the world."[167] When Pope Francis calls people to join a "revolution of tenderness" to usher in a new age of solidarity, it is hard to imagine a better example than the beliefs, actions, and relationships fostered by Fr. Greg Boyle and everyone at Homeboy Industries. Imagine how much more could be possible if others joined these efforts in their own way of "doing likewise."

[165]Heidegger writes, "The frantic abolition of all distances brings no nearness; for nearness does not consist in shortness of distance . . . Nor is great distance remoteness . . . Nearness, it seems, cannot be encountered directly. We succeed in reaching it rather by attending to what is near. Near to us are what we usually call things . . . in this discovery we also catch sight of the nature of nearness. The thing things. In thinging, it stays earth and sky, divinities and mortals. Staying, the thing brings the four, in their remoteness, near to one another. This bringing-near is nearing. Nearing is the presencing of nearness. Nearness brings near—draws nigh to one another—the far and, indeed, *as* the far. Nearness preserves farness. Preserving farness, nearness presences nearness in nearing that farness. Bringing near in this way, nearness conceals its own self and remains, in its own way, nearest of all. The thing is not 'in' nearness, 'in' proximity, as if nearness were a container. Nearness is at work in bringing near, as the thinging of the thing." See Heidegger, "The Thing," in *Poetry, Language, Thought*, trans. Albert Hofstadter (New York: Harper & Row, 1971), 165–66, 177–78.

[166]As Heidegger succinctly states, "Nearing is the nature of nearness" (ibid., 181). This is reflected in the Samaritan's movement into the ditch on the road to Jericho, as well as the work necessary to build a "revolution of tenderness" that fosters solidarity in a divided world.

[167]Boyle, *Barking to the Choir*, 204.

5

Toward a Culture of Belonging

The ethics of encounter proposes dispositions, habits, practices, and relationships to help mend the social separation and sinful inequalities that wound the family of creation. The virtues of courage, mercy, generosity, humility, and fidelity not only provide an ethical framework for "doing likewise" as the Samaritan, but they help create the conditions conducive for a culture of encounter. This includes paying attention to the personal attitudes and actions that can help with worthiness, taking steps to counteract the influence of bias, practicing tools for effective communication to bolster understanding, and attending to the formative role of the *habitus*—the local environment or system of acquired beliefs, outlooks, and actions—for creating a normative environment for more inclusive belonging. The example provided by Fr. Greg Boyle and the community of Homeboy Industries provides a blueprint for the beliefs, actions, and relationships that can heal the wounds of shame, hatred, and violence, the most daunting of all obstacles for practicing the ethics of encounter. In these ways, Christian neighbor love becomes a practice of drawing near to others, being open to receiving others, and making solidarity as inclusive as possible.

This final chapter pivots to the development of a *habitus* for practicing the ethics of encounter. It focuses on several of the most prominent spaces for formation and the future of humanity. It begins with family, the building block of church and society and the first community of belonging. Families connect the personal with the public, and provide a pathway to many other associations like schools and neighborhoods, friendships and clubs, churches and places of work. Then, it proposes how a culture of encounter can be adopted in existing communities of belonging, including local businesses and churches. Next, it explores the connections and disconnections prompted by digital technology, the internet, and social media, since we spend most of our waking hours using screens. The ethics of encounter has to analyze and adjust to how these technologies impact identity, relationships, and social capital in order to pursue more virtuous connections and communities online. To neglect nonhuman creation is to ignore human interdependence with the wider planetary community. For this reason, this chapter concludes by examining how the ethics of encounter can be applied to the natural world in order to foster a solidarity that includes nonhuman species. In light of the urgency and scale of ecological degradation, the ethics of encounter is incomplete (and perhaps even pointless) if it does not seek right relationship with the entire created order. Indeed, care for nonhuman creation (plants, animals, and the environment as a whole) as a matter of global justice and sustainability is a most vital if not the preeminent moral duty of our time.

In examining the ethics of encounter with these considerations in mind, my hope is to propose a comprehensive and integrating vision for love of God, neighbor, and nature to help realize an integral and inclusive solidarity.

FAMILY: THE FIRST COMMUNITY OF BELONGING

The ethics of encounter begins on the personal level but cannot end there. As demonstrated by the example of Homeboy Industries in the previous chapter, fostering inclusive belonging and lasting healing is most powerful and profound when it is reinforced in a *habitus* of shared practices and reciprocal relationships. For the ethics of encounter to create cultural change, it must find traction in places where trust, support, and accountability are already in place. When these networks are leveraged, they can become clusters of belonging that, through an inclusive orientation, build communities of belonging. The ethics of encounter has to be incorporated into family life, the primary place of personal, social, and moral formation. The family unit—in whatever structure it takes, not just the "nuclear family" unit as popularly conceived—is the preeminent *habitus* and the primary experience of connection today. Americans prize family like nothing else: 92 percent of Americans report that family is "very important" to them, and more than half of Americans say they would like to spend "much more time" with their family, if they could.[1] In the Christian tradition, family is understood as the building block of society, the "domestic church" where right relationship is first experienced. Love is expressed through courage, mercy, generosity, humility, and fidelity in family life.

[1]Compare this to work, for example: in 1990, 62 percent of Americans rated work as very important, while only 33 percent did in 2006. While 55 percent of Americans said they would like to spend much more time with their family in 2006, only 33 percent felt that way in 1989. See Claude S. Fischer, *Still Connected: Family and Friends in America since 1970* (New York: Russell Sage, 2011), 79–83.

Families represent intergenerational bonds of belonging, part of God's "ordering of life in the world" for sustenance and flourishing.[2] Families provide strong—and hopefully stable—attachments, reciprocal (though not always harmonious) relationships that can offer respect, support, and empowerment. Families also experience failure: obligations that are not adequately fulfilled, excessive burdens unevenly shared, breakdowns in honesty, kindness, and fidelity. Sometimes families are also home to abuse, neglect, and trauma. A good number of families experience the deep pain that results from not being loved well or instances when a marriage ends in bitter divorce. The hurt that can arise from family life can inflict unique wounds, generate anxiety and fear, and foment suspicion or resentment. Bonds once marked by trust and love can be damaged if not destroyed. However, families also learn forgiveness and reconciliation, the commitment to atone for transgressions, mend broken bonds, and heal the wounds made by failing to love.

Most if not all families struggle with unrealistic expectations, resulting in some degree of guilt and shame for being unable or unwilling to provide more for these most intimate bonds. Every parent and child wrestles with commitments in and outside of the home. And many face additional challenges posed by mental illness or chronic sickness, injury, or disability. In light of the complex relations—and sometimes divisions—that occur in families, the ethics of encounter ought to begin right here. Even though families are typically our foremost experience of love, many families could still use more humility and tenderness, gratitude and generosity, reverence and loyalty. Justice requires that each person receives what is due to him or her, which is based on ability and need. If family members are treated in an unjust manner, they may be inclined to treat others in a similar fashion. Family life is a crucial setting for learning respect and responsibility, gratitude and magnanimity, honesty and loyalty, repentance and remorse, trust and accountability.

At the same time, the ethics of encounter cannot end within the family unit. Families are "acted upon as well as acting" in culture: they are shaped by popular norms and also contribute to what people find acceptable in wider society.[3] As families practice virtues like courage, mercy, generosity, humility, and fidelity, they impact their social context and fulfill the family's duty to serve the common good through the interdependence and mutual participation of all members of society.[4] The social mission of the family bridges the personal and the political. By engaging in hospitality and service, as well as the preferential option for the

---

[2]James M. Gustafson, *Ethics from a Theocentric Perspective: Ethics and Theology*, vol. 2 (Chicago: University of Chicago Press, 1984), 158.

[3]Ibid., 166.

[4]Lisa Sowle Cahill, *Family: A Christian Social Perspective* (Minneapolis: Fortress Press, 2000), 83–110.

poor, families help transform their social, economic, and political context. This "is not optional, but fundamental to a family's identity and calling. It is what it does as a community of love in the world."[5] This is what Pope John Paul II envisioned when he proposed that "the fostering of authentic and mature communion between persons within the family is the first and irreplaceable school of social life, an example and stimulus for the broader community of relationships marked by respect, justice, dialogue, and love."[6] In this way, families can become "schools of solidarity" and "factories of hope," as Pope Francis has described.[7] Formed in love, families are equipped with the mutual power-sharing and supportive relationships necessary to resist evil and work for justice in society.

This view of family life focuses on social responsibility and solidarity, lenses that correct against the prevalence of "amoral familism" that turns families inward. Some families do all they can to survive, while others enjoy a rather comfortable lifestyle. Regardless of socioeconomic status, many families report being busy, stressed, and overwhelmed. This leaves little time or emotional energy to take responsibility for nonkin. But the image of family presented in Scripture resists divisions between kin and nonkin. Examples of the family unit as socially responsible include passages like Exodus 22:20–26, Deuteronomy 15:1–11, and Leviticus 25:23–38. Families are depicted as "structures of grace" that are "designed to mitigate hardship and misfortune . . . grounded in God's mercy."[8] Jesus affirms the overlap between the demands of discipleship and family life but minimizes the importance of blood ties. He teaches, for example, "Whoever does the will of God is my brother, sister, and mother" in Mark 3:35, Matthew 12:50, and Luke 8:21. More to the point, Jesus asserts that the demands of discipleship supersede family obligations.[9] He warns, "If anyone comes to me without hating his father and mother, wife and children, brothers and sisters, and even his own life, he cannot be my disciple" (Lk 14:25–26). Jesus also expands his followers' conception of family so that it is no longer defined by blood alone; his instruction to pray to *Abba* ("Daddy") makes everyone part of a family of believers (Lk 11:2).

---

[5]Julie Hanlon Rubio, *Family Ethics: Practices for Christians* (Washington, DC: Georgetown University Press, 2010), 53.

[6]*Familiaris Consortio*, no. 43.

[7]Pope Francis used this phrase in an address on December 29, 2014. See also Mary M. Doyle Roche, *Schools of Solidarity: Families and Catholic Social Teaching* (Collegeville, MN: Liturgical Press, 2015). Pope Francis used the phrase "factory of hope" in reference to families in an unscripted address at the Festival of Families in Philadelphia. The official version released by the Vatican uses the phrase "workshop of hope." Pope Francis, "Prayer Vigil for the Festival of Families," September 26, 2015, w2.vatican.va/content/francesco/en/speeches/2015/september/documents/papa-francesco_20150926_usa-festa-famiglie.html.

[8]John Rogerson, "The Family and Structures of Grace in the Old Testament," in *The Family in Theological Perspective*, ed. Stephen C. Barton (Edinburgh: T&T Clark, 1996), 25–42, at 36.

[9]See, for example, Mk 10:29–30; Mt 10:34–37 and 19:29; and Lk 12:51–53 and 18:29–30.

In these instances, Jesus warns against the temptation for family life to become so consuming that it eclipses the demands of discipleship, including ongoing conversion from sin (Lk 5:32) and a sacrificial costliness (Mk 8:34) in loving God and neighbor that eschews security and status. Moreover, the demands of Christian neighbor love—oriented toward solidarity and the preferential option for the poor, as discussed in Chapter 3—require placing limits on how much time and money are dedicated to the family, especially if this comes at the expense of charity and justice for the neediest among us.

The first followers of Jesus became a "new family" across previously enforced social boundaries by providing care for one another through mutual sharing and cooperation that included people who were marginalized or vulnerable.[10] The early church is described as a community of coequals who were accountable to each other's needs, as reflected in Acts 2:42–47. Gathering for liturgy proved a ritual for both religious and moral formation but less through preaching or teaching than in sharing life together.[11]

Families can and should practice the ethics of encounter within and beyond the family unit. Shared practices that encounter others in need and respond with courage, mercy, generosity, humility, and fidelity help strengthen the identity and mission of the family. It is important to note, however, that in discussing family life, we should resist the inclination to think only of parents and their children, for families take all different forms. Everyone, at every stage of life, is always a member of a family of one kind or another. When families love well, they are schools of life-giving communion. Family members learn to embody honesty, loyalty, love, justice, and other virtues that create and nurture mutually respectful and responsible relationships. These practices also foster resistance against the cultural norms that undermine faith, integrity, and discipleship. This is true for friendships as well, including the friends who become like family. Friends have a powerful influence on our personal, social, and moral formation.[12] As we consider the kind of people we are becoming, the relationships we cultivate, and the society we are building, we should analyze whether and how our friendships

[10]Richard Horsley, *Sociology and the Jesus Movement* (New York: Crossroad, 1989), 122–25.

[11]Paul writes to a divided community in Corinth, denouncing the class divisions that resulted in the wealthy eating and drinking to excess while other members of the community went hungry: "Therefore whoever eats the bread or drinks the cup of the Lord unworthily will have to answer for the body and blood of the Lord. A person should examine himself, and so eat the bread and drink the cup. For anyone who eats and drinks without discerning the body, eats and drinks judgment on himself. That is why many among you are ill and infirm, and a considerable number are dying" (1 Cor 11:23–30).

[12]"Friendship is the crucible of the moral life, the relationship in which we come to embody the good by sharing it with friends who also delight in the good." Paul Wadell, *Friendship and the Moral Life* (Notre Dame, IN: University of Notre Dame Press, 1989), xiii.

help us cross racial, ethnic, class, political party, and religious lines. Recall Gustavo Gutiérrez's claim that solidarity and the preferential option for the poor are ultimately a matter of creating friendships with the poor, the socially insignificant.[13] Families cannot be closed inward; they should overlap with other intimate bonds, including friendships, in a complementary rather than competitive claim on our time. In a time when three-quarters of white Americans don't have a single black friend and two-thirds of black Americans don't have one white friend,[14] the ethics of encounter impels us to draw near the other in a way that brings together a diverse community of family and friends.

The practice of nearing moves us toward those who look, think, and live differently than we do. Nearing is not done to judge or criticize, lecture or teach. Nearing is done in a posture of open reception to listen and learn from the other. For some, this process might begin with reading books or magazines, watching TV or movies, or listening to podcasts that open access to another perspective based on sex, gender, or sexual orientation, ethnicity, race, or nationality, age or ability, class, religion, or politics. Family trips to museums can foster intergenerational learning about the root causes of social divides and unjust inequalities; some examples are visiting the National Museum of African American History and Culture in Washington, DC, the National Underground Railroad Freedom Center in Cincinnati, Ohio, or the National Voting Rights Museum and Institute in Selma, Alabama. Spending time with others who are different and sharing life together make it possible to connect on a human level, an important way to recognize that our differences—though significant—do not always need to define us or limit our future.

One concrete practice of nearing involves direct service to the poor, vulnerable, and isolated. In a social context marked by alienation and "lifestyle enclaves," following the example of the Samaritan by changing one's social location is an essential way to bridge social divides and build a culture of encounter. Spending time with those on the margins of society—not just the economically deprived, but any person who is pushed to the peripheries because of their identity, ability, beliefs, or age—is an act of resistance in a culture that prioritizes upward mobility. It opens our eyes to personal suffering and systemic injustice; it makes it possible to cultivate compassion for people previously unknown; it reveals the unexamined privilege and luxury of those who enjoy greater financial security and social status. It can liberate people from the anxiety or fear of the "other" and foster

[13]Gustavo Gutiérrez, "The Option for the Poor Arises from Faith in Christ," *Theological Studies* 70 (2009): 325.

[14]Daniel Cox, Juhem Navarro-Rivera, and Robert P. Jones, "Race and Americans' Social Networks," Public Religion Research Institute, August 28, 2014, http://www.prri.org/research/analysis-social-network/.

more inclusive solidarity across differences, especially when service gives way to mutual giving and receiving. Service is formative less from the actions done than through the relationships formed:

> Being with those who have little and give much breaks through the numbness that is the sickness of our middle-class tribe, allowing joy, sadness, and passion to seep in. If families commit to this practice, they will find an anecdote to "emptiness in busyness" in communion—in richer relationships at home, in community with fellow believers, in service to and friendship with those in need, and in a deeper sense of gratitude and connection to the God who made us all.[15]

Charity meets an immediate need, like providing a warm meal for someone who is hungry or shelter for a person experiencing homelessness, or another practice of mercy.[16] But providing food to the hungry or medicine for the sick falls well short of what justice requires. And generosity sometimes covers for the way people benefit from others' poverty.[17] This is why such efforts must also include advocacy for the structural changes that will generate more freedom and justice for those deprived of their dignity and rights. Everyone has a responsibility to hold our elected officials accountable to civic values like equality, freedom, and justice. The Holy Spirit—which Jesus calls our advocate (Jn 14:16)—calls and empowers Christians to discern how best they can use their gifts and talents as advocates for others in need. The virtue of magnanimity, the "stretching forth of the mind to do great things," gives us moral ambition for the common good.[18]

Families should practice courage, mercy, generosity, humility, and fidelity in every setting of daily life, not just in serving the poor or needy. Charity and justice are demanded of all, including neighbors and strangers, teachers and students, co-workers, supervisors, and customers—everyone who shares in the commonweal of society. Families represent diverse identities and relationships, as well as opportunities to cross racial, ethnic, political, and religious lines. Their relationships and interactions connect to neighborhoods and clubs, schools and churches, places of business and many other hubs of social interaction like gyms,

---

[15]Rubio, *Family Ethics*, 209.

[16]The "corporal works of mercy" are inspired by Matthew 25:31–46. See James F. Keenan, *The Works of Mercy: The Heart of Catholicism* (Lanham, MD: Rowman & Littlefield, 2008).

[17]Anand Giridharadas writes that we expect that the rich will be inspired to do more good, but we do not expect them to do less harm; they should "give back" but not "take less"; and we want them to be part of the solution without ever accusing them of "being part of the problem." See Anand Giridharadas, *Winners Take All: The Elite Charade of Changing the World* (New York: Alfred A. Knopf, 2018), 155.

[18]Thomas Aquinas, *Summa Theologiae* II-II, 129, 1.

coffee shops, restaurants, libraries, museums, parks, and playgrounds. A culture of encounter can be integrated into the way one drives, uses a rideshare program, and rides public transportation, or how one interacts with others while shopping in a store. Children will learn from older relatives what it looks like to encounter another with respect and kindness, and they will see the difference it makes. Mother Teresa reminds us that "peace begins with a smile." Modeling eye contact, a warm greeting, and courteous language affirms the dignity of others, whether to someone passing by or beginning a conversation. This is an important practice when more and more people keep their eyes glued to a screen and earbuds in their ears, failing to acknowledge others nearby or tempted to see them as a distraction or interruption, rather than as a sacrament of God's presence in their midst.

When families interrupt the cycle of comfort, convenience, and complacency with the status quo, they participate in the divine life of grace, God's sharing of Godself, a Triune communion of love that is offered, received, and returned. As instruments of grace, families tap into God's sharing of divine power to cooperate in building up more inclusive and just communion on earth. It "brings into existence a community of shared religious aspiration, belief, and love that provides an environment of grace that nurtures those who live within it in an ever-deepening union with God."[19] Grace sustains life-long religious and moral growth in faith, hope, and love. As members of families practice these virtues in right relationship with one another, they share in and cooperate with these God-given gifts and serve as reminders that every encounter not only incarnates the presence of the Divine in our midst, but it helps to reconcile what divides us.

LEVERAGING EXISTING COMMUNITIES OF BELONGING

Building a culture of encounter is a religious and moral responsibility that does not fall to families alone. Families are uniquely valuable social networks for enacting the ethics of encounter, but every community and social institution—neighborhood and school, club or place of business, church or museum—can participate in this work. Regardless of religious affiliation (or lack thereof), no one is ineligible to participate in the "revolution of tenderness" that aims to mend the brokenness in and around us. Catholic schools, churches, charities, and hospitals have a special though not exclusive responsibility for integrating courage, mercy, generosity, humility, and fidelity into their mission. Focusing on

[19]Donald L. Gelpi, *Grace as Transmuted Experience and Social Process, and Other Essays in North American Theology* (Lanham, MD: University Press of America, 1988), 62. Gelpi continues, "When grace informs the social processes that create a community, it functions as an environment of grace for its individual members, even though it could never exist apart from their collaborative efforts."

local networks and institutions represents a key opportunity to exercise power from the ground up. Changing the way people relate to one another will influence how institutions exercise power. Foucault points out that where there is power, "there is resistance."[20] Power can be subversive, and when it is, the system resists change, as it is designed to perpetuate itself. Pope Francis's invitation to build a culture of encounter will not automatically make institutions change their policies and practices. People have to change their beliefs, actions, and interactions with others to put pressure on the system to change, becoming many points of resistance to the status quo. Power is both productive and constraining. Schools and churches, clubs and businesses all represent a local *habitus* that can produce and regulate the kind of power that can bring people together across differences.

Each network—whether a neighborhood or school, club or church, business or health care facility—has to decide how it will engage nonmembers. Will it be open and welcoming or closed inward, like a sect? Jean Vanier posits that a "true community becomes more and more open, because it becomes more and more humble. A sect seems to be open, but with time in fact becomes more and more closed . . . They are governed more by fear than growth towards inner freedom."[21] Communities, on the other hand, forge belongingness through openness and affection, creativity and generosity, cooperation and healing, forgiveness and patience, trust and freedom. Communities combat complacency and fight becoming closed off when its members become more sensitive and vulnerable, even dependent on one another. Vanier explains that love "makes us weak and vulnerable, because it breaks down the barriers and protective armor we have built around ourselves. Love means letting others reach us and becoming sensitive enough to reach them. The cement of unity is interdependence."[22] This is not a romantic sense of love, but rather love as self-giving; it is willing the good of the other. This is both a religious and civic duty: we have a commitment to the common good that reaches far beyond our families, neighborhoods, cities, states, and even our nation.

Given the inequality that pervades so many neighborhoods and schools, a culture of encounter can help heal divides and improve opportunities for those with less privilege and power. Ninety-five percent of Americans agree that "everyone in America should have equal opportunity to get ahead."[23] But if we do nothing to address the forces that block equal access to resources and quell social mobility, it is wrong to describe this as a sincere conviction. One way to help bridge the

---

[20]Michel Foucault, *The History of Sexuality: An Introduction*, vol. 1, trans. Robert Hurley (New York: Vintage, 1990), 95.

[21]Jean Vanier, *Community and Growth* (Mahwah, NJ: Paulist Press, 1989), 144.

[22]Ibid., 48.

[23]Robert Putnam, *Our Kids: The American Dream in Crisis* (New York: Simon & Schuster, 2015), 241.

gap is to encourage children and adults to participate in extracurricular activities and mentoring programs. Not only do these programs provide avenues for encountering others, but these opportunities are proven to cultivate the kinds of soft skills and networks of support that are essential for academic and professional success, resilience, and social mobility.[24] Volunteering to coach or supervise an afterschool activity or mentor a young person can go a long way toward mending social divides and leveling the playing field for our young people.

Businesses can and do participate in a culture of encounter by being places that welcome customers and by providing consistent opportunities for people to meet together. Bars and restaurants, barber shops and beauty salons have long been sites of intergenerational exchange. The explosion of craft breweries and taprooms has been a boon for community revitalization in many towns, as well as new locations for encountering others (in family-friendly conditions) and, in some cases, a setting for intentional practices of civility in our divided times, as is the case with "Craft Beer and Conversation" in Cleveland.[25] Corporate environments would benefit from preferring a spirit of cooperation over competition. Such an ethos is not only more amenable to fruitful encounters, but it can also boost higher morale and revenue. Adam Grant dispels the myth that those who succeed do so solely by seizing opportunities, embracing a diligent work ethic, and cutthroat ambition. He finds, in fact, that the most successful people are "givers," people who strategize to benefit others in addition to themselves. "Takers" also succeed, but what makes "givers" distinctive is that their success "spreads and cascades," creating a ripple effect that others also enjoy, rather than resent.[26] The winner-take-all mentality of "takers" pits winners against losers, "us" versus "them." A more cooperative approach does not mean settling for less achievement, but it does mean that more people are included, empowered, and fulfilled. Studies show that the more diverse a team of employees, the faster they solve problems and the more revenue they produce.[27] Morale is higher among those people who feel valued and free to contribute based on their viewpoints and expertise, who consistently receive feedback on their performance and are recognized for their efforts, and who are explicitly reminded that collaboration and team gains are

---

[24]Ibid., 258. The exception is "pay-to-play" programs, which only the elite can afford. Putnam recommends that we abolish this practice as a matter of equity.

[25]Megan Anderson, "Craft Beer and Conversation: Let's Talk, Really," Wish Cleveland, January 10, 2017.

[26]Adam Grant, *Give and Take: Why Helping Others Drives Our Success* (New York: Penguin, 2013), 10.

[27]Alison Reynolds and David Lewis, "Teams Solve Problems Faster When They're More Cognitively Diverse," *Harvard Business Review*, March 30, 2017; Anna Powers, "Study Finds That Diverse Companies Produce 19% More Revenue," *Forbes*, June 27, 2018.

valued more than being right or individual accomplishment.[28] Courage, mercy, generosity, humility, and fidelity can make a big impact in work environments, and this, in turn, can boost people's self-esteem and efficacy, likely paying dividends in other areas of life as well.

Insofar as a culture of encounter is primarily about seeing Christ in the other and being Christ for the other, every church community should be committed to this practice. Every church should foster a culture of encounter *ad intra* and *ad extra*. Churches should be places of welcome, hospitality, and reconciliation, not labeled either as "traditional" or "progressive," "conservative" or "liberal." Pigeonholing individuals or groups makes it more difficult to be inclusive and collaborative. Christians have a duty to love all (including enemies), practice forgiveness, and be peacemakers. This requires that individual disciples, families and groups, and local churches adopt solidarity, especially with the vulnerable and marginalized in and beyond their congregations. Otherwise the church will continue to rend the Body of Christ into "a body of broken bones."[29] Pope Francis describes a vision of the church that is less like a fortress and more like a "field hospital" after battle, a place without frontiers, a "mother to all."[30] He urges leaders to go to the peripheries, not only to serve the people there, but to learn from them. A culture of encounter is about equal and mutual exchange; how much can our church learn from those who have been pushed to the edges of the church and society?

Welcoming the stranger—especially migrants and refugees—ensures that hospitality and solidarity extend across borders.[31] Pope Francis's proposed "Share the Journey" campaign aims to welcome, integrate, promote, and protect migrants and refugees, especially in places where they are spurned due to xenophobia, concerns about disease, and other expressions of indifference to these people forced to flee their home.[32] Churches should make clear that any attempt to confine duty to a particular group betrays the biblical command to be agents of solidarity, unity across diversity (Gal 3:28). A claim like "America First" is totally indefensible from the perspective of the gospels, as it feeds into the dualism of us versus them, denying membership to parts of the Body of Christ. In a time of

---

[28]Tessa Ann Taylor, "Diversity, Inclusion, and Culture: How to Build Great Teams," *New York Times*, April 19, 2018.

[29]This observation is made by Thomas Merton in *New Seeds of Contemplation* (New York: New Directions, 1961), 70–79. It has been further developed by M. Shawn Copeland, *Enfleshing Freedom: Body, Race, and Being* (Minneapolis: Fortress Press, 2010), 101–05.

[30]*Misericordiae Vultus*, no. 9; Pope Francis interview with Antonio Spadaro, SJ, "A Big Heart Open to God," *America*, September 30, 2013. See also *Evangelii Gaudium*, no. 210.

[31]Kristin Heyer, *Kinship across Borders: A Christian Ethic of Immigration* (Washington, DC: Georgetown University Press, 2012).

[32]Pope Francis, "104th World Day of Migrants and Refugees," January 14, 2018, w2.vatican.va. See also https://www.sharejourney.org/.

rising anti-Semitism and Islamophobia, every church community should commit to interfaith dialogue, prayer, service, and collaboration. Pope Francis calls on each Christian to be an "artisan of peace," and there will be no peace in our world without interfaith solidarity.

In a similar vein, churches also have to combat racism in their own corporate bodies as well as in society as whole. The US Catholic Bishops' recent pastoral letter, "Open Wide Our Hearts," laments the way the church has been complicit in colonialism and slavery, white supremacy, and antiblack racism.[33] Even now, these corporate vices infect the church and divide the Body of Christ.[34] Latino and Latina Catholics report being relegated to the peripheries of ecclesial attention, concern, and influence. More than 40 percent of American Catholics are Hispanic, even while the rich diversity of local churches is not reflected in the ministerial priorities or leadership of the American Catholic Church.[35] Homophobia and heterosexism also marginalize and reject, denying LGBTQ individuals the acceptance with "respect, compassion, and sensitivity" urged in the *Catechism*.[36]

Many others feel the shame and pain of exclusion, cut off from the Eucharist or feeling unwelcome in churches because of their sex or gender, because they married someone of another religion, because they have divorced and remarried, or because they have fallen away from their faith. This also befalls those whose beliefs contradict church teaching, and those who are "living in sin," according to other members of the church. Many feel unworthy of belonging to a faith community, either because of their own scruples or the self-righteousness of others. Chris Pramuk observes, "The phrase, 'Do not fear!' appears over three hundred fifty times in Scripture, yet how many of us still struggle with that dread feeling that I have to get right with God before I walk in the door? Church is, or ought to be, where we go to find welcome and support precisely with our brokenness, relational failures, and moral shortcomings."[37] Still, many churches experience division and segregation, whether by race and ethnicity or polarization in ideology, driving wedges between parishioners and between parishes.[38] A lack of ecumenical dialogue and interfaith solidarity further points to the need for a

---

[33]US Conference of Catholic Bishops, "Open Wide Our Hearts," November 2018.

[34]Katie Walker Grimes, *Christ Divided: Antiblackness as Corporate Vice* (Minneapolis: Fortress Press, 2017), 123–45.

[35]Hosffman Ospino, ed., *Hispanic Ministry in the 21st Century: Present and Future* (Miami: Convivium, 2010).

[36]*Catechism of the Catholic Church*, no. 2358. See also James Martin, *Building a Bridge: How the Catholic Church and the LGBT Community Can Enter into a Relationship of Respect, Compassion, and Sensitivity* (New York: HarperOne, 2017), 14–20.

[37]Christopher Pramuk, *Hope Sings, So Beautiful: Graced Encounters across the Color Line* (Collegeville, MN: Michael Glazier, 2013), 145.

[38]Mary Ellen Konieczny, Charles C. Camosy, and Tricia C. Bruce, eds., *Polarization in the US Catholic Church: Naming the Wounds, Beginning to Heal* (Collegeville, MN: Liturgical Press, 2016).

culture of encounter within and between churches today. When people go "church shopping" to find a church that fits their preferences, they typically reinforce the social sorting that separates us into homogenous groups. Changing our social location in seeking more diversity—in and outside of the congregations to which we belong—can give us a better understanding of what it will take to reconcile the wounded Body of Christ.

Churches can and should be places that foster common ground for both religious and secular populations and issues. Finding common ground is made possible when people are willing to move past partisan divides and focus instead "on outcomes that can be achieved at the local level," especially those supported by "evidence-based, participatory solutions."[39] The local congregation or parish is an ideal *habitus* to bring people together across difference in the spirit of subsidiarity for effective local action. Church members can work together as peacemakers who are able "to build communion amid disagreement" because they are "willing to go beyond the surface of a conflict and to see others in their deepest dignity" and able to preserve "what is valid and useful on both sides."[40] A culture of encounter cannot be considered only in terms of going to encounter unfamiliar or unknown people; it should bring people together in mutual engagement, respect, and responsibility. Churches have to be understood as more than places where sacraments get dispensed; they should be a center of formation that enhances identity and mission. This means that the lay faithful have to embrace their coresponsibility in *being* church, in contrast to thinking of church as a place to go or get something from. If one sees a parish staff as "service providers," then parish members become "customers" or "service recipients." This consumer mindset commodifies belonging to and participating in parish life, diminishing one's baptismal duties to be church. It also feeds into an us and them dichotomy that says "it is their job to provide for me or my family."[41]

Instead, a culture of encounter relies on congregations being more intentional about the kind of *habitus* they build. Every community communicates its values through its shared repertoires. What values are expressed through the shared practices of participation in my parish? How do courage, mercy, generosity, humility, and fidelity get represented? How do these values compare to others (such as convenience or efficiency)? Parishes operate with limited resources, relying on volunteers to accomplish many thankless tasks. When so much responsibility is heaped onto the shoulders of a select few, what does that communicate about

---

[39]Julie Hanlon Rubio, *Hope for Common Ground: Mediating the Personal and the Political in a Divided Church* (Washington, DC: Georgetown University Press, 2016), xvii.

[40]*Evangelii Gaudium*, no. 228. Quoted in Rubio, *Hope for Common Ground*, 232.

[41]This may be viewed as a kind of "sacramental consumerism," as Michael Paul Gallagher describes in his essay, "What Are We Doing When We Do Theology?" *Landas* 28:1 (2014): 1–12.

who is responsible for the personal, social, religious, and moral formation of the community? Each and every group is a "community of practice" that should evaluate the messages it sends through its patterns of engagement and common repertoires.[42] If, as Putnam and Campbell have found, people are formed more through shared practices of belonging and involvement in relationships with others, then every group and faith community should assess whether and how they are forming people to practice a culture of encounter across differences.[43]

Churches, clubs, and other groups can also forge more inclusive networks to accompany and advocate with underrepresented individuals and groups. Community organizing has an extensive history of building alliances to create change on the social and institutional levels.[44] Churches have long been effective in gathering people together to encounter the Word and Sacraments; these repertoires can also be useful in moving people to care enough to speak, act, and organize for love and justice, peace and reconciliation, solidarity and the common good. In fact, this has been the case for decades in some denominations, resulting in organizing coalitions that are typically religiously, racially, ethnically, and socioeconomically diverse.[45] Faith-rooted organizing can keep people in touch with the spiritual and communal resources necessary for a long-term, sustainable commitment to social change.[46] In view of the rise of "the nones," the religiously unaffiliated, which claims nearly one in five Americans and more than one in three under thirty years old, faith-based communities need to partner with secular allies.

To be a "neighbor" has important implications for both discipleship and citizenship. A culture of encounter should strengthen "civic friendship" that cultivates trust and support among citizens, resisting the tribalism of contending interest groups.[47] Civic friendship relies on honesty and respect, and in a time when civil discourse is on the decline, we need more neighborhoods, churches, and other

---

[42]Jane Regan, *Where Two or Three Are Gathered: Transforming the Parish through Communities of Practice* (New York: Paulist Press, 2016), 30 (emphasis removed). Regan proposes practices of hospitality, conversation, followership, and discernment to bolster parish life in co-responsibility among the faithful.

[43]Robert Putnam and David Campbell, *American Grace: How Religion Divides and Unites Us* (New York: Simon & Schuster, 2010), 468–75.

[44]Jeffrey Stout, *Blessed Are the Organized: Grassroots Democracy in America* (Princeton, NJ: Princeton University Press, 2010).

[45]Examples include PICO, Direct Action and Research Training Center, InterValley Project, Ohio Organizing Collaborative, Interfaith Worker Justice, and Clergy and Laity United for Economic Justice. See Richard L. Wood and Brad R. Fulton, *A Shared Future: Faith-Based Organizing for Racial Equity and Ethical Democracy* (Chicago: University of Chicago Press, 2015), 2, 11.

[46]Alexia Salvatierra and Peter Goodwin Heltzel, *Faith-Rooted Organizing: Mobilizing the Church in Service to the World* (Downers Grove, IL: InterVarsity, 2013).

[47]See Robert Bellah et al., *Habits of the Heart: Individualism and Commitment in American Life* (Berkeley: University of California, 1985), 116, 133.

organizations to gather folks together for truthful public dialogue.[48] Finding more opportunities to gather together—marked by safety and levity—will help people feel comfortable enough to be vulnerable and honest. These interpersonal interactions can cultivate the rapport necessary for community organizing and advocacy, which help translate a culture of encounter to the institutional level, aiming to build "structures of grace" that replace self-interest, corruption, greed, and violence with love and justice, solidarity and the common good.[49] These bridge-building organizations help individuals and groups confront unjust inequality, tribalism and xenophobia, and anxiety or indifference in the face of large-scale problems. As Kevin Ahern observes,

> By forming socially engaged ethical leaders, holding governments to account for their actions, and transforming social relationships to be more in line with the gospel, Christian social movements function as counterforces to structures of sin and oppression in the world . . . [and] inspire and communicate the virtues of charity and solidarity.[50]

Through advocacy for effective legislation and accountability, these ground-up approaches can reach the highest levels of social, economic, and political organization to help with making progress from a culture of encounter toward a society that reflects a more inclusive culture of belonging.

ENCOUNTER THROUGH A SCREEN

In order for digital technology, the internet, and social media to be part of a culture of encounter, steps must be taken to avoid the manipulation, coercion, and degradation of others as discussed in the first chapter. A culture of encounter relies upon recognizing the equal dignity and freedom of the other. In some settings, the digital realm affords more equality and freedom online than offline, as power structures tend to be more egalitarian than hierarchical. At the same time, however, market influences and social stratification still create centers and peripheries of privilege and influence. To evaluate the possibilities and limits of a culture of encounter mediated through a screen, we need to consider the influence

---

[48]See, for example, the Civil Conversations Project, https://onbeing.org/civil-conversations-project/.

[49]Kevin Ahern explains that "structures of grace" (in opposition to "structures of sin") are represented by Christian social movements and NGOs as the manifestation of God present in the people who fight against sin and injustice. See Kevin Ahern, *Structures of Grace: Catholic Organizations Serving the Global Common Good* (Maryknoll, NY: Orbis Books, 2015).

[50]Ibid., 136.

of digital technology and social media on identity, relationships, and social capital.

As discussed in the first chapter, it seems more appropriate to speak of a "networked self," "connected self," or "embedded self" than Charles Taylor's "buffered self."[51] Constant contact makes available more information and potentially more experiences of affirmation and support from loved ones. But the habit of continual connection and accessing content on demand can also train people to expect instant gratification. The instant results of a Google search changes the way our brains work, making fast but superficial connections the norm, rather than deep and sustained thoughtfulness.[52] The free range of choice for whatever content we would like to consume creates an abundance of "modern Goldilockses."[53] This only exacerbates the "moral therapeutic deism" described by Christian Smith; a worldview shaped by what I find interesting, comfortable, or beneficial may not always cohere with a more complex reality, to say nothing of one's moral responsibilities to others.[54]

In every time and place, human beings desire to belong, and in our current social context, to belong is to be connected through a screen. Increasingly, identity is formed as a hybrid between the corporeal self and offline interactions in conjunction with one's digital presence and activity. Identity is mobile and protean like never before.[55] The desire to connect speaks to the social nature of being human, but we need to pay more attention to how, why, and to what end or goal people are connecting. For example, one important feature of digitally mediated communication is the possibility of changing—to whatever degree desired—one's actual identity. Some choose to distort their identity slightly, in the hope of seeming more attractive, accomplished, intelligent, or popular, for example.[56] This can be liberat-

---

[51]Sociologist Barry Wellman describes this in terms of a "networked individualism." This phrase expresses a tension between the digital ties between people tempered by a neoliberal conception of the self that maintains autonomy. He describes the resulting virtual communities as "ego-centric networks." See Barry Wellman, "The Rise of Networked Individualism," in *Community Networks Online*, ed. Leigh Keeble (London: Taylor & Francis, 2001), 17–42.

[52]Nicholas Carr, *The Shallows: What the Internet Is Doing to Our Brains* (New York: W. W. Norton, 2011).

[53]Sherry Turkle, *Alone Together: Why We Expect More from Technology and Less from Each Other* (New York: Basic Books, 2011), 15.

[54]Christian Smith with Melinda Lundquist Denton, *Soul Searching: The Religious and Spiritual Lives of American Teenagers* (Oxford: Oxford University Press, 2005), 162.

[55]John Palfrey and Urs Gasser claim that, above all, digital natives experience identity formation through insecurity and instability. See John Palfrey and Urs Gasser, *Born Digital: How Children Grow Up in a Digital Age* (New York: Basic Books, 2008), 31. Sherry Turkle describes identity formation as "newly free, newly yoked," more influenced by others, multiple, and constantly evolving due to the flow of content and impact of personal contacts (Turkle, *Alone Together*, 152, 194, 260). Michael Bugeja contends identity is more disembodied than ever before, and more blurred, since "In every facet of life, virtual habitat is intruding on real habitat," resulting in "deeply disorienting consequences." See Michael Bugeja, *Interpersonal Divide: The Search for Community in a Technological Age* (Oxford: Oxford University Press, 2005), 118.

[56]As Sherry Turkle points out, some digital users use multiple online personalities to test out

ing for those who would otherwise be judged or discriminated by their physical appearance. Some use a digital avatar to benignly escape, experience fantasy, or pretend to be someone else. Others use the internet as a cloak of anonymity, making "disinhibition" possible for aggressive or deceptive behavior, feeling immune from the consequences of what they share online.[57] Sometimes this is harmless, but many times it provides a shield of protection for vile behavior online, including "flaming."[58] The harsh comments at the bottom of articles and videos contribute to demonizing and dividing people into categories of "us" and "them." This raises important questions about the limits of free speech, especially when civility, tolerance, and social unity are at stake.[59] Strong virtual communities establish norms to discourage and even punish such behavior, although the anonymity of the internet makes accountability difficult to enforce.[60] A virtuous use of digital technology, the internet, and social media would surely benefit from a greater commitment to practicing courage, mercy, generosity, humility, and fidelity. For personal well-being, other values should be adopted as well. Donna Freitas recommends several, including appropriate vulnerability to engage others honestly; authenticity to dispel myths of perfection; toleration to make room for difference and dissent; forgetting, in order to let memories fade; being present instead of dwelling on past highlights or hurts; play and silliness; digital fasts, time spent in solitude, untethered from technology; and even quitting some social media in order to empower the self to interact with others in more substantial and meaningful ways.[61]

Insofar as personal connections are now more of a matter of choice, interper-

---

various dimensions of themselves, akin to various "windows" into their emerging identity. See Sherry Turkle, *Life on the Screen: Identity in the Age of the Internet* (New York: Simon & Schuster, 1996), 14.

[57]When deception is employed to attract a potential romantic partner, this behavior has been referred to as "catfishing." See Paula Fleming, "Online Dating Scams: What Is Catfishing?" Better Business Bureau, January 24, 2013.

[58]The most hostile online content is referred to as "flaming." It is routinely denounced as part of a "culture of narcissism" that feeds extremist positions, exacerbates a wide trend in a loss of civility, and contributes to a thinning public discourse. See Nancy K. Baym, *Personal Connections in the Digital Age* (Malden, MA: Polity, 2010), 57; Felicia Wu Song, *Virtual Communities: Bowling Alone, Online Together* (New York: Peter Lang, 2009), 122.

[59]Lee Rainie, Janna Anderson, and Jonathan Albright, "The Future of Free Speech, Trolls, Anonymity and Fake News Online," Pew Research Center, March 29, 2017.

[60]Song offers examples from various online communities. But she admits such examples only point to possibilities that "are often not pressed into plausible potentials because the structure of virtual communities—that is, the field that it becomes for public life—is one merely open to these possibilities but not configured to actually encourage and constrain members toward these essential democratic goods" (Song, *Virtual Communities*, 123). The challenges of exercising sanction against offenders means that communities must rely heavily on members' good will, as there is little incentive or organizational structure that counters the "ethic of individual choice" to behave as they wish, join or leave groups as they so desire (ibid., 124).

[61]Donna Freitas, *The Happiness Effect: How Social Media Is Driving a Generation to Appear Perfect at Any Cost* (Oxford: Oxford University Press, 2017), 256–64.

sonal interactions and relationships need not be determined by geographical or social location. Finding others who share similar interests is a powerful way to feel like one belongs. This can reduce isolation in those who feel like they do not quite fit in their physical surroundings. It can also lead to promising developments for those looking to find a romantic partner: today, nearly one in five brides report finding their spouse online or through a dating app. Even among those who interact in a more platonic fashion, these associations being cultivated online have potential to bolster the social fabric and produce democratic goods.[62] Although people used to talk about connecting the world across "six degrees of separation," now the number is closer to three degrees of separation.[63] We can connect with others wherever we are and wherever they are, bringing new meaning to William Wordsworth's phrase from 1807: "The world is too much with us."

These new possibilities for mobile connection are relevant in light of the deterritorializing effects of globalization and the manner in which rising use of digital tools and structures have contributed to the sociological trend known as "displacement."[64] On the one hand, this new sense of being partially or completely set free from one's physical location might "become quite counterproductive in the effort to cultivate a lively civic culture."[65] This could be disorienting for people who do not feel grounded in any particular place. On the other hand, it could be emancipatory for some people who find community online more easily than they could offline. In virtual communities, they discover belonging, solidarity, and efficacy that they could not in their physical surroundings.[66] Many have

[62]Mark Warren tests the assumption that all associations are beneficial for democracy in his helpful study, *Democracy and Association* (Princeton, NJ: Princeton University Press, 2001). He proposes six kinds of goods that can be fostered through virtual associations to improve personal identity and inclusive social bonding (ibid., 133).

[63]Jonah Engel Bromwich, "Six Degrees of Separation? Facebook Finds a Smaller Number," *New York Times*, February 4, 2016.

[64]Displacement is described as the chaotic clash between real and virtual environments, a loss of connection to one's physical place, and the blurring of roles and relationships, including between business and family life. See James Howard Kunstler, *The Geography of Nowhere* (New York: Simon & Schuster, 1994); and Howard Rheingold, *The Virtual Community: Homesteading on the Electronic Frontier* (Cambridge, MA: MIT Press, 2000).

[65]Song notes that "Online communities are not linked together like neighborhoods or street blocks that require you to drive through, or even be cognizant of the existence of, an impoverished or wealthy part of town. Instead, online life can be hermetically sealed within the particular modes of interaction that are chosen within one's groups." Insofar as digital users are free to engage in the content and groups of their choosing more so than unexpected encounters offline, it is easier for digital users to remain in a rather homogenous digital enclave that too easily "promotes a self-absorbed state of being that cares little for the collective good" (Song, *Virtual Communities*, 125–26).

[66]This is especially true for young people from "resource-poor" backgrounds. See Ricardo D. Stanton-Salazar and Stephanie Urso Spina, "Adolescent Peer Networks as a Context for Social and Emotional Support," *Youth & Society* 36, no. 4 (2005): 379–417. The authors focus on the ways in which Latino students discover *confianza* to offer support and buffer against environmental stress

made use of the low threshold to participate in online conversations, empowering greater numbers to access a plurality of voices and activate their own agency to be included among them. However, insofar as cultural meaning is locally created, a more ambiguous shared "space" makes it more difficult to construct and maintain shared beliefs and values necessary to create the moral norms for solidarity. As people spend more and more time online, the wireless enclaves of digital connections can supplement and potentially even become more meaningful than the ties in one's geographical neighborhood.[67] Yet it is also difficult to predict the psychological and sociological effects of being physically in one place but mentally or emotionally present elsewhere. A culture of encounter must overcome any semblance of a "culture of elsewhere" that splits a person's presence between the physical and digital.

Alternatively, digital technology, the internet, and social media help make it possible to demonstrate Christian neighbor love to people across great physical distances. Drawing near to others is no longer contingent upon physical proximity.[68] The "networked self" or "connected self" has more possibilities for solidarity than any previous generation, even in a time of decreasing social capital.[69] People may be opting out of corporeal connections in favor of their screens, but this is still a means of social connection.[70] The danger arises when screens replace—rather than complement—meaningful connections. There are some indications that

---

through peer networks. This corroborates other data illustrating that virtual communities offer a "safe space" for minority groups. For example, research shows that LGBTQ youth are more likely than their heterosexual peers to use the internet to make and sustain friendships. See Tori DeAngelis, "Is Technology Ruining Our Kids?" *Monitor on Psychology* 42, no. 9 (October 2011): 62. This kind of support is important in light of the discrimination, bullying, and even violence youth might face in their local communities.

[67]Some, like Michael Bugeja, are concerned that "cabled enclaves" may ultimately undermine community life, insofar as personal attachments and associations will too easily be reduced to a "cluster" of those who share the same "likes" (Bugeja, *Interpersonal Divide*, 23–28, 99–104). In some cases digital networks reinforce geographical ties, as is the case with the Nextdoor web platform that offers private social networks for specific neighborhoods.

[68]To some extent this has been true since the invention of the telephone. But today's smartphones—owned by more than 80 percent of American adults as of June 2019—combine traditional telephone abilities with digital camera functionality to share images and video. Accordingly, Rich Ling points to these phones as essential for socialization and social cohesion through the ritual interaction of texting, calling, and video conferencing that ultimately "result in social solidarity." See Rich Ling, *New Tech, New Ties: How Mobile Communication Is Reshaping Social Cohesion* (Cambridge, MA: MIT Press, 2008), 83.

[69]See Baym, *Personal Connections in the Digital Age*, 73.

[70]I am not criticizing social disengagement per se, as it can be part of a healthful balance between solitude and sociality. Rather, I use Taylor's emphasis on the pusillanimous social disengagement of the buffered self to critique capricious, inordinate, or irresponsible social disengagement (virtual or physical), especially in the face of another person in need (much like the *antiparechomai* embodied by the priest and Levite in Luke 10:31–32).

the ease of digital interaction will make some people avoid physical interaction, finding it cumbersome and perhaps obsolete.[71] Years ago, it was laughable that people would choose robots over other humans for their romantic partners, but now this is becoming all the more common. A robot will not argue, criticize, or abandon you; neither will a robot say "no" to one's requests, including for sex, among those properly equipped.[72] In the future, a culture of encounter will have to more robustly consider what humans owe intelligent machines as well as whether and how solidarity can be possible with artificial intelligence.[73] In our current context, it is worth contemplating how we speak to digital assistants like Siri and Alexa, since speaking harshly to these nonhuman voices can still establish norms for how we encounter the other. For example, if children observe adults being condescending or rude to a female-voiced digital assistant like Siri or Alexa, they may internalize a sexist disposition that treats women as inferior.

As physical and digital life collide, more connections are possible through a kind of "copresence" that integrates the physical and the digital.[74] A growing number of smartphone apps consult users' geographical location to tailor content to help users become more "location aware" of their physical surroundings, including the people and local businesses nearby.[75] An orientation toward enacting solidarity online could reinforce bonds through a screen among those who happen to live in the same neighborhood.[76] In other cases, being tethered to a screen can impede

---

[71]Sociologist Juliet Schor presciently observed that "Once people become acclimated to the speed of the computer, normal human intercourse becomes laborious." See Juliet Schor, *The Overworked American: The Unexpected Decline of Leisure* (New York: Basic Books, 1991), 23. Song explores whether "face-to-face communities" might be "outdated and obsolete" following higher rates of mobility and divorce which "have progressively weakened the sense of local and familial bonds." She adds, "Even without the internet, it is typical for the modern person to belong to nonlocal social networks that are multiple and specialized rather than solitary and geographically bounded" which contribute to a shift in the sense of community as no longer a "special relation or a kinship group" (Song, *Virtual Communities*, 25).

[72]Turkle, *Alone Together*, 23–147.

[73]Turkle adds a fourth category in her work to "reclaim conversation" that includes artificial intelligence and digital assistants; see Turkle, *Reclaiming Conversation*, 51–53.

[74]Rich Ling concludes, "While the mobile telephone may be fraying the fabric of some co-located social interactions, it seems to be supplementing it in others," especially as they make possible more consistent "connected presence" via multiple, quick check-ins (Ling, *New Tech, New Ties*, 169, 171).

[75]Eric Gordon and Adriana de Souza e Silva point out that since January 2010, Google has been factoring in IP address information or mobile phone GPS coordinates to order search results by users' actual locations. Since that time, smartphone apps—from news services to dining and shopping guides—help digital users become more "location aware" of their physical environment. See Eric Gordon and Adriana de Souza e Silva, *Net Locality: Why Location Matters in a Networked World* (Malden, MA: Blackwell, 2011), 2, 56.

[76]This is precisely what Keith Hampton and Barry Wellman found in their study of one Toronto suburb. See their report, Keith Hampton and Barry Wellman, "Neighboring in Netville: How the Internet Supports Community and Social Capital in a Wired Suburb," *City & Community* 2, no. 4 (December 2003): 277–311. Hampton and Wellman found that online interactions between

respectful and meaningful interaction offline. No one enjoys someone nearby speaking loudly on their phone, and an even more dangerous example is texting while driving, which is so distracting that it produces an impairment similar to being under the influence of drugs or alcohol.[77] It might be easier for parents to give their children a tablet to be distracted while they wait at a restaurant or at the doctor's office, or even to fill time in the car. When children tune out from their surroundings—including their parents and siblings—it robs them of an opportunity to connect with loved ones. At home, the norm is increasingly becoming the case that family members head to their own room to watch their preferred content, losing a chance to take in an episode or movie together (as well as work on the negotiating skills involved in deciding together what to watch), a shared experience and memory that foster the feeling of being connected to each other. Digital tools and structures make more connections possible, but a culture of encounter that increases its scope in range cannot come at the expense of being fully present to those nearby—especially family and friends—who rely on us for attentive listening, supportive words, and gestures of love and acceptance.

A culture of encounter that is mediated through a screen can and should leverage the contacts and connections made possible through "copresence" and "connected presence" that bridge our online and offline relationships. By and large, people are selective in making time for others online, leading to smaller social networks, online and offline.[78] People are also being shaped *by* these technologies and social media, part of the "impact imprint" of using these tools. For example, the lack of facial cues and tone in text and email can impoverish interactions, making it hard to understand the full picture of what the other person is trying to share. Without more practice to read body language and imagine what the other person intends to communicate, people lose important opportunities to develop their emotional and social intelligence.[79] A digitally mediated culture of encounter

---

physical neighbors increased offline interactions compared to neighbors who did not have access to the internet. Hampton found corroborating evidence in a more recent study, described in his essay, "Neighborhoods in the Network Society: The e-Neighbors Study," *Information, Communication & Society* 10 no. 5 (October 2007): 714–48.

[77]John Morgan Wilson, "Texting While Driving Is as Dangerous as Driving Drunk. We Need to Treat It Accordingly," *LA Times*, April 4, 2018.

[78]See the report issued by Miller McPherson, Lynn Smith-Lovin, and Matthew E. Brashears, "Social Isolation in America: Changes in Core Discussion Networks over Two Decades," *American Sociological Review* 71, no. 3 (June 2006): 353–75. The authors find smaller discussion networks from 1985 to 2004, with three times as many people reporting they have no one with whom to discuss important matters, as well as a substantial reduction in kin and non-kin confidants, and fewer contacts through voluntary associations and neighborhoods.

[79]Daniel Goleman outlines how being attentive to others' bodily cues helps us to understand their emotional state and respond appropriately. For example, if someone whispers to us, we automatically whisper back, even regardless of the context. If we fail to heed these cues, we can easily get anxious and awkward, creating a mismatch that is sure to "torpedo rapport." See Daniel Goleman,

should be framed by courage, mercy, generosity, humility, and fidelity. Sticking with the example of text and email, this means applying generosity—giving the other person the benefit of the doubt, for example—in interpreting another person's tone or mood (even if this can be mitigated, in some situations, with emojis).

Digital technology, the internet, and social media are important tools for bringing a culture of encounter into the civic arena, potentially to advance love, justice, and solidarity. They have proven to be powerful tools for advancing democracy, capable of changing the landscape of social and political imaginations. Facebook, Twitter, and YouTube have incredible potential to raise social consciousness. Hashtags collect posts from all over the world, uniting people by shared cause. #BlackLivesMatter and #MeToo have burst the bubbles of those oblivious to racial- and gender-based violence. Even more than raising awareness, these trends have resulted in actual policy and legal changes.[80] The #IceBucketChallenge raised more than $115 million for ALS research, resulting in a medical breakthrough. Hashtags can galvanize support for a range of causes, from mental health to human rights, from environmental protection to interfaith solidarity. Hashtags prominently connect posts as people reflect and respond to tragedies, even if "the half-life of online empathy" is "tragically short."[81] Writing a post, clicking "like" or "favorite," or sharing another post, petition, image, or video can seem like a promising way to overcome the "globalization of indifference." Indeed, for many, this is a first entrée into social and environmental issues that they might not otherwise encounter. Laudable as it is to become more informed, it is important to add that awareness does not automatically generate concern or commitment to creating change. For these reasons, this "hashtag activism" or "clicktivism" is more aptly described as "slacktivism," a simplistic and superficial level of engagement compared to what is required by social or environmental "activism."[82] Digital activism is still largely unilateral, a doing-for rather than a being-with. It does not involve transparency, mutuality, and accountability, as genuine solidarity requires. Because it caters to a person's interests and does not really require them to change their behavior or social location, this temptation to click "like" or "favorite" or "share" is, in the eyes of some, a cowardly act.[83] Moreover, in some cases, "slacktivism" hurts more than

---

Social Intelligence: The New Science of Human Relationships (New York: Bantam Books, 2006), 30.

[80]Janell Ross, "How Black Lives Matter Moved from a Hashtag to a Real Political Force," *Washington Post*, August 19, 2015; Brittany Packnett, "Black Lives Matter Isn't Just a Hashtag Anymore," *Politico*, September/October 2016; Rebecca Beitsch, "#MeToo Has Changed Our Culture. Now It's Changing Our Laws," Pew, July 31, 2018.

[81]Caitlin Dewey, "The Tragically Short Half-Life of Online Empathy," *Washington Post*, November 17, 2015.

[82]For more on "slacktivism," see Laura Seay, "Does Slacktivism Work?" *Washington Post*, March 12, 2014.

[83]In an essay adapted from the commencement address he gave at Kenyon College, Jonathan

it helps, since it convinces people they have fulfilled their social duty by adding a filter to their profile picture or sharing an article or petition, without taking more action to support what is needed on the ground or draw near to others in need.[84]

If digital users do not move from awareness to meaningful, responsible action for justice and peace, it will not be possible to resist the "spectator culture" that produces more bystanders than activists. "Spectator culture" relies on endless entertainment, streaming videos, and social media algorithms to produce the exact kind of newsfeed that will spark your interest and engagement (this is what advertisers are paying for, after all). While the internet and social media can be powerful tools to connect people to new content and connections, it can also be used as a crutch for mindless diversion, a way to "amuse ourselves to death."[85] Screens can appease, buffer, and disempower; users can choose to engage only what entertains and/or confirms their worldview without confronting other content or connections that might challenge them. This allows people to ignore other parts of reality or even hide from it. Elisabeth Vasko explains that Christians have a moral responsibility to confront the reality of "sin as hiding" via "apathy and mindless conformity." This can be seen in some versions of life mediated through a screen that function as a hiding "from God, one another, and ourselves" in a "lack of self-assertion" and segregation by participating "in the ongoing creation of separate and unequal worlds. Privilege creates myopic vision wherein the periphery is hidden from view. It encourages a culture of escapism where time and attention are delivered from the suffering of others to the trivial."[86] A culture of encounter is undermined by escapism and entertainment, a "spectator culture" that renders people bystanders and observers, rather than active participants. A culture of encounter relies on intimacy, rapport, and love through a willingness to be vulnerable. While digital technology, the internet, and social media can provide gateways to share new perspectives, practice vulnerability and intimacy,

---

Franzen laments the Facebook "like" as a cowardly way to avoid controversy and rejection. He writes, "since our technology is really just an extension of ourselves, we don't have to have contempt for its manipulability in the way we might with actual people. It's all one big endless loop. We like the mirror and the mirror likes us. To friend a person is merely to include the person in our private hall of flattering mirrors." Love, on the other hand, splatters dirt "on the mirror of our self-regard." See Jonathan Franzen, "Liking Is for Cowards. Go for What Hurts," *New York Times*, May 28, 2011.

[84]Shaunacy Ferro, "Just Liking a Cause Doesn't Help: Internet Slacktivism Harms Charities," *Popular Science*, November 8, 2013.

[85]This was Neil Postman's concern about television in *Amusing Ourselves to Death: Public Discourse in the Age of Show Business* (New York: Penguin, 1985). But at least with television programs, people would have something to talk about as a shared social experience (given limited channels and programs from which to choose), whereas streaming platforms and YouTube make it possible for people to watch only what interests them, which may undermine shared engagement across differences.

[86]Elisabeth Vasko, *Beyond Apathy: A Theology for Bystanders* (Minneapolis: Fortress Press, 2015), 143–44.

and cultivate rapport, these experiences find more traction when they lead to or flow from interactions and experiences offline. Digitally mediated interactions can be helpful for those who do not have access to such encounters in their physical surroundings, but the former should not replace the latter.

These concerns do not imply a Luddite rejection of technology, but they do temper hopes that digital connections can make up for the collapse of community and the decline of social capital in America. While the potential for meaningful and diverse connections is latent in these digital tools and structures, the reality is that countless hours are spent shopping, gaming, and consuming sports, movies, and other forms of entertainment in ways that do not require substantial interaction with others. Robert Putnam's theory about the decline of social capital in the United States made an exception for the capital forged through online groups.[87] Some studies have shown that the internet and social media increase civic engagement.[88] Leveraging the "fandom" of those with shared interests—whether a YouTube channel, sports team, consumer product, or hashtag campaign—will be a vital way to cultivate civic identity and community going forward.[89] At issue is Putnam's "time displacement hypothesis" for determining whether digital technology, the internet, and social media contribute to or detract from social capital. This depends on whether digitally mediated content and connections replace or supplement offline interactions, and if these digital platforms can take the step from shared interest to the rapport and accountability necessary for long-term, sustainable commitments.[90]

Digital tools and structures have to be considered as extensions of the market economy. This is what Pope Francis signals in warning about the effects of the "technocratic paradigm" that conditions users to cycles of production and con-

---

[87]Putnam alleges, "Social capital is about networks and the Net is the network to end all networks." See Robert Putnam, *Bowling Alone: The Collapse and Revival of American Community* (New York: Simon & Schuster, 2001), 171.

[88]See Aaron Smith, "Civic Engagement in the Digital Age," Pew Research Center, April 25, 2013, http://www.pewinternet.org/Reports/2013/Civic-Engagement/Summary-of-Findings.aspx.

[89]See the insightful—and hopeful—analysis of Ashley Hinck's *Politics for the Love of Fandom: Fan-Based Citizenship in a Digital World* (Baton Rouge: Louisiana State University Press, 2019).

[90]This is not to suggest that bridging these virtual and corporeal connections is always to be desired, especially if trying to engage both at the same time, which is usually to the detriment of one or both. It should also be noted there are different motives for making these connections and different kinds of connections. For example, Putnam distinguishes "weak ties" from "strong ties." Weak ties require less maintenance but also offer less support than strong ties. Updating Putnam, strong ties are those that experience regular contact online and offline, whereas weak ties typically share less of one or even both. Felicia Wu Song is among several scholars who explore these different kinds of connections—including "latent ties"—to consider the impact of virtual connections on them. She concludes that it is a mistake to pit online and offline ties against each other, given the hybrid nature of most Americans' interactions today. See Song, *Virtual Communities*, 13–21.

sumption to maximize profits for stockholders.[91] Digital technology and social media are designed to produce revenue and user data to make advertising ever more effective in increasing market share. The logic of the market caters to "networked individualism," which orients users to "public life in terms of personal fulfillment, rather than viewing personal fulfillment in terms of public life."[92] Digital technology, the internet, and social media thereby "promote a culture of autonomy and choice that not only appeals to people but also makes them efficacious." However, given the "inexorable role that the market plays in both shaping the community and its members," it is possible that the "very dynamics of this autonomy and choice will reduce the civic sphere to a state of consumption built upon a foundation of self-interest." This leads to the conclusion that "the strengths and most exciting characteristics of virtual communities are, in turn, the greatest weaknesses that threaten to undermine their democratic potential."[93] Put differently, those who tout the many advantages of increased rates of connectivity need to more closely examine the kinds of contacts, content, and connections being engaged, especially in a context so heavily tipped toward consumption. This is one way that Taylor's "buffered self" becomes the "networked self" who sits at the center of one's own community of choice, opting in and out at will. A culture of encounter and especially the aspiration for an inclusive culture of belonging pivot on the ability of individuals to show up to others' experiences, to be curious about their lives and invested in their well-being. It means fostering relationships of mutual respect and responsibility, ensuring transparency and accountability. This involves examining the motives, methods, and goals of our digital activity and evaluating to what extent this models courage, mercy, generosity, humility, and fidelity.

When social media serves as a bridge to connect people in mutual engagement and accountability, it makes it possible to create new spaces for shared knowledge and expands the boundaries for community. When used virtuously, it can positively influence identity, relationships, and social capital. This means disrupting market forces to produce and consume content based on interest (and potential for making a purchase), and instead using it to resist the spectator culture that puts

---

[91]Pope Francis, *Laudato Si'*, nos. 109–112 (hereinafter *LS*).

[92]Song, *Virtual Communities*, 129. Song continues, "virtual communities do not so much introduce a completely new dynamic of membership to the public sphere but actually reinforce a set of assumptions about the self and community that . . . becomes fully realizable and augmented in radically new ways through the novel experiences of social interaction and collective action online. The technology itself functions to grant further legitimacy as its design and configuration implicitly justify and 'hardwire' these assumptions into the very entities we choose to call 'communities' " (ibid., 130).

[93]Song adds, "If virtual communities are to be the harbingers of the future, then their greatest service to American public life may be to function as canaries in a coal mine" (ibid., 129).

entertainment and convenience ahead of human dignity, rights and responsibilities, love and justice, solidarity and the common good. Users should consider their choices of what content and connections fill their time, who benefits from these choices, and who suffers as a result of them.[94] They should reflect and discern whether and how their time with a screen helps or hinders a healthy sense of identity, the quality of their relationships with others, and to what extent it helps them to encounter others across differences. Recall that Luke's presentation of Jesus's story about the Samaritan should not be separated from Jesus's visit with Mary and Martha (10:38–42). In that visit, Martha's busyness distracts her from what really matters (being present to her guest, Jesus). Today, we might consider how we are distracted by screens in a way that makes it easier to miss opportunities to love God and neighbor.

A digitally mediated culture of encounter is further tasked with trying to reconcile the "digital divide," or the inequalities in technological access, resources, and literacy. Although progress is being made in resolving some of these asymmetries, a more nuanced view sheds light on the work left to be done.[95] Instead of thinking in terms of a binary divide between the "tech haves" and the "tech have nots," it is more accurate to think in terms of a continuum of technological access, resources, and literacy.[96] These disparities—which can be found across gender, age, race and ethnicity, and physical ability—provide a sobering contrast experience to much of what is consumed and produced by digital users in the United States. If the majority of what one reads, sees, and responds to is related to shopping, entertainment, fashion, sports, or gaming, it is hard to make room for more serious matters. Given the widespread reports of the self-absorbed state of being of

---

[94]These questions (Who decides? Who benefits? Who suffers?) come from a model of social analysis developed by Joe Holland and Peter Henriot, *Social Analysis: Linking Faith and Justice* (Maryknoll, NY: Orbis Books, 1980), 28.

[95]Some have simply called for more digital tools and internet access in developing countries, and although this is happening, it does not always ameliorate the situation on the ground. Pippa Norris offers a more developed account of the "digital divide" in three parts: (1) the global divide between industrialized and developing nations, (2) the social divide between those with or without access in each country, (3) the democratic divide between those who do or do not use digital technology and social media to participate in public life. A more effective approach responds to all these issues, taking into consideration the desires of the people involved. See Pippa Norris, *Digital Divide* (Cambridge: Cambridge University Press, 2001), 4.

[96]See Mark Warschauer, *Technology and Social Inclusion: Rethinking the Digital Divide* (Cambridge, MA: MIT Press, 2003), 6. Warschauer also notes that the rhetoric of the "digital divide" can be patronizing and exclusionary, if not overly simplistic. Taking into account the real disparities in technological access, resources, and literacy at the micro-, meso-, and macrolevels, Warschauer proposes several helpful strategies to marshal screens for social inclusion, including leveraging the resources and connections already in place as well as designing digital technologies and social media to encourage prosocial motives and behaviors (ibid., 163, 210–11).

the networked self, experiences of deprivation and suffering may be the kind of wake-up call to social consciousness and social commitments that many people of privilege and security need.[97] This raises the question of "virtual morality," which requires more deliberate thought and action than the impulse of picking up one's phone to fill time. Insofar as the networked self is conditioned more by personal interests than geographical place, and more by consumer sovereignty than social bonds, this underscores the need for a more robustly shared moral culture that includes well-established foundations for moral obligation.[98] This requires attention to the personal and social formation that happens by adapting to these tools and methods for connection, how we modify these technologies, and the "impact imprint" of engaging these resources, practices, relationships, and the resulting "virtual morality."[99]

The digital realm is a crucial place for a culture of encounter to take place. This is not only because it is where we spend so many of our waking hours, but also because it is an important arena for individuals and communities to exercise agency, learn about and interact with others, and discover what we share in common. The "networked publics" are important opportunities for exchange across a number of differences, from race to religion, class to age. But given the way social media are designed for greater homogenization than heterogenization,[100] it takes a concerted effort to make these "networked publics" places of equity and diversity.[101] This means that the "flaming" and echo chambers that exacerbate social separation have to be battled with more than civility and tolerance. It is not enough to just make room for others with whom we disagree. Although this is a good first step, it is insufficient for healing the wounds that degrade and exclude. A more virtuous

[97]It cannot be overstated how necessary it is to confront the dangers of self-absorption. Daniel Goleman insists, "Self-absorption in all its forms kills empathy, let alone compassion. When we focus on ourselves, our world contracts as our problems and preoccupations loom large. But when we focus on others, our world expands. Our own problems drift to the periphery of the mind and so seem smaller, and we increase our capacity for connection—or compassionate action" (Goleman, *Social Intelligence*, 54).

[98]Song contends that the narrative of communal decline cannot be reduced to the structural erosion of local neighborhoods and civic life, because this is also a result in a significant shift in people's beliefs and values about public life. In fact, she wagers, "the more significant shift may lie in the *very meaning* of communal action and civic practices" (Song, *Virtual Communities*, 64).

[99]Song posits, "What this technology gives us, then, is a means of adapting our existing relationships to challenges posed by the social realities of geographic distance and the task-cluttered lives that contemporary Americans seem to have. The irony, however, is that while these technologies help us confront the challenges of modernity in these ways, they also serve to exacerbate these conditions and even radicalize them" (ibid., 136).

[100]Dan Rockmore, "Getting to Know Your Online Doppleganger," *The Atlantic*, May 22, 2017.

[101]danah boyd, *It's Complicated: The Social Lives of Networked Teens* (New Haven, CT: Yale University Press, 2014), 31.

approach to digital tools and structures requires the same disciplines discussed in the previous chapter: courage in risking vulnerability and changing one's own behavior; mercy in acknowledging one's bias and blind spots; generosity in giving others the benefit of the doubt (especially via text and email); humility in forming a *habitus* for prudent and temperate uses of technology among one's family and friends; and fidelity in trying to reconcile bonds that have been broken by stigma and shame, hatred and fear-mongering. In this way, we can better use these tools for collective flourishing for the common good, not just to kill time.

A digitally mediated culture of encounter begins with a commitment to use these tools and participate in these structures with respect for self and others. It means fighting the temptation to post anything that one would not say or share in person, to "tweet at others the way you would want to be tweeted," for example. It means refusing to hide behind the anonymity afforded by the internet, unless it is necessary for one's personal safety or mental health. It means authentically and gently sharing what you honestly believe and being willing to listen to those with whom you disagree. It means being more intentionally diverse in the content and connections that fill your time; as you scroll through the people you follow, ask yourself how many of them belong to the same social groupings by sex, gender, and sexual orientation; race, ethnicity, and nationality; age group and ability; class, political affiliation, and religion. What can you learn by following others who see the world differently than you do, because of their identity or experiences? How can you help broaden others' horizons by sharing content that your friends and followers might otherwise miss?

A digitally mediated culture of encounter also requires a consciousness that serious conversations—whether about personal or political matters—are seldom successfully accomplished online. If you have an issue with someone, it is better to call or speak in person than write to or about that person online. A culture of encounter aims for mutuality and accountability, and this requires equal partnership in power sharing. How do you use your time with a screen or your social media platform to bring more love, peace, and justice into the world? People should consider how they—and the virtual communities they join—share images and messages about worthiness and belonging. How do they love their digital neighbors? By being a neighbor to those in need, showing up and sharing life with those on the margins, and advocating for the kinds of relationships, practices, and structures that reconcile social sins like discrimination, exclusion, and unjust inequalities. It is on all of us to use digital technology, the internet, and social media as tools for more inclusive solidarity and justice in our networks and in our world, online as well as offline. Sometimes, this also means putting our screens away so that we can draw near others, mediating tenderness and solidarity through physical interaction and relying less on the virtual.

ENCOUNTERING NATURE FOR INTEGRAL SOLIDARITY

Given the escalating destruction of Earth's life systems, it is easy to identify climate change as one of the most important moral issues of our time. Not only is there scientific consensus that these changes are caused by human activity, but human indifference to this issue exacerbates many related trends: habitat destruction and the extinction of species, the warming and rising of oceans, worsening drought and flooding as well as other extreme weather conditions, pollution and exploitation of natural resources, and other conditions that are forcing human and nonhuman species to migrate.[102] News about climate change is grim: the UN Convention on Biological Diversity concludes that up to 150 species are made extinct on a daily basis to due climate change and habitat loss.[103] Over 140 million people are or will soon be forced to migrate because of problems related to crop failure, water shortage, and sea-level rise.[104] A 2015 study by the Institute for Environment and Human Security of the United Nations University predicted that between two hundred million and one billion humans will be climate refugees by 2050.[105] Among those affected now, the poor—mostly women and children—are impacted by climate change first and worst. These are just some of the human and nonhuman costs to climate change caused by overconsumption, burning fossil fuels, the clearing of land for agriculture and industry, and methane emissions from cattle. One of the best ways to reduce one's carbon footprint, in fact, is to eat less meat.[106]

The "globalization of indifference" to human suffering that Pope Francis laments extends to environmental issues as well. The University of Chicago found that only 36 percent of Americans identify global warming as a "moral issue," and nearly 40 percent reported that they are "not too worried" about its effects.[107] Globally, only 54 percent consider climate change a "very serious problem."[108]

---

[102]For an overview of the scientific evidence, causes, effects, and frequently asked questions about climate change, see https://climate.nasa.gov/evidence/ and related webpages.

[103]https://www.cbd.int/doc/speech/2007/sp-2007-05-22-es-en.pdf.

[104]Laura Parker, "143 Million People May Soon Become Climate Refugees," *National Geographic*, March 19, 2018.

[105]Baher Kamal, "Climate Migrants Might Reach One Billion by 2050," Inter Press Service News Agency, August 21, 2017.

[106]Oliver Milman, "Why Eating Less Meat Is the Best Thing You Can Do for the Planet in 2019," *The Guardian*, December 21, 2018.

[107]"American Attitudes toward the Pope Following His Visit to the United States," Associated Press–NORC Center for Public Affairs Research, November 3, 2015.

[108]Bruce Stokes, Richard Wike, and Jill Carle, "Global Concern about Climate Change, Broad Support for Limiting Emissions," Pew Research Center, November 5, 2015.

Widespread human ignorance or apathy only makes matters worse. Moreover, it points to a vicious anthropocentrism that places humanity at the top and center of creation, instead of bound together with it, in a mode of interdependence. In some regards, Christianity has contributed to a posture of domination over nature, rather than respect and responsibility for it, in the spirit of stewardship.[109] Even today, some Christians presumptuously believe that "God will save us" from the mess that we have made on Earth, even though such an intervention would violate the credibility (and accountability) of free will. Too many Christians remain unfazed by the suffering and destruction caused by unchecked human production and consumption.[110]

Human exploitation, degradation, and pollution are examples of sinning against the Creator (who made everything "good"), our neighbors (including those who will follow us, forced to suffer from the consequences of our decisions and inaction), and nonhuman creation. Sinful social structures impede the moral perception, desires, and agencies of people and communities. While his 2015 encyclical *Laudato Si'* does not explore these structures of moral formation and deformation, Pope Francis's call to resist "throwaway culture" and build a culture of encounter for a culture of solidarity is a crucial path to reconcile the breach between humanity and nonhuman creation, restoring right relationship, love, justice, peace, and sustainability in order to integrate solidarity with the entire created order.

Nearly thirty years ago, Pope John Paul II declared that "Christians, in particular, realize that their responsibility within creation and their duty towards nature and the Creator are an essential part of their faith."[111] These and other statements were echoed by Pope Benedict XVI, dubbed "the Green Pope" by secular media for his consistent emphasis on care for creation as central to discipleship.[112] Even more than his predecessors, Pope Francis has highlighted the links between love of God, neighbor, and ecological solidarity. For example, in *Evangelii Gaudium,* he reflects,

> There are other weak and defenseless beings who are frequently at the mercy of economic interests or indiscriminate exploitation. I am speaking of creation as a whole. We human beings are not only the beneficiaries but also the stewards of other creatures. Thanks to our bodies, God has joined us so closely to the world around us that we can feel the desertification of the soil almost as a physical ailment, and the extinction of a species as a

---

[109]Lynn White Jr., "The Historical Roots of Our Ecologic Crisis" *Science* 155 (March 10, 1967): 1203.

[110]John M. Clements, Chenyang Xiao, and Aaron M. McCright, "An Examination of the 'Greening of Christianity' Thesis among Americans, 1993–2010," *Journal for the Scientific Study of Religion* 53, no. 2 (June 2014): 373–91.

[111]John Paul II, "Peace with God the Creator, Peace with All of Creation," January 1, 1990, no. 15.

[112]Daniel Stone, "Benedict XVI, The Green Pope," *Newsweek,* April 16, 2008.

painful disfigurement. Let us not leave in our wake a swath of destruction and death which will affect our own lives and those of future generations.[113]

In 2015, Pope Francis released the first-ever encyclical focusing largely on the environment. He urged Catholics, Christians, and all people of good will to hear both the "cry of the earth and the cry of the poor."[114] In this document, *Laudato Si'*, "On Care for Our Common Home," Pope Francis alludes to solidarity more than a dozen times, a solidarity that calls every community to honor their "duty to protect the Earth and to ensure its fruitfulness for coming generations."[115] Francis wonders how humans will be judged based on the commandment, "Thou shall not kill" when "twenty percent of the world's population consumes resources at a rate that robs the poor nations and future generations of what they need to survive."[116] He then dedicates six paragraphs to calling for an "ecological conversion" to acknowledge our sinful excess and indifference that are expressions of our irresponsibility before God, neighbor, and nonhuman creation.[117] This conversion begins within, with a spirituality rooted in a sense of God's love for us strong enough to overcome the temptation to buy our way to contentment, acceptance, or social status. He quotes a 2005 homily from Pope Benedict XVI: "The external deserts in the world are growing, because the internal deserts have become so vast."[118] As with social separation and unjust inequalities, for any progress to be made, individuals will have to make conscious choices to live their way into new patterns of being courageous, merciful, generous, humble, and faithful. Francis beseeches us to exercise creativity and enthusiasm in trying to address these environmental problems, even if they exist on a global scale.

A culture of encounter has to include an encounter with the natural world, which is always and everywhere around us. This is a call to move beyond human neighbors to embrace the nonhuman members of creation as well. Nature is a sacrament of God's presence and activity in the world. Wonder and awe might be more easily generated by stunning sunrises or sunsets, a pristine beach, or gorgeous flowers, but every element and detail of the created order reflect the loving artistry of God, who ushered everything into existence. Drawing near to nature—putting away our screens, taking a pause from our busy and rushed routines—can put us in touch with God who delights in every dimension of creation. As ecotheologian Thomas Berry reflects, an encounter with nature is an opportunity to experience

[113] *Evangelii Gaudium*, no. 56.
[114] *LS*, no. 49.
[115] Ibid., no. 67.
[116] Ibid., no. 95.
[117] Ibid., nos. 216–21.
[118] Ibid., no. 217.

intimacy and rapport with the Earth community, feeling "wonder and beauty and the full depth of its meaning" to enable "an integral human relationship with the planet." He continues, "The fulfillment of the Earth community is to be caught up in the grandeur of existence itself and in admiration of those mysterious powers whence all this has emerged. Nourishment of both the outer body and the inner spirit will be achieved in intimate association with each other or not at all."[119]

A personal and physical encounter with nature can help mend humanity's broken relationship with nonhuman creation because being in and with nature—plants, animals, the environment—has the potential to generate feelings of tenderness and unity with nonhuman creation. This reflects Jesus's own encounter with nature in his journey into the desert after his baptism and before beginning his public teaching and healing ministry. The gospels recount that Jesus went out to pray among the "wild beasts" (Mk 1:12–13), where he likely sought perspective, peace, and purpose in this retreat-like experience. As Berry explains, to encounter nature is "to establish a rapport among the divine, the natural, and the human."[120] Feeling connected with nature is instructive for knowing ourselves as members of creation, learning about the rest of the created order, and experiencing God who reveals Godself as both immanent and transcendent, or "above all and through all and in all" (Eph 4:6). It also reminds us that God made human beings responsible to "cultivate and care for" creation (Gn 2:15) and holds us accountable as covenant partners with God and other humans as well as "every living creature" (Gn 9:9–10).

Encountering nature can produce wonder and awe at the intricacy and enormity of the natural world, which reaches back 4 billion years and includes 8.7 million species (6.5 million species on Earth, 2.2 million species in the sea), all dynamically evolving and complexly interconnected.[121] To encounter the natural world offers the humbling perspective that these creatures and elements existed long before, and in most cases, will long outlast any human resident. This provides a stark contrast experience to the ecological degradation and waste produced by human activity. Countries like the United States disproportionately consume natural

---

[119]Thomas Berry, *The Great Work: Our Way into the Future* (New York: Broadway, 2000), xi.

[120]Thomas Berry, "The Universe as Divine Manifestation," in *The Sacred Universe: Earth, Spirituality, and Religion in the Twenty-first Century*, ed. Mary Evelyn Tucker (New York: Columbia University Press, 2009), 146.

[121]Carl Sagan offers a sobering perspective: if one were to map out the history of the cosmos in a calendar year, beginning with the Big Bang on January 1, the sun and planets wouldn't come into existence until early September, dinosaurs appear on Christmas Eve, and the first humans don't show up until December 31 at 10:30 pm. "All recorded history occupies the last ten seconds of December 31." See Carl Sagan, *The Dragons of Eden: Speculations on the Evolution of Human Intelligence* (New York: Ballantine Books, 1977), 17.

resources; some estimates suggest that if everyone on the planet consumed at the rate of an American, we would need at least six planet Earths worth of resources. As a result of this exploitation and pollution, from 1975 to 2000, 10 percent of all living species went extinct.[122] Those of us who are buffered from this kind of environmental suffering may be blind and deaf to such harmful experiences, which is why theologians like Ivone Gebara call for a greater sense of ecological relatedness as "the primary reality" that is "constitutive of all things."[123] Leonardo Boff insists, "Only a personal relationship with Earth makes us love it. We do not exploit but respect and reverence the one we love."[124] Tenderness and solidarity are impossible without a personal encounter. In other words, Pope Francis's call for an "ecological conversion" will remain unrealized unless and until people encounter the natural world firsthand.

Ecological conversion will require courage, mercy, generosity, humility, and fidelity. It will also require "doing likewise" as the Samaritan. This may seem surprising, since there is no ecological concern in Luke's passage. But as Hart indicates, this story is about right relationship with God and others, intended to expand the definition of neighbor, and transforming the concept of neighbor from object to subject. In other words, through this story, Jesus demonstrates that the proper question is not "Who is my neighbor?" but rather "To whom am I neighbor?"[125] If such a boundary-breaking shift can extend neighbor love to humans previously considered to be nonneighbors or enemies, can it also be extended to nonhuman creation?

Hart contends that a major point of this parable is to replace the limit-seeking question of the lawyer ("Who is my neighbor?" implies a nonneighbor to whom I owe less or perhaps even nothing at all) with the boundary-breaking, loving-without-limit example of the Samaritan being a neighbor. He writes,

> Jesus teaches that people should not await someone's cry for help to respond to a call to be a neighbor; they should make themselves neighbors to those who need them. From the parable might be drawn two ideas for ecological ethics: first, assist those who are in need; second, choose to be consistently a neighbor to others. Humans are not the only neighbors who are suffering

[122]One study finds that species extinction is one thousand times worse because of human activity. See S. L. Pimm et al., "The Biodiversity of Species and Their Rates of Extinction, Distribution, and Protection," *Science* 344:6187 (May 30, 2014): 1246752.

[123]Ivone Gebara, *Out of the Depths: Women's Experience of Evil and Salvation*, trans. Ann Patrick Ware (Minneapolis: Fortress Press, 2002), 98.

[124]Leonardo Boff, *Cry of the Earth, Cry of the Poor*, trans. Phillip Berryman (Maryknoll, NY: Orbis Books, 1997), 118.

[125]Canon Morris, *The Gospel According to St. Luke* (Grand Rapids: Eerdmans, 1974), 190.

> and need help. Earth and the biotic community are in crisis and in need of assistance. People are called to make themselves neighbors to humankind, to Earth, and to extended biokind.[126]

The Samaritan's example provides an imaginative framework for each of us to consider how we can be neighbors to nature. This paradigm situates Christian neighbor love within creation, not above it. This better reflects the interdependence of the created order, Earth's life systems, on which humans desperately rely. This is a belonging that is "prior to our choice." If we ignore or reject this bond with nature, it will be "at our peril" because we belong to all creation "as part of our sanctification, for this realm of nature ultimately is destined to be filled with Christ's life (Ephesians 1:10, 23)."[127] To clarify, interdependence is not reducible to interrelationship or equality. I do not argue for ecological kinship or egalitarianism, as some do.[128] Nevertheless, humans bear a special responsibility "to be a reflection of the ultimate Lover, to be one who loves *all* that God loves—which covers 'all that participates in being.'" Because "God's love is unbounded, loyal Christian love is similarly inclusive or universal. This love resists confinement of any sort."[129] That human love ought to reflect divine love is an inspiring ideal, but it does not account for the realities of finitude and sin.[130] As noted earlier, prudence will be crucial for helping each person to discern what is within their capacities, no more and no less.

A culture of encounter that includes nature must obviously begin by drawing near to the natural world. This should also include drawing near to those who are most negatively impacted by Earth's deteriorating life systems. Environmental

---

[126]John Hart, *Sacramental Commons: Christian Ecological Ethics* (Lanham, MD: Rowman & Littlefield, 2006), 218–19 (emphasis removed).

[127]Edward Vacek, *Love, Human and Divine* (Washington, DC: Georgetown University Press, 1994), 81, 82.

[128]For example, Thomas Berry writes, "On the planet earth, all living things are clearly derived from a single origin. We are literally born as a community; the trees, the birds, and all living creatures are bonded together in a single community of life. This again gives us a sense that we belong. Community is not something that we dream up or think would be nice. Literally, we are a single community. The planet earth is a single community of existence, and we exist in this context." See Thomas Berry, *Befriending the Earth* (Mystic, CT: Twenty-Third Publications, 1991), 14–15.

[129]James Nash, *Loving Nature: Ecological Integrity and Christian Responsibility* (Nashville: Abingdon, 1991), 141–42.

[130]Nash tries to account for this romantic and rather abstract claim by arguing for and describing love of nature in terms of beneficence, other-esteem or empathy, receptivity, humility, understanding, and communion (ibid., 151–61). He accounts for sin elsewhere, describing it in an ecological context as "the refusal to act in the image of God, as responsible representatives who value and love the host of interdependent creatures in their ecosystems, which the Creator values and loves." The result of sin is the "breaking of bonds with God and our comrades in creation" (ibid., 118–19).

racism results in people of color and indigenous communities often bearing the worst effects of environmental degradation.[131]

When this is not possible firsthand, an environmental culture of encounter can also make use of digital technology, the internet, and social media to approximate this encounter through learning about nature or advocating on its behalf.[132] It can use these technologies to lift up voices of marginalized people who are not always cited in mainstream media.[133] Collecting narratives from the margins, especially of those impacted by climate change, can help educate those who might be skeptical about the gravity or scope of the environmental crises, which is particularly important in the United States, given Americans' "increasing distrust of science."[134] Digital contacts and networks might be effective in overcoming what Pope Francis laments as widespread "self-absorption and a lack of commitment" and the "absence of peace with God, with our neighbor, and with the environment."[135] This is an important step because one of the difficulties in trying to galvanize support for environmental responsibility is that the scale of the problem makes it hard to know where to begin. And without a clear "identifiable victim" to help, the issue seems more abstract than concrete to many people.[136] A culture of encounter with the natural world is oriented toward a common good that integrates sustainability and solidarity with the Earth, taking seriously not just the dignity of creation, but "Earth rights" as well as human rights.[137] It understands what is good for humans as interdependent with the order of the entire cosmos,[138] a "planetary common

---

[131]Vann R. Newkirk II, "Trump's EPA Concludes Environmental Racism Is Real," *The Atlantic*, February 28, 2018.

[132]Examples include protecting mangroves in Singapore or whales off the coast of Japan and documenting the appearance of certain endangered species in North America. See, for example, the article by Daniel R. Richards and Daniel A. Friess, "A Rapid Indicator of Cultural Ecosystem Service Usage at a Fine Spatial Scale: Content Analysis of Social Media Photographs," *Ecological Indicators* 53 (June 2015): 187–95; and John Still, "Five Greenpeace Campaigns against Companies: Lego, Barbie, and Shell," *The Guardian*, August 7, 2014.

[133]One example would be the Navajo Nation in Arizona, whose people are climate refugees now that their land is being overrun by sand dunes. See Laurel Morales, "Navajo Nation Witnesses Changing Landscapes: Growing Sand Dunes," NPR, May 28, 2015.

[134]Aaron Blake, "Americans' Increasing Distrust of Science—and Not Just on Climate Change," *Washington Post*, January 30, 2015.

[135]See, for example, his 2016 World Day of Peace Message, "Overcome Indifference and Win Peace," January 1, 2016, no. 3, w2.vatican.va.

[136]P. Sol Hart, Dan Lane, and Sedona Chinn, "The Elusive Power of the Individual Victim: Failure to Find a Difference in the Effectiveness of Charitable Appeals Focused on One Compared to Many Victims," *PloS ONE* 13, no. 7 (July 18, 2018).

[137]Daniel P. Scheid, *The Cosmic Common Good: Religious Grounds for Ecological Ethics* (Oxford: Oxford University Press, 2016), 6, 24.

[138]Pope John Paul II, "Peace with God the Creator, Peace with All Creation," 1990, no. 8, w2.vatican.va.

good,"[139] seeking the flourishing of all life and all creation.[140] This commitment to the global common good defies both presumption and despair. It requires that each and every person work to break down ignorance and indifference. It hinges upon long-term, sustainable collaboration among families and neighborhoods, schools and churches, business and government.

As Pope Francis has observed, formation takes place not through mere connection but through true encounter.[141] True encounter requires sharing time and space together; it involves an intentional, mutual exchange that expands one's cognitive perspective and emotional state to the extent that it invites a change within and among those involved. A culture of encounter with nature means that we try to be more proactive about our carbon footprints and make a more concerted effort to reduce the environmental impact of our lifestyles, in the spirit of accountability. It also includes advocating for legislation that limits environmental degradation, conserves natural resources, and protects fragile ecosystems, habitats, and species. It sees nature not just as a gift for enjoyment or profit but as a sacrament of God's presence and continuing activity in the world.

The ethics of encounter with the natural world is framed by courage, mercy, generosity, humility, and fidelity. It exercises courage in making hard choices to reduce one's carbon footprint.[142] This must also involve the courageous reduction in one's pattern of consumption, as capitalism deserves the most blame for environmental degradation.[143] Mercy for nonhuman creation will help Christians more consistently practice respect for all life. This includes standing up for water rights, which are essential for all life.[144] It also means rebuffing a kind of "speciesism" that puts humanity at the center and above other members of creation, including animals.[145] Generosity can take the shape of direct aid to those in need or in being willing to pay more for products that are socially and environmentally responsible.[146] Humility and fidelity reinforce bonds of interdependence, starting

---

[139]US Conference of Catholic Bishops, "Renewing the Earth," 1991.

[140]US Conference of Catholic Bishops, "Global Climate Change: A Plea for Dialogue, Prudence, and the Common Good," 2001.

[141]Pope Francis, "World Communications Day," June 1, 2014, w2.vatican.va.

[142]This can be done at the following website: https://www.carbonfootprint.com/calculator.aspx/.

[143]Simon Pirani, *Burning Up: A Global History of Fossil Fuel Consumption* (London: Pluto Press, 2018).

[144]Christiana Zenner describes access to clean drinking water—which one in ten people on the planet do not have—as a "right-to-life issue" in *Just Water: Theology, Ethics, and Fresh Water Crises*, rev. ed. (Maryknoll, NY: Orbis Books, 2018), 68–85.

[145]Charles Camosy, *For Love of Animals: Christian Ethics, Consistent Action* (Cincinnati, OH: Franciscan Media, 2013), 11–13. Camosy writes that this is a matter of justice, "being consistent and impartial," and that it is wrong to discriminate between animal species we love (like dogs) and kill to eat (like pigs).

[146]For a ranking of the most socially and environmentally responsible companies, see https://betterworldshopper.org/.

with those most estranged from us. If humility finds even the "lowliest human as an equal," perhaps it can inspire more people to find all creatures as worthy of moral consideration.[147] This is an important step toward making the "cry of the earth and the cry of the poor" our cry as well. These virtues inspire a commitment to compensate for a history of weak responses to climate crises as well as a shared commitment to build "a legal framework that can set clear boundaries and ensure the protection of ecosystems" for freedom, peace, and justice in our political systems.[148] Pope Francis calls for gestures of generosity, solidarity, and love in order to work in a spirit of "tenderness in protecting this world, which God has entrusted to us."[149] Following this line of thinking, one can begin to imagine the changes that might take place if more people embraced nature love as an extension of neighbor love: expanding recycling programs; ending or at least constraining the (extremely profitable yet wasteful) practice of selling bottled water; decreasing toxic waste and more properly disposing of it; limiting pesticides and fertilizers and using ones that are less hazardous to the environment; donating to preserve local habitats and protect endangered species; advocating to end hazardous practices like mountain-top removal mining and fracking, offering direct aid and advocacy for present and future victims of climate change, including those forced to migrate; promoting energy efficiency; and rewarding economic practices and policies that are sustainable, rather than profit driven.[150]

Nature is a special place to encounter the Divine in our midst, just as Jesus's time away from civilization left him "filled with the power of the Holy Spirit" (Lk 4:14). Certainly, the natural world can also be discovered in urban settings; we are charged to care for the entire natural order, not just pristine forests and streams, majestic mountain ranges and lakes. This includes all plants, animals, and insects that comprise our complex and interdependent ecosystem as well. The creation story in Genesis reminds us that humanity could not be created until the rest of creation was well in place, a nod to our dependency on Earth's dynamic and sometimes delicate life systems. When it is appropriate, an ecological encounter means using digital technology, the internet, and social media to facilitate love for and solidarity through wonder and awe, gratitude and responsibility. As Thomas Berry contends, the point is to design and use "our human technologies" in a

---

[147]Nash, *Loving Nature*, 156.

[148]*LS*, no. 53.

[149]Ibid., nos. 58, 242.

[150]This is just a short list of possible outcomes. For more business-related examples, see Paul Hawken, *The Ecology of Commerce* (New York: HarperCollins, 1993). For faith-based ethics for religious communities and personal practice, see Ilia Delio et al., *Care for Creation: A Franciscan Spirituality of the Earth* (Cincinnati, OH: St. Anthony Messenger, 2008); or Walter Grazer, *Catholics Going Green* (Notre Dame, IN: Ave Maria Press, 2009).

way that is "coherent with the ever-renewing technologies of the planet itself."[151] Rather than continue the "radical discontinuity" that has been constructed between the human and natural ecologies, Berry calls for a "reciprocal relationship," since, as he explains, "We are touched by what we touch. We are shaped by what we shape. We are enhanced by what we enhance."[152] An encounter with nature is an opportunity to mend the broken relationship between humanity and nonhuman creation, erase any sense of entitlement and superiority, and replace it with intimacy and rapport with all of God's creation. In this way, an ecological culture of encounter engenders tenderness and solidarity with the planetary common good to which we belong.

[151]Berry, *The Great Work*, ix.
[152]Ibid., 72, 81.

Conclusion

Hope for the Future

A culture of encounter is ultimately a practice of hope. Even when it seems to be unlikely to be effective or meaningful, an encounter means being willing to take risks as an act of love. The ethics of encounter refuses to be complacent with a status quo marked by social separation and unjust inequalities. Instead, the ethics of encounter embraces hope not as fantasy or escapism, but rather as the virtuous midpoint between presumption and despair. Hope trusts that God makes good on God's promises, and that love and communion will triumph over fear and division. Hope looks for the ways that God is at work in the world, giving us reason to enlarge our vision of what is possible.[1] Hope is not merely theoretical or hypothetical; it is a responsibility to continuously remake the world. Hope implies partnership with the Holy Spirit, creating new life and new forms of community; hope reminds us that we are never alone. Hope looks at Easter not as a historical event but as a transformed reality, giving us the audacity and urgency to live now—already—as risen beings who can do more as a "new creation" (2 Cor 5:17).[2] Hope keeps our eyes fixed on our future who is God, coming to us from the future, drawing us toward our destiny, which is the loving communion of all, the ultimate culture of solidarity.

The ethics of encounter is a practice of hope meant to "constantly arouse the 'passion for the possible,' inventiveness and elasticity in self-transformation, in breaking with the old and coming to terms with the new" with a truly "revolution-

[1]William Lynch writes, "Hope is, in its most general terms, a sense of *the possible,* that what we really need is possible, though difficult, while hopelessness means to be ruled by the sense of the impossible. Hope therefore involves three basic ideas that could not be simpler: what I hope for I do not yet have or see; it may be difficult; but I *can* have it—it is possible." See William F. Lynch, *Images of Hope: Imagination as Healer of the Hopeless* (Notre Dame, IN: University of Notre Dame Press, 1974), 32.

[2]Jon Sobrino quotes his slain Jesuit brother Ignacio Ellacuría with the admonition "that we should live as already risen beings." See Jon Sobrino, *Christ the Liberator: A View from the Victims,* trans. Paul Burns (Maryknoll, NY: Orbis Books, 2001), 12–13.

ary effect."[3] This means resisting comfort and complacency with things as they are, choosing instead to aspire for greater growth, resilience, and creativity. The famous peace activist Dan Berrigan insisted, "If you want to be hopeful, you have to do hopeful things." The ethics of encounter signifies hopeful action, the practice of neighbor love that seeks solidarity. The effect of love is union: it draws us near others, moving from encounter to accompaniment to exchange to embrace and ultimately to a commitment to inclusive belonging. This is what God most deeply desires for creation.

As Thomas Merton writes,

> Christ lives in us and leads us, through mutual encounter and commitment, into a new future which we build together for one another. That future is called the Kingdom of God . . . True encounter with Christ liberates something in us, a power we did not know we had, a hope, a capacity for life, a resilience, an ability to bounce back when we thought we were completely defeated, a capacity to grow and change, a power of creative transformation.[4]

When Christian neighbor love illuminates our interdependence and generates mutual respect, responsibility, and tenderness, it helps to dismantle illusions, divisions, and unjust inequalities. Drawing near to others to share life together erodes the barriers of self-interest, deception, indifference, cynicism, and abuse. It makes it possible to encounter others as related to and representatives of the divine in our midst. When we build communities of inclusive belonging that reach across difference, we heal wounds left by stigma, shame, fear, hatred, and violence. Practicing courage, mercy, generosity, humility, and fidelity online and in person creates virtuous individuals and communities, networks for love, peace, and justice. This exercise of agency on the individual and interpersonal levels resists and repents for personal and social sin, the beliefs and actions, systems and structures that keep us from living like we belong to each other.

Drawing near to others in a spirit of tenderness means being willing to risk conflict and harm. For this reason, a culture of encounter relies on God's presence and power in every encounter, no matter how uncomfortable. It requires mutual respect, freedom, equality, responsibility, and self-care. It means recognizing the other as a sacrament of God's powerful presence in our midst, just as we are sacraments to everyone we meet. The ethics of encounter calls us to share life together in accompaniment and aim for exchanges that enrich and empower. Ritualizing these exchanges in purposeful gatherings creates the conditions for personal, social,

---

[3]Jürgen Moltmann, *Theology of Hope: On the Ground and the Implications of a Christian Eschatology* (Minneapolis: Fortress Press, 1993), 35.

[4]Thomas Merton, *He Is Risen* (Niles, IL: Argus Communications, 1975), 1–2.

and institutional transformation for the common good, sustainability, and solidarity with all creation. The ethics of encounter relies on exercising imagination, not only to better understand others across difference but to expand what we desire and dream. In order for a culture of encounter to realize a culture of solidarity, we must share in a commitment to never settle for anything less than what God makes possible. In every time and place, God gives Godself to us: a communion of love that is offered, received, and returned. God beckons us to share in this encounter in order to build a world of ever more inclusive belonging.

Index